TOMORROW TO
BE BRAVE

Susan Travers

'Distrust yourself, and sleep before you fight
'Tis not too late tomorrow to be brave.'

DR JOHN ARMSTRONG,
THE ART OF PRESERVING HEALTH, 1744

CORGI BOOKS

TOMORROW TO BE BRAVE
A CORGI BOOK : 0 552 14814 8

Originally published in Great Britain by Bantam Press,
a division of Transworld Publishers

PRINTING HISTORY
Bantam Press edition published 2000
Corgi edition published 2001

1 3 5 7 9 10 8 6 4 2

Set in 11/12¼pt Sabon by
Falcon Oast Graphic Art Ltd.

Corgi Books are published by Transworld Publishers,
61–63 Uxbridge Road, London W5 5SA,
a division of The Random House Group Ltd,
in Australia by Random House Australia (Pty) Ltd,
20 Alfred Street, Milsons Point, Sydney, NSW 2061, Australia,
in New Zealand by Random House New Zealand Ltd,
18 Poland Road, Glenfield, Auckland 10, New Zealand
and in South Africa by Random House (Pty) Ltd,
Endulini, 5a Jubilee Road, Parktown 2193, South Africa.

Printed and bound in Great Britain by
Clays Ltd, St Ives plc.

CONTENTS

'As a matter of fact, one woman did serve in the Legion and without masculine disguise. She was an Englishwoman, Miss Susan Travers ... No writer of romance ever has imagined anything to equal Miss Travers' adventures with the 13th in Europe, Asia and Africa throughout the course of the Second World War.'

CHARLES MERCER, *THE FOREIGN LEGION*
(Arthur Barker, 1964)

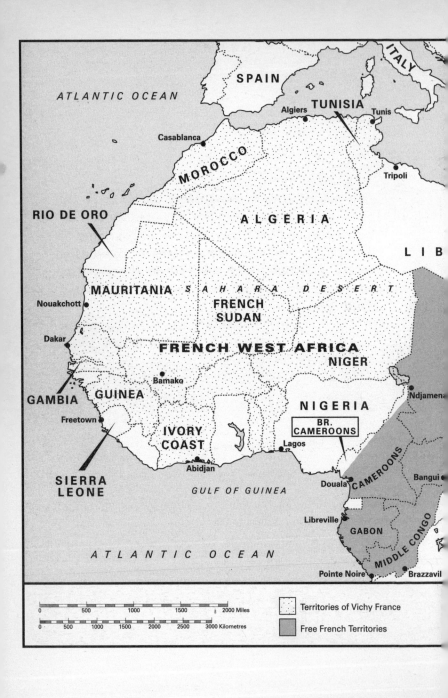

SPAIN

ATLANTIC OCEAN

ITALY

Algiers   TUNISIA   Tunis

Casablanca

Tripoli

MOROCCO

RIO DE ORO

ALGERIA

LIB

MAURITANIA   SAHARA DESERT

Nouakchott

FRENCH
SUDAN

Dakar

FRENCH WEST AFRICA

NIGER

GAMBIA   GUINEA

Bamako

NIGERIA

Ndjamena

Freetown

IVORY
COAST

BR.
CAMEROONS

Lagos

CAMEROONS

Bangui

SIERRA
LEONE

Abidjan

GULF OF GUINEA

Douala

Libreville   GABON

ATLANTIC OCEAN

MIDDLE CONGO

Pointe Noire   Brazzavil

0   500   1000   1500   2000 Miles

0   500   1000   1500   2000   2500   3000 Kilometres

Territories of Vichy France

Free French Territories

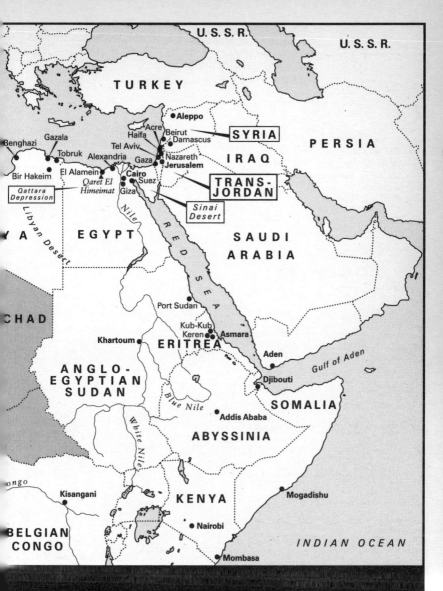

NORTH AFRICA AND THE MIDDLE EAST

TOMORROW TO
BE BRAVE

PROLOGUE

I sit alone in an armchair in my little apartment in Paris, staring out of the window. My beloved cat Pinky is on my lap. I told her that one day they would come, those who wanted to hear my secrets.

Others had been before, but I hadn't been ready and I turned them away or told them only scant details. They all had to be dead, you see – especially dear Nicholas. His death in 1995 gave me the freedom to speak, to unlock the memories of that remarkable time; memories that have never been erased, although I had destroyed my diaries to keep them from him. The thin leather-bound volumes contained handwritten accounts of events which might have hurt him, recollections too private to share of a time before, when my life – all our lives – had been so very different. I burned them to protect him, as he had always protected me. It was only after his body had been committed to the soil of his beloved France that I could begin to think of them again.

The fuss really began after I was widowed, thank goodness. First came the medal, which was offered out of the blue. In truth, I think they were a little surprised to find me still alive. During that simple ceremony, watched by my family and the few remaining veterans they could muster, I stepped up rather shakily with my walking stick to receive my award. General Hugo Geoffrey leaned forward, kissed me on both cheeks and pinned the Légion d'honneur – so coveted by those of us who'd served – to the lapel of my brown tweed suit. He was watched by another familiar face, now that of a five-star general, Jean Simon.

Peering into my heavily lined face with his one good eye, trying to remember the fresh-faced 'La Miss' he'd first met all those years before, Simon smiled politely at the peculiar old Englishwoman before him. I allowed myself a shrug of pride, nodding my acceptance of the accolade, albeit nearly sixty years late. I would add it to my other medals, eleven in all, including the most treasured – the Croix de Guerre with star – with which I was decorated in front of the entire brigade in Cairo, and the Médaille Militaire, presented to me on that heart-wrenching day in Paris.

Holding this latest award in my fingers, I studied the ornate green-and-white silk ribbon and thought of poor Nicholas, who had longed for it so badly but never received it. I thought, too, of my father, the indomitable Captain Francis Travers, awarded his medal after the First World War. He and I were probably the only father and daughter in the history of France to have both received the Légion d'honneur, and yet we were both English.

At the small reception held for me afterwards in the dining room of the sheltered home where I live, my fellow legionnaires – men I hadn't seen for several decades – shuffled shyly over to where I sat with my family, to offer their congratulations. There had never been a better time for teary-eyed reminiscences and yet none was forthcoming. There were few words to express what we felt. Watched by my curious fellow inmates – the old French ladies with whom I slowly decay – we must have made a strange spectacle. Stooped with arthritis and the pain of memory, each one of us still burned with the pride of having belonged to the 13th Demi-Brigade, Légion Etrangère.

We had all been there together, in Bir Hakeim. These men knew what it had been like, half-starved and parched

14

and yet determined not to surrender. They knew of the role I had played, and why.

It was only when everyone had gone and I was left alone with my medals, that the others came – those who wanted to know. They are here now, asking me to tell them my story, tell them what it was really like. Their faces are young and fresh and untainted by death and war. They are dipping into my well of memories, before it dries . . .

1

A WELL OF MEMORIES

*'I shall remember while the light lives yet
And in the night time I shall not forget.'*
SWINBURNE, 'EROTION'

The Stukas were the worst. I could hear them several miles away, like a vast swarm of bees droning in the distance, heading directly for us across the endless desert sky. At first sight they looked like a plague of silver locusts hovering above us, with nothing to prevent them from swooping down and picking at our bleached bones. My heart would begin to pound in my chest as the humming got nearer. My legs would quiver as the fear rose from the pit of my stomach, clutched at my throat and squeezed tighter and tighter.

A key weapon in Adolf Hitler's massive military machine in the North African Campaign, the dreaded Stukas, or dive-bombers, were specially equipped with wind-activated sirens to make a screaming sound as they plummeted to earth at high speed. Flying in formation in waves of up to a hundred planes at a time, without warning they would break away independently to hurtle headlong towards us, shrieking, spinning and whistling. At the exact moment when the bombs were released from the special mounts under their wings, the screaming would stop and they would soar silently, almost gracefully, back up into the sky, freed from the burden of their load. For their near-defenceless target on the ground, the echoing quiet which followed was almost as unnerving; an interminable five seconds while the bombs they'd dropped spiralled silently down.

I would count the seconds in my mind, one, two, three, four, five . . . like a frightened child trying to calculate the next clap of thunder in a storm. And then it would come, that horrible crump and the blinding flash of white light, making me jump every time even though I'd fully anticipated it. The earth would shudder and debris filled the air as the armour-piercing shells exploded on impact, maiming and scorching and disfiguring all around me. And still more planes were on the way, sweeping leisurely over the horizon before slowly circling round, their flanks adorned with black swastikas. The humming they made drew closer and closer until it seemed to be inside my head.

It was the screaming that terrified me more than anything else in that godforsaken spot; the screaming that I could hear long before the ground shook and the grey Libyan dust rose up in a great pillar to mingle with the lethal matter; the screaming that I still heard in my mind long after they had gone. 'Please let it be over, please let it end,' I would murmur softly to myself, but the droning would start again in the distance and I knew that they were coming back.

Sitting alone on the floor in the middle of my dugout – a narrow grave four feet deep into the floor of the Western Desert, piled up at the edges with sandbags and a thin scrap of khaki canvas stretched over the top – I would put on my tin helmet and wait. My hands up around the back of my neck, my legs bent and clamped together beneath me so that my chin was tucked well into my knees, I flexed my muscles and held my breath. In my mind's eye, I imagined that I was in a vast underground bunker, much more substantial than this shallow little scraping in the sand. My tin helmet became a huge metal umbrella and if any of the bombs fell on me, I forced myself to believe, they would simply ricochet off like harmless hailstones.

My helmet would protect me by providing an impenetrable barrier against what I had seen the Stukas do to the men around me. The faceless, limbless and dying all called out for their mothers in their native tongue, '*Maman!*', '*Mutti!*', '*Madre!*' And I, leaning over them afterwards, the only woman among nearly four thousand men, would duly play the role. I tended to them after the air raids, I helped carry those still alive to the overcrowded hospital tent, I slid shut the eyelids of those beyond help. Then, after each raid, I crept back to my dugout alone, closing off my mind, pressing my own eyelids shut against the grisly sights and sounds and smells I'd just witnessed, and waited once again for the next attack as forty thousand German and Italian troops closed in on our position.

We'd been in this hell on earth for over three months, in a theatre of war that had become pivotal to the outcome of the Axis invasion of North Africa. As the world watched and waited, holding its breath, the legendary German commander Erwin Rommel and his Afrika Korps were pounding us to dust, using every war machine at their disposal. Each day brought fresh artillery shells whining across the desolate no-man's-land of coiled barbed wire and anti-tank minefields to erupt in the sand. Heavy-calibre machine-gun bullets rained on us almost constantly. The scorching desert sun – sometimes as hot as 51° Celsius (120° Fahrenheit) with no shade – sat unchallenged in the sky for fourteen hours a day, baking us dry. We were pestered by sand and flies, had no shade and little water, hardly any food, and had been under continuous attack for just over two weeks. Some of the men were so thirsty that they drank from the radiators of the few remaining vehicles.

The nights brought little respite from the glaring heat. Almost as soon as the sun dipped below the horizon, it became bone-achingly cold, the temperatures plummeting to well below zero. We shivered in our pits, the cold depriving us of any sleep we might have been able to snatch between the incessant night raids.

Despite their best efforts, the RAF were unable to do more than pester the relentless waves of Stukas, Messerschmitts, Heinkels and Savoia bombers. The German panzer and Italian Ariete tank divisions were rolling closer and closer across the vast desert plain towards the slit trenches where we were dug in like hares. We were outnumbered ten to one. The noose was tightening.

Rommel, having confidently predicted that we could be crushed in fifteen minutes, had been fighting us for fifteen days. Unaccustomed to such a setback in his hitherto glorious campaign, he had vowed publicly to deal with us himself. Breaking away from the rest of his forces, which were locking horns with the Eighth Army further north, he had come in person to supervise our annihilation. And, despite the gallant efforts of our general and his men, who were constantly badgering the enemy at the periphery of our beleaguered encampment, his determination was paying off.

'Over here, padre,' an officer named Simon called out to Père Mallec, our Yugoslav chaplain, summoning him to administer the last rites to a mortally wounded man on that final evening. 'This man needs your blessing.' Simon and his men had just survived a tank barrage as fierce as any yet, emerging dusty and sweat-stained but grinning from a shattered Bren-gun carrier as fires raged all around.

The chaplain, a thick-set Slovene with an indefatigable spirit, looked up from his sad task. 'No need,' he called, his voice cracking with fatigue. 'By the end of this night, we'll all be in Paradise.' As his hands made the sign of the cross over the shell of the man he was kneeling by, I found I too was crossing myself, despite being an agnostic. The chaplain saw me in my moment of weakness and I retreated hastily back into my hole.

In some strange way, I wasn't afraid to die. I had only myself to blame for being at this previously insignificant place, this compass bearing on the map of Africa on which the future of the entire continent now appeared to rest.

The sun turned the colour of blood and began its slow descent that June night in the summer of 1942, silhouetting the shredded tricolour that still fluttered proudly at the heart of our makeshift garrison. I knew it was only a matter of time before I might have to use the Beretta pistol I now kept permanently to hand. With the same curious sense of calm that had cloaked me as I sat day after day in my dugout under its canvas wing, I quietly accepted that my big adventure might well end soon. Here, at a place called Bir Hakeim . . .

2

LONELY ARE THE BRAVE

'Your children are not your children.
They are the sons and daughters of Life's longing for itself.'
KAHLIL GIBRAN, *THE PROPHET*, 1923

It is my greatest regret that I wasn't born a boy. I simply didn't feel like a little girl should. I was a natural tomboy, constantly seeking thrills and adventures. I preferred books to dolls, bathing to sewing, and talking with the gardener to studying. Unfortunately for me, as both the girl and the youngest child, I was forced into the most awful bonnets and frilly clothes, which I wore under great duress because all I really wanted were shirts and breeches.

My arrival in the world, on 23 September 1909, was a matter of great satisfaction for my father, who had always wanted a daughter, even if he didn't have the first idea what to do with me. It was an unpleasant surprise for my elder brother Laurence, who would very much have preferred to remain an only child. He resolved from an early age to treat me in exactly the same way Father had always treated him – with loathing and contempt. That situation was never to change.

My father was a handsome man and a true Victorian. He could be most amusing when he wanted to be, but in his later years he was often irritable and moody. He'd revelled in the bachelor life at sea; in his last vessel, the

Robin Redbreast, he'd toured the ports and cities of the world, visiting lady friends and generally amusing himself. Towards the end of his service, he was posted to Dartmouth College on HMS *Britannia* (where he met my mother at a party) and remained there until his retirement. But I think he missed the cut and thrust of his former life, with its high drama and changing horizons.

Unhappy at home and in retirement, he was inclined to be rather disagreeable, especially to my mother. He was eighteen years her senior, a considerable age gap for any couple, and he treated her shabbily. He had almost certainly married her for her money, for he had none of his own, and once he had secured his future and sired two children he felt little need to have anything more to do with her.

They had separate rooms and led separate lives, meeting only at meals and for occasional social outings. I'd never been close to my mother; as a small child I would see her only once or twice a day – when she came up to the nursery to say goodnight, or occasionally when we used to go down after tea to the drawing room to sing songs with my aunt Hilda. From the age of six, however, I saw her every day because I was allowed to take luncheon with my parents on the strict condition that I was seen and not heard.

I remember watching them at either end of the polished mahogany dining table, drinking their consommé with hardly a word spoken between them. My brother sat opposite me, as rigid and silent as they, while I fidgeted in my uncomfortable high-backed chair, fantasizing about making loud slurping noises or creating a forbidden clatter with my silver spoon. But I never dared.

There was little hint during my pampered yet disciplined childhood of the unusual path my life was later to take. My first five years were an unremarkable blur. On 4 August 1914 I was a month short of my fifth birthday and staying at my grandmother's home in London when the Kaiser's forces descended on Belgium, outflanking French defences, and the First World War began.

23

Rising to the occasion and the Travers family motto, *Nec Temere nec Timide* (Neither Afraid nor Timid), Father came out of retirement, volunteered for war service and was soon afterwards dispatched to the port of Salonika in northern Greece, to help supervise the fleet of battleships en route to bombard the Turks. My mother and grandmother, fearing Zeppelin raids on London, fled to my grandmother's house in the seaside resort of Torquay, taking me and my brother, plus assorted staff and pets.

At the heart of the 'English Riviera' with palm trees and lush greenery in its many parks and gardens, Torquay in those days was inhabited largely by old ladies like my grandmother, all dressed in black and living in huge villas. Some of them still owned a carriage and a pair of horses. My grandmother must have been slightly more modern because she had a car, although that was soon relinquished when the chauffeur left for the Western Front.

The Priory, my grandmother's Victorian villa in Parkhill Road at Daddyhole Plain, on one of seven hills overlooking Tor Bay, was dignified but rather faded. Covered with ivy and Virginia creeper, which at times seemed to be holding it together, it was nonetheless a delightful house for a child. My grandmother was a great hoarder, and her house was filled with large trunks of clothes to dress up in, vast cupboards stuffed with interesting items, and books everywhere, especially children's books which had belonged to my mother and her elder sister, my aunt Hilda, by then a wealthy spinster who lived in some splendour in Abingdon Court, off Kensington High Street.

The house had a vast dusty library belonging to my great-great-uncle, Thomas Turnbull, which nobody but us ever entered. Thomas had been an eccentric clergyman and traveller who collected anything from books to shells from all over the globe, and it was always a great treat to be shown some of his prized possessions.

'This is extremely valuable,' my grandmother would say, carefully unwrapping some fossilized African treasure from its tissue paper as I stared in wide-eyed anticipation.

I would study these ancient artefacts from far-off lands and try to conjure up an image of the intrepid explorer and his wondrous travels. How I longed for pith-helmeted journeys like his, to places few had visited, to see sights rarely shared.

My grandmother was a delightful and gentle old lady who adored us and was kindness itself, filling in the emotional void my parents appeared unable to address. Patently aware of my mother's sadness and her consequent withdrawal from life, my grandmother and my aunt Hilda did their best to make it up to us, although my grandmother clearly favoured my brother, whom she called Larry. This was just as well because nobody else seemed to like him, least of all my father and me. I much preferred our black Labrador, Duchess, who was bought as a gun dog for Father but turned out to be terrified of loud bangs and was thereafter confined to the nursery in disgrace.

Grandmother's house had a long and featureless garden, just lawn and laurel hedges, but I used to play endlessly in it, spoiling my layers of frocks. The scent of wet laurels can still take me right back to those days. We had an old gardener called Vinnicombe who came twice a week and made marvellous bonfires in which he let me roast potatoes – never fully cooked, always raw and smoky – which I used to eat with pride. When he'd tired of me and thought he'd done enough in the garden, Vinnicombe would retire to a ruined potting shed to smoke his pipe and have a nap. I loved him dearly.

Days were spent at Meadfoot Beach, a sheltered, magical spot at the foot of the cliffs, a place where I learned to swim and play happily alone. To the consternation of my nurses, I used to climb trees and slide down the steep rock slopes, ripping my petticoats. The beach was a wonderful place, scattered with pebbles and rock pools. And then there were the bathers. It was still the era of wooden Victorian beach huts set atop cart wheels, which would be hauled right down to the water's edge by hapless male servants, so that the local gentlewomen could

25

slip into the water unseen and bathe discreetly in frilly, flouncy costumes and drawstring caps. I would watch them with a mixture of fascination and joy, feeling even then that I was being allowed a glimpse of a bygone age.

My schooling was initially conducted at home by governesses. Sitting side by side at our little wooden desks in the nursery, Laurence and I learned to read, write and do sums on slates. We were also taught French from a very early age. One learned it as a matter of course in my generation, whereas in my mother's childhood they'd learned German. When I was old enough, I was sent to a local primary school in Babbacombe, travelling there by tram with the three Payne brothers who lived nearby and became my most spirited companions. All my childhood friends were boys, never girls.

I had a series of nurses who washed, dressed and fed me. My favourite was Bessie, who also played games with me and made marvellous clothes for my toy monkey, Münch, from whom I was rarely separated. I adored Münch; he was dark grey and my aunt Hilda had given him to me when I was four. He was one of six toy monkeys I had, whom I thought of as 'my little family'. In return for Bessie's kindness to me and my 'pets', I tried to teach her French, to no avail. Try as she might, her broad South London accent always got in the way. 'G-er m-a-r-pelle Bessie,' she'd recite and I'd raise my eyes to the heavens and sigh.

She and I used to go for walks with Duchess and another nanny, her two dogs and her small charges, chatting incessantly and traversing enormous distances up hill and down dale without ever seeming to get tired. For much of my early childhood, she was the first person I saw in the morning and the last person I saw at night. I adored Bessie and was devastated when she was eventually sent away. I wasn't even given a chance to say goodbye. No explanation was offered for her departure. The first I knew about it was when the new nurse, a young mademoiselle who it was thought would improve my

French, arrived to take her place. I hated her. I never saw Bessie again.

Most of my childhood was spent in Devon, but there were still regular trips to London. My grandmother refused to allow anything as inconsequential as the First World War to interfere with her social life and she continued to take a house in the capital for the 'season' each winter, just as she'd always done. My mother, brother and I went along too and my memories are of large, dark London townhouses with innumerable stairs and a permanently musty smell. I also recall being out in a thick yellow fog when I couldn't see my hand in front of my face and had to feel my way home along the wrought-iron railings. On fine days, Mademoiselle used to take me on walks in Kensington Gardens with all the other nurses and their young charges, perpetually scolding me for wanting to run ahead.

Our life appeared to be unaffected by the war. There were a few Zeppelin raids further up the river, and some of the first German attacks by aeroplane killed a hundred people and injured four hundred in the East End, but nothing seemed to be in short supply and we lived exactly as we always had, with linen sheets, fine clothes, servants and three meals a day. Whether my grandmother deliberately flouted Government calls on the wealthy to be frugal and live simpler lives, I don't know. I imagine she simply thought that they couldn't possibly be referring to her.

I heard little or nothing from my father during the four years of war. Anything I was able to glean came from Bessie or my aunt Hilda, who assured me he was doing 'sterling' work. After some years in the Middle East, he was posted to Marseilles as commander of maritime transport, which is where he remained until hostilities ended in November 1918. It was for his services to France in Marseilles that he was awarded his Légion d'honneur. His own father had been the British consul in Marseilles in the mid-1800s and had a long-standing connection with the city, so I think Father felt quite at home there.

27

Grandfather had returned to England from France with a pair of bronze statues of kepi-wearing members of the French Foreign Legion, elegant figurines in their distinctive 'flat box' hats, which my father had inherited and which I'd known throughout my childhood.

The war ended when I was nine. I remember being told sombrely at school that ten million people had died in a four-year campaign which had seen some of the worst fighting in history. But I had only a child's perception of what that meant – several schoolfriends' fathers never came back, one of our former teachers was missing and my grandmother's chauffeur returned half-mad and blind after a mustard-gas attack.

My father had been lucky. His age and service experience had kept him from the front lines and yet he had served his country honourably and well. When he eventually returned home with his coveted medal, he retired once more on his naval pension and we moved *en famille* to a large Victorian house called Little Hill on the outskirts of the small market town of Chudleigh in Devon. It was a cold, austere, double-fronted property with huge windows and views across Exmoor. The atmosphere inside was equally chilly. Laurence was sent to a boarding school in Norfolk and I hardly saw my mother, who, when she wasn't off visiting my grandmother or aunt, continued to spend most of her days alone in her room.

Father would sit downstairs in an armchair by the fire reading the newspaper and seldom talking. He seemed to be kinder to animals than he was to my mother and brother. With them he would become unreasonably cross, flaring up at the slightest thing. I was often afraid of him.

Like most daughters, I adored him nonetheless, and he became my only true role model. There were no heroines in my life, only heroes, and to my mind he was the greatest hero of all, having volunteered for war service. I dreamed of honour and adventure, and of emulating him one day. How grand it would be to follow in his footsteps and make him proud of me.

I was never happier than when he paid me some small attention or allowed me to be with him for a while.

'Come and sit here, Susan,' he would say, patting a tapestry footstool at his feet. 'Why don't you read something to me?'

He loved to read, often returning from the library with armfuls of volumes, and he encouraged me to do likewise. Desperate to please him, I would devour book after book, especially the classics and stories such as *Beau Geste*. I vividly remember reading the exotic tale of the jewel theft and the Foreign Legion and thinking how wonderful it would be to have such an adventure one day.

'What was it like travelling the world, Father?' I'd ask him, sitting at his feet, hoping for one of his rare smiles.

A faraway look would enter his eyes and he'd tell me a little of the wonders he had seen, of the great seascapes and magical lands he'd visited, before stopping himself and allowing the coldness to return. Shaking out his newspaper impatiently to read about the latest crisis in Russia or the civil war in Ireland, he'd dismiss me abruptly from his side. 'Now run along and leave me to my paper in peace,' he'd say crossly, stabbing at the fire with a poker. 'And tell the maid to bring in some more coal.'

I expect I was a source of irritation to him, unaccustomed as he'd been to children in the previous four years. I tried to be good and quiet and keep out of his way, but I would often find him glaring at me from a window somewhere as I played in the garden, tapping on the glass impatiently with his pipe, urging me to behave in a more ladylike fashion. In any event, my brief time with him and my mother in Devon was interrupted, not long after he'd returned, when a mass flu epidemic swept Britain, killing thousands. I was suddenly sent away to a redbrick boarding school, St Mary's in Wantage in Oxfordshire. It was an experience I detested.

I'd always been a loner, and I didn't really know how to interact with children my own age. At boarding school I knew nobody and all the other girls were beastly. The teachers were unkind and the matron, Mrs Buckle, was a dragon, announcing on the first day that she 'only liked little girls who could put their hair into a plait and look after themselves'. I'd never had to do either so I didn't know how and she seemed to hate me for it. Boarding school was nothing like the Angela Brazil books I'd read, with the tomboys of the Upper Fourth having fun in the dorms. My only consolation was sport, at which I'd always excelled.

Away from the sports field, I was miserable and often cried myself to sleep. There was no-one I could turn to – Mother and Father were remote and unapproachable and I knew they'd be furious if I wrote to Grandmother to complain. She and my aunt Hilda sent occasional letters and cards to try to cheer me along, but they were of little comfort. Instead I hardened my heart and, clutching Münch to my side every night, prayed for the day when I could eventually leave and be in control of my own destiny.

It was three years before that day came, three long years in which I only ever returned to Devon for the summer and Christmas holidays. Laurence was equally unhappy in Norfolk, but he later won a music scholarship to Lancing College in Sussex, a place he came to adore. Thereafter, when he returned to Chudleigh, his unhappiness at being with me and our parents was as obvious as my sadness at having to return to my solitary life in Wantage. In the end he persuaded Mother to allow him to stay with Grandmother in nearby Torquay during the holidays, an arrangement which suited everyone.

By the time I was twelve years old, I'd resigned myself to my fate and settled better to school life, even making a few friends, but my teenage years as a boarder still stretched ahead of me. But then a remarkable thing happened. Father suddenly declared that I was to be taken out of boarding school for good.

'Your mother and I are moving to France,' he announced. 'We think it might broaden your education if you were to accompany us.' There was no mention of Laurence.

My parents had chosen to emigrate to Cannes on the French Riviera. The decision had apparently been planned over some considerable period of time. Money was tight in Britain after the war; there were miners' strikes and mass unemployment and the mood was gloomy. In comparison, France was a cheap place to live and seemed far more attractive. Father, who'd spent many of his happiest years there, hankered after the warmth of the south to ease his arthritis and sour temper. My mother's feelings didn't come into it.

Thus it was that in 1921 I said goodbye to England without much sadness, and embarked for the first time for the country which would remain my home, spiritually and physically, for the next eight decades.

3

DREAMS OF FREEDOM

'The desire of the moth for the star,
Of the night for the morrow,
The devotion to something afar
From the sphere of our sorrow.'
SHELLEY, 'ONE WORD IS TOO OFTEN PROFANED'

We travelled by boat and train and arrived in France late at night, checking into a hotel, Des Orangers, in Le Suquet, the old town, five minutes from the old port and La Croisette, the lengthy boulevard along the seafront. A south-facing, Provençal-style building, the hotel was set in a garden of oleander, olive trees and lavender. I remember waking up in the morning and throwing open the red-shuttered windows of my room, to be utterly dazzled. I felt as if my eyes had been opened for the very first time; my senses were assailed from all sides. The view was exquisite – the Mediterranean sea was the deepest azure blue, the scent of pines and thyme and lavender impregnated the air, and sailing vessels of every description rode the waves. In the far distance, the Esterel mountains rose mauve in the morning haze. The food was divine, cooked as it was in olive oil with garlic, tomatoes and herbs. Everything seemed so very different from Devonshire, crisper and brighter and, oh, so much richer. If this was France, I was completely entranced and never wanted to leave.

My parents took a pretty green-painted villa called Casa Longa on the Chemin Bella Isola just off the Boulevard Carnot, on the hill above the old port. It had six bedrooms and several reception rooms and came complete with a kindly middle-aged housekeeper called Jeanne Martin, of whom I became very fond. Not long after we arrived, she presented me with a kitten, which I christened Chipmunk. 'This is for you, *ma chérie*, so you'll always have someone to play with,' Jeanne told me. I was touched. It was the kindest thing anyone had done for me since the days of Bessie.

I attended a private day school, the Ecole Cours Fénelon (named after François Fénelon, a priest and writer under Louis XIV), where I found the schoolchildren far friendlier than they'd ever been at my boarding school in England. At first I was in the minority once again, not knowing anyone and feeling rather out of place, but this time I had novelty value, being English, and my fellow pupils went out of their way to be kind. My knowledge of the language improved quickly and I soon made friends, whole-heartedly embracing the life of a French schoolgirl, complete with pigtails.

Between the ages of twelve and sixteen, I was a model daughter. I did well at school and grew accustomed to living alone with my parents, keeping largely out of their way. The climate seemed to lift my father's mood. He spent most of his time out, at various clubs with new friends. My mother, however, missed my grandmother and aunt Hilda tremendously and was inconsolable at being so far away from the home she knew. She'd never been much of a social butterfly and, now that she was trapped in a strange house in a strange land, she all but cocooned herself away.

Her isolation only served to confuse me about my true identity. Was I French or English? I'd been brought up in England, certainly, but I was now living in France, speaking French and living the life of a Cannes schoolgirl, even though my friends perceived me as entirely British. With both my parents so withdrawn from my daily sphere, I began to acquire a sense of otherness which was to remain with me for the rest of my life. I was an outsider, destined to remain on the fringes of the society in which I found myself. I had no concept of 'home'. From now on, home would always have to be where I made it.

Father remained emotionally aloof from both my mother and me and I rarely saw him until, to my great delight, I reached my thirteenth birthday and he resolved to make a sportswoman out of me. Tennis was one of the few socially acceptable sports for a girl of my class and Father had been a keen player in his youth. It was the era of Suzanne Lenglen, the greatest woman tennis player of all time, the French and Olympic champion, an example to aspiring sportswomen (and their parents) everywhere. Mademoiselle Lenglen had caused a great stir in England three years earlier when, as a twenty-year-old prodigy, she won the first women's final at Wimbledon after the war wearing a short, loose dress and baring her arms. She became the first Wimbledon winner from a non-English-speaking nation. Thereafter every father wanted his daughter to be a tennis champion, for the cachet alone, and mine was no exception.

Mademoiselle Lenglen lived locally in Cannes and I was lucky enough to see her play many times. She was mesmerizing. A very ugly woman with a large beak of a nose, she had a beautiful figure, dressed immaculately and was wonderfully graceful. When she walked onto the grass, it was akin to watching a great dancer come onto the stage. Her appearance simply made a tennis tournament. The clubs competed for her favour and her word was law. She played singles only in her own club, the Nice Lawn Tennis Club, which belonged to her father. We belonged to the smartest of all clubs, the Cannes Lawn Tennis Club, which was owned by my mother's cousin Henry Atkinson, who kept two professionals to play only with him. The lady secretary was rather severe and insisted that all the young ladies should play in white woollen stockings but not, thankfully, long skirts – Suzanne Lenglen had seen to that. They were magical days.

I enjoyed tennis immensely, especially my daily lessons with the rather dashing professionals, who provided me with my first real contact with the opposite sex and enabled me to improve my game. What I didn't like so much was the interminable practising with my father, with whom I played badly, simply through nerves. Try as I might to impress him, I was often all fingers and thumbs in his presence, missing shots I'd normally have no problem with and double-faulting regularly. Time and again I'd hear the words, 'You're not trying!' or 'What do you call that?' bellowed at me from the other end of the court. Invariably he would beat me and then rant at me for my poor return of service all the way home. His criticism was crushing. I felt physically winded each time he shouted at me. Tennis was the one area of my life where I'd hoped to impress him, to make him proud. But I soon came to realize that my father's praise was something I would never be able to earn.

The early 1920s were the years of the Riviera's great elegance, when everyone who was anyone went to Cannes for the winter. *Tout* Paris, *tout* Londres, rich Americans, destitute grand dukes, the *monde* and the *demi-monde*, plus the usual hard core of respectable, retired English like my parents. It was the time of Charlie Chaplin and Rudolph Valentino, Josephine Baker and Noel Coward. Jazz was the new musical rage, although the Charleston was also causing quite a stir. Coco Chanel was transforming the way women dressed, giving them a new freedom with her straight, boyish lines. The Catholic Church warned that the 'scandalous' new fashions would herald a moral decline.

Doctors declared that modern young women were in danger of 'straining their nervous system' with nights of frivolity, days of excitement, and the poisons of tobacco and alcohol. Determined to shake off their whalebone stays, women became ever more willowy and adopted the new styles fervently, bobbing their hair and raising the hems of their skirts. I was no exception. My long, dark hair, so fondly brushed and gathered up into enormous silk ribbons by my grandmother throughout my childhood and plaited throughout my schooldays, was cut into a severe Eton crop. Later it was permanently waved into a shingle, which remained more or less its style for the rest of my life.

With hindsight, Cannes was a totally unsuitable environment for a child to grow up in, surrounded as I was by rich, bored adults. I didn't even have my brother for occasional diversion. My cousin Diana was there and I was fond of her, but she was two or three years older than me, which seemed an unbridgeable chasm at that age. So I remained trapped and frustrated with just my parents for company. They were very strict with my liberty: there was nothing for a young girl to do if she wasn't at school or playing tennis and I was never allowed out in the evenings. My overwhelming childhood emotions were loneliness and a sense of abandonment.

I felt the pangs of adolescence keenly. I was becoming quite a striking young woman, slim and dark, with piercing blue eyes and a sculptured face, and yet I was constantly treated as a child. I'd escape to my bedroom to read rather than endure the stultifying atmosphere downstairs.

Fiction again became my magic carpet to faraway lands. Books borrowed from schoolfriends or the Cannes library made me realize that there was another life outside the four walls which imprisoned me, a world where dragons were slain, damsels saved and great adventures could be had. It didn't matter to me if the books were in French or English, I was fluent in both languages by then, but the French ones were far more explicit and I'd digest them avidly by lamplight under my bedclothes. My parents would have snatched some of them away in horror if they had found them. I remember one called *La Garçonne* by the Algerian writer Victor Margueritte about a girl who had a series of affairs and tried to live like a man. It was filled with graphic sexual detail, and I gleaned a great deal. My imagination fuelled, I could barely wait to put all I'd learned into practice.

Apart from the odd moment of intense excitement when one of the tennis pros put his arms around me to show me how to improve my serve, my only chance to experiment with my burgeoning sexuality came through contact with Max, my ballroom dancing tutor, on whom I had an enormous crush. He was a gigolo, thirty years old to my fifteen, but I was deeply flattered when he pulled me towards him during one of our first waltzes and told me how lovely I was. After a time I allowed him to kiss me, nothing more, and I marvelled at how it made my lips tingle. 'Oh, Su-*zanne*, Su-*zanne*,' he would moan, nuzzling my neck with his warm breath. I felt as if I'd died and gone to heaven. He was Greek, very handsome, and he slept with women for money in between teaching young girls how to tango and foxtrot. I knew what he wanted from me – in a way I wanted it too – but I was too afraid to give in to him in the close confines of the community in which I lived. Thoughts of what my father would do to me, and to Max, if he ever found out played a formidable part in my refusal to succumb fully to his persistent advances.

Needless to say, by the time I was sixteen and coming to the end of my schooling, I felt like a caged animal, watching and waiting for my chance to escape. I wanted excitement, romance and adventure. I wanted to travel the world and meet the man of my dreams. All my childhood had been spent, it seemed, waiting for the day when I could be free. I longed to spread my wings. My tomboy dreams of dashing travels and heroic exploits overseas were usurped by wild notions of love and sex and marriage. My schoolgirl heart now wanted nothing more than to be betrothed to some rich industrialist who would finance my adventures and shower me with diamond bracelets, while I secretly enjoyed a string of passionate

37

affairs with wholly unsuitable men whose kisses would set me alight.

Most of all, I wanted to be wicked. A wicked lady, flirting with danger and scandal, like the daring heroines of the books I'd read so voraciously. It was all a great departure from the humdrum reality of my strictly regulated life, with its relentless luxuries and conventions. But surrounded by the beautiful ladies of Cannes at the height of the Roaring Twenties – adorning the arms of ageing millionaires in their divine clothes, dripping with jewels – I could hardly be blamed for such exotic fantasies. All that ever mattered in Cannes was money and sex. Nobody seemed to work and everyone played. It was years before I discovered (with some considerable shock) that not everybody lived like that. It was an intoxicating environment and one into which I longed to plunge myself.

To my great relief, salvation was at hand. After some lengthy behind-the-scenes discussions, my parents called me to the drawing room one evening to inform me of a dramatic change in circumstance.

'You will be leaving Cannes when you have finished your studies,' my silver-haired father told me, standing ramrod straight by the ornate mantelpiece, sucking on his briar pipe and fingering his gold pocket-watch.

As I stood to attention before him, my arms pinned to my sides out of a lifetime of respect, my heart sank and I wondered if I would shortly be on a ship back to England and boarding school again. But Father had far grander ideas for me.

'We have decided to send you to a finishing school in Florence so that you may acquaint yourself with some social refinements. We've chosen a reputable establishment run by a Miss Penrose and recommended by your current headmistress. You will be leaving within the month,' he declared, clearly satisfied with his plans.

My heart skipped a beat. Florence, home of the Medicis, the most beautiful city in Italy, seemed the perfect antidote to the sterility of my existence. Finishing school, a place to complete my education before being thrust towards marriage and social convention, beckoned. 'Thank you, Father,' I said, my eyes shining.

My mother barely looked up from her sewing.

Dismissed from the room by a formal nod of my father's head, I closed the door quietly behind me and leaned breathlessly against it, my hand clasped to my chest in delight. Picking up Chipmunk as she passed, I danced into the entrance hall with the bewildered cat in my arms.

As Jeanne helped me pack my belongings into a large valise in those last few days before my departure, I could barely control the urge to fly headlong down the stairs and out of the house in case my parents changed their minds. I felt suddenly as if a door had been opened and my future was spread out before me like a vast ornate carpet. All I had to do was take the first tentative step across it.

4

THE WICKED LADY

*'The body searches for that which
has injured the mind with love.'*
LUCRETIUS (C. 99–55 BC), 'ON THE NATURE OF THINGS'

In Italy, I finally found the freedom I'd dreamed of. Florence and, later, Rome gave me the chance to be myself and not the dutiful daughter or the would-be débutante. My head spun with the intoxication of the place. It was a far cry from the well-groomed, orderly streets of Cannes. In the city the Italians call Firenze, there were sights and sounds and smells which bewitched me. Humanity was everywhere, on foot, in cars or carriages, on bicycles – eating, drinking, smoking, laughing, fighting. Italian housewives hung their washing out on lines strung nonchalantly between buildings, shutters slammed shut against the sound of shouting lovers, and sweaty men brawled openly in the street. Everywhere there was the smell of cooking. Food was eaten voraciously, almost sexually, with the fingers or using bread to wipe the plates, and everything was washed down with copious amounts of wine. The city was throbbing with life. Ordinary people lived, worked and played within its huge, beating heart.

Swelling their numbers were the tourists, thousands of them, halfway through their grand European tours, cramming the narrow streets. People of every nationality,

English, American, French and German. Strangers ourselves, we, the new girls in Miss Penrose's care, queued alongside the rest to admire Botticelli's 'Primavera' in the Uffizi Gallery and climbed the hill to Fort Belvedere and San Miniato al Monte. Miss Penrose was our educational guide, a formidable spinster and an experienced disciplinarian, well used to clipping the wings of flighty young birds desperate to flee the nest. We were always accompanied in public, and rarely left alone – not least because of parental concerns that we be kept well away from the Fascist Blackshirt rallies which were becoming a common and alarming feature of Italy at that time.

Of indeterminate age, with short grey hair and spectacles resting on a long, thin nose, Miss Penrose marched us around the little side streets in tight formation, pointing out ancient churches and historical landmarks. We whispered in the Duomo, gazed at the Baptistery doors, watched the swirling brown water of the River Arno beneath the Ponte Vecchio, and strolled with our floral parasols in the Boboli Gardens. We saw artisans at work, blowing glass and making ornate gilt picture frames; we visited the premises of pastry chefs and cheese makers; we drank espresso in trattorie and gobbled up freshly made ribbons of pasta.

'This is the famous Campanile, designed by Giotto,' our tutor would tell us, her eyes bright, and eleven of the twelve be-hatted young heads bobbing along behind her would look up dutifully. 'Please note the particularly fine carvings.'

My eyes, however, almost always remained firmly at ground level. The sight that most interested me was the trail of young Italians we usually accumulated behind us, with their cloth caps and braces. They'd whistle their appreciation and flash their dark eyes at us in a way I'd never previously experienced, gesturing with their hands for us to run off with them. As I giggled with my new friends, twirling my parasol and pretending to be embarrassed and outraged by their attentions but all the

41

while signalling my desire that the boys should keep up, I'm afraid that much of Florence's venerable history was completely lost on me.

It was only later, when I was back in the large, shuttered rooms of the gently peeling villa that formed the main body of the school, that my ardour for Florence's less-talked-about attractions was able to cool. Miss Penrose and her *signorine* taught us how to sit and walk and talk, how to hold a knife and fork or drink from a glass, and how to spend our weekly allowances and budget accordingly. I always found these indoor classes immensely boring, not least because I already knew most of these things automatically, but chiefly because I would have much preferred to be back on the pavements, blushing under the burning stares of the local boys.

We did have occasional treats, such as life painting classes in an atelier under the auspices of a humpbacked old Frenchman, when a very pretty Italian youth called Eugenio was allowed in to paint with us. Despite the tempting array of naked men and women which one was supposed to sketch, I could hardly take my eyes off Eugenio; he was so beautiful with his long dark eyelashes and coy smile. I was transfixed. My paintings were nearly always incomplete. I even got to kiss him once or twice, secretly, and found that his lips tasted of vanilla.

On another memorable occasion, Miss Penrose hosted a party in the villa and invited some well-bred local boys along for us to dance with and practise our Italian. She and her ladies watched us all, eagle-eyed, ready to catch us out on our poor manners, bad posture or incorrect dance steps. Eugenio was among the young men. We were like bees round a honey pot. I'm sure the poor boys didn't know what to make of this blushing, chattering crowd of willowy foreign teenagers desperate for secret assignations.

The only consolation of being locked into the villa at night was when, as we lay awake in the echoing dormitories, the Angela Brazil stories of my childhood really sprang to life. The new friends I'd made helped to make my time in Florence truly memorable. I remember an American girl called Carol and a nice English girl called Lois Robinson, whose family came from Oxfordshire. There were pillow fights, midnight feasts, scary ghost stories and the usual sniggering under the sheets, but it was also here that I realized for the first time that my sexual frustrations were far from unique. All we ever talked about were boys, boys, boys. I heard more dirty stories at finishing school than I did anywhere else in the rest of my life. Many of the other girls were equally keen to taste life, to learn about and experiment with sex; and experiment we did.

I was not alone in wanting to be wicked, it seemed, and I relished the opportunity to sate my curiosity. We so wanted to be grown up, plucking up our courage to examine each other's bodies and explore the erogenous zones with an almost medical fascination. There were many girls who, I'm sure, left Miss Penrose's care as fully committed lesbians. Their eyes had been opened to the pleasures of female sex and for them there was no turning back. But for me the experience only heightened my sense of lost satisfaction. It was male company I craved; the love of a man had become an obsession for me, virtually ignored as I'd been by my father and brother. More than anything now, I realized, I wanted to lie in the arms of a man and be utterly seduced. Little did I know how soon I would have my chance.

'You'll be leaving for Rome tomorrow,' Miss Penrose announced in her strident tone one morning after breakfast towards the end of the first term. 'You will remain there for one week and utilize that time to continue your studies of the mighty Roman Empire. From there you will travel to your respective homes for the Christmas break, as it is easier to make connections from Rome. I shall not be accompanying you, but you will be constantly chaperoned by one of your tutors, Miss Hartley.'

43

Had I misread her bespectacled expression, or had she stared specifically at me at the mention of a chaperone?

I was going to Rome, city of emperors, home to Romulus and Remus, and Miss Penrose wasn't coming. I quivered with anticipation as I packed my hand-tooled valise.

We journeyed south by train and arrived at the sprawling Stazione Termini in the middle of the afternoon. I disembarked with the other girls under the close supervision of our elderly chaperone, and we wandered together towards the taxi rank. Within seconds I'd elicited my first Roman wolf-whistle, my cheeks reddening slightly at the sound.

Catching my own reflection in a plate-glass window, I studied the image before me critically and smiled. I was a slight young woman with a gamine beauty. Prior to embarking for finishing school, my mother and my aunt had taken me to Paris and to Eve Valère in Knightsbridge to purchase an entire new wardrobe, with which I was delighted. I had just turned seventeen and looked as slim as ever in my favourite white dress, cape and natty cloche hat. I was by now at least two inches taller than my female companions and looked and felt completely grown up.

As we booked into our little *albergo* in the streets behind the Forum, the dashing middle-aged manager, a man with the incongruous name of Hannibal and the dark Latin features of the south, caught my eye. My cheeks burned further when he flipped back his mop of black hair and winked at me openly.

I shared a room with another girl, an American called Amy, and we whispered much of the first night away, swapping our secrets and fantasies about Italian men. In the daytime we wrapped up warm and toured the sights – the Vatican, the National Museum, Piazza Venezia, the Capitoline and Palatine Hills – dining at cafés in between, where we were even allowed the odd sip of *vino da tavola* by our indulgent spinster chaperone. Day after day we walked and walked, wide-eyed at all that Rome had to offer. Each evening after supper we'd return exhausted to our hotel, collect our keys from Hannibal – he of the wandering eyes – and retire to our respective rooms.

It was on almost the last night, at around one o'clock in the morning, that my life was to change. I was awoken by the sound of gentle but insistent tapping on my bedroom door. Slipping on my silk robe, I crept out of bed and opened the door gingerly to find Hannibal standing smiling in the corridor, holding a bottle of champagne and two glasses.

'Signorina Travers,' he said softly, a wicked gleam in his eye, his jacket draped over his shoulders and his tie loosened, 'Su-*zanna*, I bring this especially for you, *bella inglese*. You like, yes?'

I was flattered by his attention and impressed by his audacity. I'd never drunk champagne before and I thought what fun it would be to try. Whispering for him to be quiet so as not to waken Amy, I ushered him in and we sat side by side on the edge of my bed in the half-light. Making far too much noise, Hannibal popped the cork and poured me a glass, allowing it to cascade over the rim. Raising it to my lips, I giggled as the bubbles tickled my nose.

Hannibal, his dark eyes shining in the moonlight that flooded into the bedroom from the unshuttered window, encouraged me to drink up. Two glasses later the alcohol had gone straight to my head. Laughing uncontrollably, I felt like dancing and singing and running through the streets of Rome in my silk night robe. My head spun with the intoxication of the moment, I felt set alight by Hannibal's burning gaze and I longed for him to kiss me. My glass overspilling, I suddenly found myself clenched in his arms in a passionate embrace, tasting the champagne on his lips. By the time the bottle was empty, I'd lost my virginity.

Making love to a man for the first time was certainly not the earth-shattering experience I'd imagined it to be. It wasn't particularly memorable, in fact, and I was more than a little disappointed. There was no lingering embrace

45

or waiting together for the dawn, as I'd read in the novels. In no time at all, it seemed, Hannibal was standing up, adjusting his clothing and scurrying from my room with a rather ignominious '*buona notte*' and a hastily blown kiss. As I watched him go, I felt cheated. Was this all it took to be wicked? Would moments of passion always be followed by such hollow feelings of emptiness? For the first time in my life I began to entertain doubts about some of the wilder romantic notions I'd come to regard as my essential truths. In the fantasy world I'd created in my mind, based on all the books I'd read, I truly believed that the intimacy I'd shared with Hannibal would lead to everlasting love. As my hopes crumbled, I realized with a shock that I had been deluding myself all along.

Amy had been asleep throughout the entire episode. I lay awake until dawn, listening to her steady breathing and wishing I could turn the clock back. If I saw Hannibal again, maybe everything would become clearer, I reasoned. Perhaps he would apologize for his quick exit and promise to spend more time with me during my final days in Rome. I imagined us strolling hand in hand by the Trevi Fountain or in the pretty Campo de' Fiori, as I'd seen other young lovers do.

But when I went to find him at reception later that morning, to see when we could meet again, he kept his distance and pretended to be too busy to talk.

'I can't see you now,' he hissed at me, half under his breath lest anyone should overhear us. 'Maybe later.'

He never did manage to find the time, and I – feeling like a fool – didn't press. It was, I think, with relief that he bid me farewell when we checked out two days later.

Travelling back towards Cannes on the train from Rome, I stared out of the window at the bare winter landscape. Pondering long and hard about what had happened and how different it had made me feel, I realized that my childhood had been swept aside in a matter of a few minutes. I'd finally lost the burden of my virginity. There was no going back to my old life now. I couldn't possibly stay on at Casa Longa with my parents. I'd tasted of the forbidden fruit and the experience had already set me apart from the other girls. In the 1920s, if a woman wasn't respectably married, she could only be a governess, a secretary or a nurse. I didn't want to be any of those, nor did I want to be locked into a loveless marriage like my mother.

No, I decided, I'd made my bed and I would have to lie in it. Wicked was what I had longed to be, and wicked I'd become – albeit rather unexpectedly. The only course left to me now was to carry on in the same vein, to fill my cup to overflowing and to cram all life's experiences into the years ahead of me. If I flirted with danger in my youth, then I could settle down later happy in the knowledge that I had really lived, unlike Mother whose youth and beauty had been completely wasted on my father. Men would become my salvation, I resolved, my ticket to travel and wealth and happiness. Without any serious money of my own, and in a world where women were second-class citizens, I would follow the example of the rich mesdemoiselles of Cannes and use my charms to my greatest advantage. It was a road to self-destruction, forged from a lonely childhood, and it would lead only to heartache and tears, but I was far too young to realize it.

I had first persuaded my parents to give me driving lessons when I was seventeen. Laurence was not the driving sort, my mother had never wished to learn and my father was getting older and finding the roads too busy. Only boys had cars in those days, girls didn't (I knew of only one girl who had a car and she was very rich), but when I reached eighteen I became one of the few. I drove my father's old Cottin-Desgouttes, a venerable French car he loved and was forever messing about with. He taught me a few basics such as how to check the suspension, change a tyre and check the oil – lessons I was later to be very grateful for – and allowed me to use it as often as I liked.

On occasional family trips home to see my grandmother

47

and aunt or my parents' friends, I would drive them all the way from the South of France to England and back. The car would be hoisted up onto the boat at the seaport. We always went via Le Touquet to pick up my father's bull terrier, Betsy, who spent the summer there because it was too hot for her in Cannes.

Driving brought me greater independence than I'd ever known before and I thrived on it. My friends appreciated it too and used me as a chauffeur. One English girl I became friendly with was a very bad influence on me. She was called Hersey Piggott. Her family were well off and she and I used to go out and pick up a couple of Americans and drink far too much. Hersey drank whisky, which was then a man's drink, neat or in Manhattan cocktails. She was a rebel who wanted to be even more wicked than I. We visited nightclubs which didn't open their doors until 11 p.m. There we'd dance the Charleston and the foxtrot, the waltz and the tango. The vogue at the time was for drop-waisted pleated dresses, flapper-style with the hem just above the knee, which were very flattering. I almost always wore a hat.

The years between 1929 and 1939 were, for me, a heady decade of socializing and playing tennis across Europe. I divided my time between Vienna, Belgrade and Budapest, largely living at other people's expense. It was a different era, a time of calling cards and printed invitations. If one was a good enough player, one would be invited to compete in leagues all over Europe and others would pay all the travelling and hotel expenses. There were no professionals then, everyone was an amateur and the prize was generally little more than a token silver cup. I won several. Mostly I travelled alone, but I often met up with another friend, Lily Sarkene, for doubles. I stayed with her mother in Budapest and remained friends with Lily right up until her marriage in the late 1930s.

I embarked on several affairs with wholly unsuitable men, which usually ended with me broken-hearted. To my great dismay, none of the men I fell in love with ever asked me to marry them – probably because I went to bed with them. I would have accepted a proposal just for the financial security and independence marriage would have given me. Perhaps sensing my inner desperation, they were all very careful not to get me pregnant, for fear that I might then have a more substantial claim.

I developed a penchant for champagne and Turkish cigarettes (smoked through a holder) and evaded all my parents' attempts at a midnight curfew by claiming that their old car was unreliable and kept breaking down. They strongly disapproved of my lifestyle and did all they could to dissuade me from my chosen path. Father, particularly, tried to rein me in, telling me gravely that I was in danger of becoming '*une fille facile*', but I was as wilful in my late teens as I had been compliant in my earlier years, and I'd laugh off all his protestations. Exasperated, they resolved to send me away from Cannes, hoping that in a less heady environment I might see sense and settle down. I think they were glad to get rid of me. They dispatched me to stay with my aunt Hilda, who became a welcome companion in what had been quite a lonely existence.

In London, we were wined and dined by her many high-ranking friends and had some wonderful evenings out. Aunt Hilda lived in some style in a well-appointed apartment in Kensington. She loved music; she played the violin in a local orchestra. She was also a talented water-colourist. It was she who took me to see an operetta called *Bitter Sweet* by a young playwright called Noel Coward, a spectacle of melody and colour which changed my life. The story centred around a woman called Dolly Chamberlain whose love life was as complicated as my own. The drama of her elopement from high society with a musician was set amid swirling Viennese balls. I cheered Dolly's liberation, applauded her courage and wept at her despair. My aunt loved the play too and for the first time I began to realize what a free spirit she was.

'Why did you never marry, Aunt Hilda?' I asked her once, recalling some distant tale of a young suitor who was killed on the Somme in the First World War.

'I lost the man I wanted to spend the rest of my life with and I never found another,' she sighed. Then, with a glint in her eye, she added: 'But I'm still looking.'

After a brief and happy spell with Hilda in London, I decided that it was time for me to move on. Not back to Cannes, where I knew my parents would try to stifle my growing taste for adventure, but to Austria, where my aunt knew people.

'I've had a letter back from my friends in Vienna,' she announced cheerfully one morning over breakfast. 'They'd be happy to have you. I know you're keen to learn German. Lord knows, we might all be speaking it soon.'

Adolf Hitler was the new Chancellor of the German Reich and promised a mighty German empire. What with Mussolini and the Blackshirts becoming increasingly active in Italy, she feared that Europe was a slightly worrying place to send me back to.

Waving me off on the boat-train at Waterloo station, she seemed emotional at having to say goodbye. 'Adieu, my little one, adieu,' she said, tears in her eyes, as I hugged her and thanked her for her many kindnesses. A few days earlier, she'd told me that she had generously arranged to give me a monthly allowance which would effectively free me from my parents and allow me to do exactly as I pleased. Smiling at her through the clouds of steam billowing up from under the carriages, I blew her a kiss with my gloved right hand as the train pulled out of the station.

My parents, reading my letters from all over Europe, soon abandoned any hopes that I might lead a conventional life. Laurence was also out of their control, living in Vienna and working as a concert pianist, although we rarely saw each other when I was in Austria. (He remained single all his life and never had a girlfriend to my knowledge, although I suspect he may well have had boyfriends.) In the end, my parents took the view with both of us that what they didn't know couldn't hurt them. They were growing older and getting tired of the expatriate lifestyle. When my grandmother died (aged eighty, in bed in Torquay, still barking instructions to a nurse) and the pound nose-dived, making it a far less attractive prospect to live in France, they left Cannes and moved to Seal, near Sevenoaks in Kent, while Laurence and I stayed on in Europe.

Every winter I dutifully returned home to Kent for another dreary Christmas with my parents. It was a chance for me to sleep and read and catch up on their news, what little there was of it. Our relationship had improved slightly – at least they treated me as an adult now – and they seemed to have mellowed into a companionable sort of marriage in their later years. Laurence had moved back to London by then and was working as a divorce barrister. I saw him only if his annual visit to our parents happened to coincide with mine.

Then I would be off on my rounds again – to Hausbrück in the high Tyrol in March sunshine for six weeks of the most exquisite skiing, Budapest in the spring to play tennis, a few weeks perhaps in St Moritz, then on to Vienna to see my friends at the tennis club and find out where all the other tournaments were to be held that year. I travelled mostly by train, but I did fly once between Belgrade and Budapest, just to see what flying was like. It was an Air France flight and I was the only passenger so the service was exclusive. I enjoyed the flight and regarded it as a convenient way of getting somewhere. The air turbulence meant that it was a little rough, but I suspected that, despite the discomfort, flying was a fad which would catch on.

Flitting between the chateaux, country houses and smart hotels of chic European resorts, I suppose I must have acquired something of a reputation. Had I been a man, I would have been fêted as an urbane and sophisticated house guest, a well-travelled aristocrat with a penchant for good living. Being a woman, I was probably regarded

51

somewhat suspiciously as an embarrassment to my family and, with my disregard for propriety and social standing, a dangerous bohemian. Apart from my aunt Hilda, who, I believe, secretly admired my unconventionality, the others who befriended me were mainly rich divorced women who cared not a fig what other people thought.

It was the era of Mae West, Virginia Woolf, Amelia Earhart, Greta Garbo, Marlene Dietrich and Isadora Duncan. Women were freeing themselves from the shackles of the previous century, nowhere more so than in France, the birthplace of haute couture, where bold new fashions such as backless frocks and slimline, shorter dresses were all the rage. Wearing men's clothes was even in vogue for a while and, impervious to public opinion, I was among many young women who defied the European law against attracting 'undue attention by walking the streets in male attire'.

Pampered and protected from the real world, I nevertheless found little truly to excite and stimulate me among the shallow men of my own class. They promised the earth but delivered nothing. Each one I hoped would be the special person, the man I'd end up marrying and loving for ever. Like my aunt Hilda, I was 'still looking'. I began to realize, with some bitterness, that I'd never known how it felt to be loved purely for myself. Ever since Hannibal had conquered me in Rome, I'd been unable to say no to a man for fear of his rejection (even though I almost always ended up being rejected anyway).

To my own annoyance, I would frequently fall head over heels in love and hope each time that things would be different. But once the initial heady days of an affair passed, we'd part, generally with great sadness for me, and I would be alone once more, vowing never to succumb so easily again. But of course I always did.

My only solution was to seek grander, bolder men with whom I could have greater adventures and who would never grow bored with me. An officer, perhaps, or a nobleman with a taste for travel? I'd know him when I met him,

I reasoned, but until I did, I'd just have to keep on looking.

By the summer of 1939, change was in the air. Reservists were called up all over Europe, the railways were requisitioned and we knew that war was likely. There was a frisson of excitement, a sense that 'something new' might come along and stir things up a bit. Few of us truly believed that, after the wholesale slaughter of the last war, a new conflict would amount to anything more than a brief burst of hostilities, or that it would directly affect us. How little we knew.

I was staying with a good friend, a wealthy American divorcee called Gladys Ashe, in her chateau, Beaudiment, at Châtellerault, near Poitiers in western France. I'd first met Gladys many years earlier in Cannes through my parents. They wanted a bull terrier and Gladys bred the feisty little dogs. She also kept huge glasshouses in which she grew all manner of exotic flowers. Gladys took an instant shine to my parents and then to me and we'd remained friends ever since. She'd been married three times – always for her money – and was currently divorcing her last husband. Her maiden name was Crocker and she had that very dry sense of humour that many Americans have. She was considerably older than me but seemed to enjoy my company, often inviting me to join her in her various homes or hotel suites. Her mother lived in some splendour in Paris and her red-haired son Gerald, who was the same age as me, stayed with us often.

I spent all of that last summer of peace with Gladys at Beaudiment. Her home was a small turreted chateau, moated and rather pretty. Most of the time it was closed up, but when Gladys and I arrived with a few friends that July, it became the hub of social activity in the area, with tennis and hunting parties in the day, glittering dinner parties and balls at night, and friends dropping in unexpectedly from all over Europe. I liked chateau life; it suited me very well.

The approaching war was all anyone seemed able to

talk about. My friends in Vienna and Budapest insisted that I didn't come that year; in their telegrams and letters they all seemed very fearful, especially those who were of Jewish extraction, so I reluctantly cancelled my plans and remained in France instead. Friends there assured me that it would all be over almost as soon as it began, and that in any event none of it would have any bearing on us in Poitiers. I had no reason to doubt them.

In her languid American drawl, Gladys told me: 'Now, honey, if I'm staying put then you can bet your bottom dollar that it'll be safe here, even if I seem to be just about the only American left in France since Prohibition was lifted.' She had incorrectly assumed that I might be fearful. I wasn't. If anything, I was excited.

I idled away much of that late summer by having an affair with Gladys's son Gerald, who was kind and sweet. When he eventually returned to Paris, bored with me, Gladys and I were left alone to play cards, go riding or amuse ourselves. She taught me to play baccarat and I taught her to shoot a rifle. Despite the shadow of war, life went on much as it always had. Then, three weeks before my thirtieth birthday, on 1 September, Germany and Russia invaded Poland. Over the next two days, despite the most intense diplomatic activity, Hitler refused to respond to an ultimatum from Britain and France to withdraw.

In the early evening of Sunday, 3 September 1939, I was resting on my bed when there was a gentle tap at the door. Gladys entered in a state of great agitation.

'I've just heard the news on the wireless, my dear,' she said, sitting by me in a cloud of perfume and cigarette smoke. She peered anxiously into my eyes. 'It's started, Susan. We're at war.'

5

LADY IN WAITING

'Thousands at his bidding speed
And post o'er land and ocean without rest:
They also serve who only stand and wait.'
JOHN MILTON, SONNET 16,
'WHEN I CONSIDER HOW MY LIGHT IS SPENT'

Cocooned from the rest of the world, glued to the wireless and drinking Manhattans, Gladys and I listened intently to the news broadcasts that Sunday evening as the French Prime Minister, Edouard Daladier, reluctantly declared war. In London a few hours earlier, the British Prime Minister, Neville Chamberlain, had driven to the House of Commons to make a solemn announcement. 'This country is now at war with Germany. We are ready.' The two governments had then issued a joint declaration stating that it was not their intention to use poison gas or germ warfare.

In the initial weeks of the conflict, Gladys and I stayed in her chateau, waiting for news and experiencing little of what it meant to be at war. Soap and decent cigarettes were in short supply, we had to keep the curtains closed at night under the strict blackout rules, and our headlamps now had special slatted fittings. But the wine still flowed (although it already fetched a frightful price on the flourishing black market), the usual guests arrived each evening in their diamonds and furs, and dinner was always served, even if it now tended to be game birds shot on the estate rather than the finest cuts from the *boucher*.

My parents wrote to me from Kent about life under the myriad new rules and regulations – the mass evacuation of children from the towns, the introduction of food rationing, coupons, digging for victory; the various inducements to buy war bonds, not to travel, to waste nothing and to stifle rumour and gossip. Stumbling around the blacked-out streets of their cities, towns and villages, the British appeared to be far more alert to the consequences of war than the French.

Father had, of course, signed up immediately with the local Home Guard (having been rejected for military service on the grounds that at nearly seventy-five he was too old). He was in his element organizing all the local defence volunteers. Mother – who'd been to London to visit Aunt Hilda – said the streets were crammed with military vehicles and the skies over the towns, ports and docks were crowded with barrage balloons designed to deter aerial bombardment. Her spare time was spent helping to make bandages and organizing food and clothing parcels for the men at the front.

Neither of my parents seemed unduly worried about me staying on in France. 'Do keep in touch, dear,' their letter instructed, but I felt sure that it was more out of a sense of duty than love. I was my own worst enemy when it came to my family. I'd become completely independent of them, and they were so accustomed to my wilful ways that they knew there was nothing they could do once my mind was made up.

It had been eighteen years since I'd lived in England; more than half of my life had been spent in France. I suppose I felt more French than anything, although my accent and upbringing still marked me as English. Fearing a loss of independence if I returned to my parents' home, I decided to stay in the country where I felt most at home, although I had little idea what I could usefully do.

Social life was at an end – men had been mobilized, the chateau staff were deserting to sign up and few of my young friends were left. Making enquiries, I quickly discovered that the most acceptable thing for a well-bred young woman to do was to sign up with the Croix Rouge, the French Red Cross. All the young girls from the right families were doing just that.

'The uniforms are so becoming,' one girlfriend told me excitedly, her eyes bright. 'And think of all those grateful young men.'

Although I would have much preferred to be doing something of value on the front lines – I could drive a car and shoot a rifle after all – I knew that, as an upper-class woman with few skills and no military training, my choices would be limited. Still, I didn't have to be a nurse, I reasoned; I could drive an ambulance. I went to the Red Cross station immediately and volunteered. To my dismay, I discovered that even to qualify as an ambulance driver I needed a nursing diploma first.

'You might well have to give emergency medical attention to wounded soldiers,' an imperious woman clerk told me at the local *hôtel de ville* when I tried to protest. 'You'd hardly be any good to us if all you could do was drive.'

Under her beady eye, I reluctantly signed up for a three-month nursing course, the sole Englishwoman amongst thirty volunteers.

A medieval hilltop town overlooking two rivers, Poitiers rested in a huge plain of wheatland and sunflower fields. Within its narrow network of lanes, I found lodgings with an Englishwoman married to a French army officer. She had been left alone to bring up their children and manage on the money he sent. I paid for my bed and board and it suited us both very well. Unpacking my case, I stopped to re-examine my newly acquired nurse's uniform, which consisted of a starched white overall, an apron and a cap. It was, indeed, extremely becoming. Hanging it up in the small oak wardrobe in my room, however, I still wondered at the wisdom of my choice.

I began my nursing course with the greatest unwillingness, learning the basic principles of health and hygiene in the austere conditions of the gloomy Poitiers hospital. The wards smelled of disinfectant and carbolic soap and my tasks were menial and humiliating. My hands, unused to manual labour of any kind, were soon raw and my perfectly manicured nails split and ridged. After a month of scrubbing floors, washing sheets and dressing minor wounds, I was finally instructed to put all I'd learned into practice, spending fifteen days on a ward with the seriously ill, and fifteen days nursing those who were not so ill.

The nursing course dragged on and on and what I minded most was having to undertake so many tedious tasks just so that I could drive an ambulance one day. It seemed a ludicrous waste of time and money to me, especially as I was completely hopeless as a nurse and already an experienced driver. I had no patience what-soever with those I had to help and resented having to look after them. I was also poor in practical matters. As part of my training, I once had to administer anaesthetic to a man who was having a hernia operation. The surgeons operated on everybody they could lay their hands on. They adored operating; they were miserable if they couldn't and I even knew of one surgeon who operated needlessly on a dog just to keep his hand in. War mania was affecting everybody.

During the hernia operation, I was in charge of the mixture of chloroform and ether which was administered by a mask connected to a contraption I had to push down to increase the dosage. Matron, as formidable as the one who had terrorized my boarding-school days at Wantage, told me firmly: 'Travers, for goodness' sake be careful. Don't administer too much or you'll kill the poor patient. *Faîtes attention!*'

Afraid of ending up with a corpse on my conscience, I

hardly pushed down on the contraption at all. Needless to say, the hapless fellow woke up in the middle of the operation, clutching at his mask and gasping horribly. Quite taken aback, I stepped away from him and the machine, instinctively wanting to run from the operating theatre.

Fortunately for the man now flailing his hands in the air and trying to get up, the surgeon acted immediately. Reaching across the operating table, his eyes narrowing with fury at me above his green theatre mask, he plunged the anaesthetic contraption down with his bloodied right hand and the patient slumped back, oblivious once more. Matron thereafter made her views widely known. She called me 'un danger publique'.

I was certainly no Florence Nightingale, but despite my ghastly mistake I surprised myself and everyone else by gaining my diploma. They must have been desperate.

February 1940 was bitter, one of the coldest winters on record, and the war was gaining in intensity. A cruise liner with 152 people on board was sunk by a mine off the south-east coast of England as Hitler declared that all shipping was fair game for his U-boats. The British, after calling up two million men aged nineteen to twenty-seven, had landed 158,000 of them in France to help bolster the French defences against a possible German invasion. Australia had pledged aeroplanes and 3,000 airmen. In Finland, the gallant little military force, fighting in sub-zero temperatures, were frustrating the Red Army at every turn and humiliating them into a stand-off. Only when faced with overwhelming numbers and arms did the Finns begin to fall back. By February they were appealing to the world for help as they made their last stand.

Newly qualified and desperate for some action, I saw this as a golden opportunity to get to the front lines. I immediately contacted the Croix Rouge ambulance service to volunteer my services as a new driver.

'You and a hundred others,' came the disappointing

reply. 'We've got enough volunteer drivers to outnumber the entire Finnish army!'

My name was taken, along with my details, but the man to whom I spoke held out little hope for me. Many of the rather grand ladies of Paris had, it appeared, offered their services as nurses and drivers – volunteering had become the fashionable thing to do. But when the time came and they were called to action, the majority suddenly found that they were otherwise engaged. Leave Paris? Abandon their husbands, lovers, children and friends, and travel thousands of miles to a place where temperatures were brutally cold? The prospect held minimal appeal. Those of us with genuine intent were eventually given our chance, although sadly for me it was my nursing skills they wanted, not my driving capabilities.

And so, on 3 March 1940, I set off for Finland from Paris with a French expeditionary force which included six ambulances, several drivers and six nurses. It was part of what was called Operation Petsamo, under the Croix Rouge France/Finland Alliance to assist in the war against the Russians. An armed French force had been sent eight weeks earlier. We travelled to Amsterdam by train, stayed overnight and then continued by air to Copenhagen and Stockholm (avoiding German air space). I was thirty years old, in a uniform of sorts and heading for the front line at a time when most were fleeing from it. I had to pinch myself to believe that this was really happening. I'd shrugged off the social-butterfly life I'd come to resent and was setting out into the unknown. Perhaps I would finally achieve something worthy of the Travers motto.

But my dreams of high adventure in a faraway land were soon scuppered. As we landed in Stockholm, news came that the vicious fourteen-week Winter War was over. On 13 March, under the sheer weight of enemy numbers, the Finns had been forced to capitulate, surrendering much of their territory. An estimated one million Russian soldiers had died, along with thousands of Finns. Half a million people were evacuated from the Karelian isthmus, the scene of the worst fighting.

The Swedes had no idea what to do with us. There was a lengthy hiatus as negotiations took place over the future of our enthusiastic little band of volunteers. I couldn't contain my frustration at not being where the action was. I'd come to Scandinavia for drama, not a holiday. Until a decision was made, we had no choice but to remain in Stockholm. Set on some twenty islands and peninsulas beside the Baltic Sea, the Swedish capital with its medieval streets and seventeenth-century burghers' houses was very beautiful, but I found it all rather dull – not least because of the strange tradition that you couldn't take a sip of your drink at parties unless someone caught your eye and toasted you. I nearly died of thirst.

I stayed with a very kind family called the Lindfors. The father was the mayor of Stockholm and his pretty daughter Margo was fascinated by us nurses in our uniforms, declaring with great passion that she would come with us to Finland to tend the wounded. 'I *must* do something to help,' she insisted, her blue eyes bright. Her father's expression led me to believe he'd never allow it. In an attempt to liven things up a bit for her while we were there, I took her out onto the hard-packed ice in an ambulance as I tried to teach myself how to get out of a skid. It was absolutely terrifying in such a heavy, unwieldy vehicle and her shrieks of fear and delight nearly deafened me as we veered right and left without any control whatsoever.

The Scandinavian authorities eventually arranged for us to go to Finland after all. Poor Margo was terribly upset when her father refused her permission to join us. She bid me farewell in tears, reminding me of myself as a young teenager, desperate to break away from my parents. Squeezing her hand, I told her: 'Don't worry, someone or something will come along one day and set you free.' Boarding a fishing vessel, we set off for the principal Finnish seaport of Abo in bitterly cold conditions. Our little boat got stuck in the pack ice a few miles off the coast and an icebreaker had to come and cut a way through for us. We were the first ship through the ice floes of the Baltic Sea that spring, arriving on 3 April.

Abo, Finland's third largest city, on the Gulf of Bothnia to the west of Helsinki, had been its capital until it was destroyed by fire in 1827. We stayed within its frozen heart for a few days before being billeted to a hospital in Helsinki, where we lived in a spartan dormitory, awaiting further instruction. Helsinki felt bleak and bitterly cold and there was little to amuse us. It was also one of the noisiest cities I've ever known, with seagulls whirling and screaming overhead all day as the fishing boats came in, and trams clattering across cobbled streets. At night it was worse as we tried to sleep through the incredible snoring of our head nurse, a woman called Docpress. 'You just have to get off to sleep before she starts,' a fellow nurse warned me, 'or else it's hopeless.' I found a good slug of cognac did the trick.

Six days later, on 9 April, just a few hundred miles from where we waited, the Germans invaded Denmark and Norway so that they could sweep down on British shipping in the North Atlantic. The 'phoney war' was well and truly over. The Norwegian waters were mined and all communications with England were cut. There was news of several big naval battles, and at Narvik the French Foreign Legion forces, along with the British, sank ten German destroyers and pushed the Germans back into the snow-covered mountains. Bored and frustrated once again, I was stranded in the land of the midnight sun as storm clouds rolled across Europe.

Dispatched to a small town called Norrmark, we set up a makeshift hospital and cared for convalescing Finnish soldiers. Many of them had had frostbite and had lost fingers and toes; others were suffering from exposure and a few had been shot or hit by shrapnel. The men spoke perfect English and told grisly tales of fighting the

Russians in bitterly cold temperatures and of comrades freezing to death. I could barely imagine the horrors they'd witnessed.

On 10 May 1940 the war took a dramatic turn. Germany invaded Holland and Belgium 'to protect their neutrality' against any British attack. France was now in the gravest danger and our priorities had altered. If the Germans could invade Holland and Belgium so easily, what was to stop them driving on to Paris? The great port of Rotterdam had been pulverized in an aerial bombardment, killing eight hundred people, and there was widespread bombing of airfields, communications and military strong points. In England, a discredited Neville Chamberlain resigned and Winston Churchill became the new Prime Minister, offering 'blood, toil, tears and sweat'.

Anxious to get back to France, we were obliged to wait through several more weeks of negotiations and false starts before we finally found a passage home. The Finnish soldiers held a party in our honour and presented us each with a little book of poems. Their farewell was quite emotional; some of the wounded were in tears and they sang the Marseillaise as we departed, their deep voices resonating across the lobby of the hospital that had been our home.

I knew that I had to get back to the front as soon as possible. Italy had joined Germany and declared war against the Allies. A week later, the French government, under the new Prime Minister, Paul Reynaud, capitulated (having provided his new under-secretary of state for war, a young brigadier-general called Charles de Gaulle, with documents and funds to flee to England in the hopes of starting up an Anglo-French alliance). On Reynaud's resignation, Marshal Philippe Pétain, the aged Commander-in-Chief of the French Army and hero of the First World War, was invited by the Germans to form a government in the spa town of Vichy. Many of the French supported the new government at first. They believed it was madness to try to fight the Germans and would rather have allied themselves with them than with their old enemy, Britain. The first seeds of what was to become a civil war were sown.

My fellow nurses and I listened on a crackling wireless to the emotional and powerful broadcast by General de Gaulle, who'd gained the backing of Mr Churchill. In defiance of the new Vichy government, he invited all French soldiers, technicians, engineers and any others who wanted to help in the fight for France, to join with him and his 'Free French' against the Germans and the Vichy French. 'France is not alone. She has behind her a vast empire. She can join with the British Empire which rules the seas and is continuing the struggle. Like England, she can draw . . . on the immense might of the United States. This war is not limited to the unhappy territory of our dear country. The outcome of this war has not been settled by the Battle of France. This is a world war,' he declared. 'Whatever happens, the flame of the French resistance must not go out and it will not go out.' They were stirring words.

I'd spent most of my adult life in France and now that my adoptive country was in enemy hands I felt as affronted as any French citizen. A German swastika fluttered from the Eiffel Tower, Nazi troops were marching in the Champs-Elysées, and I was still stranded in Scandinavia.

The long journey home was through a calm, quiet sea, jade and silvery grey. We travelled so far north that we entered the ice field and the ship had to alter course, into a minefield. Not only was there the constant danger of hitting a mine or being torpedoed by the Germans, but the weather became so atrocious that the ship rolled alarmingly at night and set off the air-raid sirens by mistake, which was most perturbing. We all rushed onto the deck in our night attire to muster to the lifeboats, our Mae West lifejackets the only buffer against the icy winds, and stood there fearfully dreading a descent into the chilly depths below. We docked at the huge shipbuilding port of Greenock on the Clyde on 6 July 1940.

I arrived exhausted on my aunt's doorstep in Abingdon Court, Kensington, in my crumpled nurse's uniform and carrying a small suitcase.

'Hello, Auntie,' I said wearily, as she opened the door. 'Any chance of a bath and a gin?'

Her mouth dropped open. She threw her arms around me and ushered me inside, eager to hear all about my adventures and to find out what on earth I planned to do next.

London was the last place I wanted to be. I was more determined than ever to find my path to battle, hoping very much to get to France, but my hopes were dashed when my aunt brought me up to date on the war news. The British Expeditionary Force, along with French and Belgian troops, had been driven back to Dunkirk. Bombarded daily, facing total annihilation, they had been evacuated by an extraordinary flotilla of fishing vessels, river cruisers, ferries and pleasure boats. I thought of the beaches of the west coast where I'd played as a child, and I wondered at the madness of the world we now lived in. Day by day the news worsened. With Scandinavia, Holland, Belgium and France now in enemy hands and the Russians and Italians allied with Hitler, Britain was left to fight on alone. It seemed only a matter of time before the German invasion of the British Isles would begin.

The impending threat spurred me on. I contacted everyone I knew in London to see if they could pull any strings for me, but no-one was remotely interested in the personal ambitions of a thin little rich girl. Then my dear cousin Diana told me that General de Gaulle had set up his headquarters in former government offices in Carlton Gardens, St James's, central London, and that the Free French were desperate for volunteer nurses, drivers and soldiers. They hoped to take their campaign to French Africa and elsewhere to enlist support.

'Why not go up there and see if they'll take you,' she

suggested. 'It could be just the opportunity you're looking for.' I only had time to give her a thank-you kiss on the cheek before jumping on the next double-decker bus to Pall Mall.

Walking up the steps to the grand building, I felt optimistic that I might at last be able to serve. Inside, there were people everywhere, secretaries rushing across the polished linoleum floor holding great sheaves of documents, soldiers in greatcoats, women in feathered hats. Military police manned the doors, refusing to take any chances after de Gaulle had been convicted of treason and sentenced to death *in absentia* by the Vichy government.

When I asked someone where I should go, I was pointed in the direction of a Miss Ford, a woman I'd known vaguely in Paris who was now organizing the nursing services. There followed what must have been the fastest job interview in the world.

'Yes, Miss Travers,' she said briskly, 'General de Gaulle has been given the use of twenty ambulances and we need nurses, so you can be of some assistance. You'll need a full medical and you'll have to equip yourself with a uniform and belongings suitable for the tropics. Here are some forms to fill in and a list of the inoculations you'll require. If you pass the medical, you will be taken on at the rank of sergeant on two-thirds of a regular sergeant's pay. Report to headquarters on 30 August.'

Having filled in the forms and passed the necessary tests, I had two weeks to kill, so I took a train to Folkestone to see my parents. War hadn't altered my family at all. I might just as well have returned from a local tennis tournament as a voyage to the Arctic Circle and back. Mother seemed ever more distant, and I didn't get on very well at all with her during that visit, which was to be my last trip back to England for five years. She certainly wasn't interested in my adventures in Scandinavia, wanting to know only if my aunt Hilda was well when I last saw her.

Laurence was a different matter entirely. Mother told

me proudly that he'd secured himself a desk job in London working for British Intelligence. 'He can't tell us what he does, of course,' she whispered conspiratorially. 'It's all to do with national security.'

Father took a different view. He called Laurence 'little more than a secretary', and considered his decision not to go to the front lines as 'only one step up from being a conscientious objector'. Father had, of course, been promoted to senior officer of the local Home Guard and was taking his position most seriously. He paraded proudly in front of me in his khaki uniform and regaled me with tales of how he was introducing military discipline to the local volunteers so that they could repel all invaders and guard key installations. They'd crafted makeshift weapons from farming implements, kitchen knives and gardening tools. They had a few old Lee Enfield rifles between them and Father still had his pistol from the Great War. 'No Hun's going to get through my defences,' he boasted. 'I've made sure of that.' I'd never seen him so animated.

In the small back garden of their house, Father and I watched the dogfights of the early days of the Battle of Britain in the skies over the harbour. I had a feeling of detached fascination as the little planes wheeled and circled overhead. An estimated one thousand German planes were sent daily to Britain in the next few weeks and some seven hundred Luftwaffe aircraft were downed. Churchill paid legendary tribute to the RAF in a speech to Parliament. 'Never in the field of human conflict was so much owed by so many to so few,' he declared. Not surprisingly, there were numerous air raids when I was there and the Travers family had to retreat to a tiny corrugated-metal Anderson shelter in the garden, dogs and all.

I returned to London by train during the first massive aerial bombardment of the city. Buildings were ablaze, men, women and children were running everywhere and the air was full of the smell of woodsmoke and burning rubber. The streets were filled with rubble, every window was covered in tape, hundreds of people were made homeless and most spent the nights in the Underground stations and tunnels, waiting for the bombing to stop. Yet somehow life went on. The red double-decker buses wove their way through the mayhem, picking up passengers eager to get to work, and milkmen still delivered milk and postmen the mail. Taxis waited patiently at their ranks, even during air raids.

Having visited the Army and Navy store in Victoria to purchase a canvas bath, a folding bed and suitable clothes for the tropics, I reported to headquarters and checked in my few pieces of luggage. I boarded a bus for Euston then a train to Liverpool. Watching the suburbs of the city speed by my window that late August evening, the little houses all cheek by jowl, their gardens full of flowers, I marvelled at the indomitable British spirit and wondered if I possessed it too.

Despite my cut-crystal accent – picked up at home and at boarding school – I'd never felt terribly English. After nearly twenty years abroad, I was rootless. As a child at school in Cannes I had learned of the epic adventures of the French Foreign Legion, in Mexico and elsewhere. The legion motto, I remembered, was *Legio Patria Nostra*. The Legion is Our Country. As an itinerant teenager, unsure if I was French or English, that motto had resonated deep within me.

Catching sight of my own reflection in the glass, I saw a slim young woman with cropped brown hair and piercing blue eyes wearing a simple black felt hat and a plain grey jacket. Gone were the trappings of my former life, the fancy hats, fine silks and chic Parisian suits, all left behind in a Europe that no longer existed, with friends I might never see again. My new attire was, I realized with a strange sense of satisfaction, far more appropriate to the person I really was, and perhaps had always been.

6

AFRICAN DREAM

'Round the cape of a sudden came the sea,
And the sun looked over the mountain's rim,
And straight was a path of gold for him
And the need of a world of men for me.'
ROBERT BROWNING, 'PARTING AT MORNING'

I shall never forget that moonless summer's night, pulling out of the massive Liverpool docks, the ship's lights extinguished as the German planes swept in overhead to rake us with gunfire. We were confined to quarters below decks and a blackout was enforced for safety. I'd been billeted on an unarmed Dutch liner called the SS *Westernland*, the sister ship to the SS *Pennland* on which nearly a thousand men of the newly raised 13th Demi-Brigade (DBLE) of the French Foreign Legion, the Légion Etrangère, were stationed. These were the men with whom I was to become inextricably linked.

Our ship flew the Cross of Lorraine (the adopted emblem of the Free French) along with the tricolour and the Dutch flag. General de Gaulle was on board, together with his advisers, chiefs of staff and several British liaison officers under Major General Sir Edward Spears, Churchill's personal representative. Ahead and behind us was a fleet of nearly thirty ships including three French sloops, two armed trawlers and four French cargo boats, and carrying the pilots of two air squadrons.

The British contingent, which was intended to escort us safely to Africa and then turn away, included two battleships, the *Barham* and the *Resolution*; four cruisers; the brand new aircraft carrier *Ark Royal*; some destroyers and a tanker, all under the command of Admiral Sir John Cunningham. The combined forces totalled more than fifteen hundred men. We had Winston Churchill's blessing and the protection of the Royal Air Force on our mission to persuade those under the control of the Vichy French to join us.

We all shared a tremendous sense of responsibility. As we set sail on what de Gaulle called our '*beaux voyages*' on 31 August 1940, we were leaving an island nation virtually under siege and carrying the fortunes of France with us to distant lands. The day we left we heard that the French colonies of Chad, the Cameroons, Equatorial Africa and Tahiti had declared for our side. Good news indeed.

I was one of ten nurses, six of whom were English, the remainder either Belgian or French; all of us under the close supervision of Miss Ford, who insisted: 'Tunics and hats must be worn at *all* times. You will dine in a separate dining room to the rest of the ship's company and you are strictly forbidden to fraternize with any of the men.' None of us expected that last rule to be adhered to for more than a day or two.

The three nurses I became most friendly with were May Kelsey, the English head nurse, Nadine Cane, a pretty young French girl, and her Belgian friend Simone. I shared a cabin with Rosie Curtis and Elizabeth Burchall. Kelsey ruled the roost: she was a most impressive woman, thin and dark, with a dominant personality but a soft centre when you got to know her. Nadine was pretty and plump, an attractive blonde. Simone was a big woman, older than me, and with large features.

The motley armed force which accompanied us, assembled by de Gaulle, included British troops convalescing after Dunkirk, French servicemen abroad and others, including disaffected Germans, who had volunteered for service rather than spend their war in English prisoner-of-war camps. There were also some Royal Navy officers and two battalions of the 13DBLE of the Foreign Legion. We had no clear idea of our destination, although we'd all been told to prepare for the tropics and we suspected we were heading for the French colonies of West Africa. As the sun set on the starboard side of the ship day after day, our suspicions were confirmed.

The journey was to take several weeks, as we had to make a wide detour to avoid German U-boats and aircraft, and to keep pace with some of the smaller cargo boats travelling with us. On the second day we were allowed up onto the deck for the first time. The sea was literally covered with ships, three abreast with destroyers sweeping round them.

We were lined up on deck by our ship's commander, the kindly Dutch Captain Lagaay, and formally introduced to General de Gaulle. He moved along the line towards me, shaking hands, towering over us all, formidable in manner as well as appearance. With his huge beak of a nose, he was every inch a general.

'*Bonjour, merci de votre assistance*,' he repeated flatly, greeting us with a stiff but courteous smile. His handshake was firm, his gaze steely. De Gaulle's dislike for the British was well known. He needed nurses, he didn't care what nationality they were and he didn't go out of his way to be friendly. One of his aides, however, did.

His name was Tony Drake, a young lieutenant working as a liaison officer with the Spears Military Mission. He was rather dark and came from Jersey in the Channel Islands. At least four years younger than me, he had the same kind of background as I did. Fastidiously dressed, he had a quick smile and kind eyes. I can't even remember how our affair began, I only know that it was he who made the first move, and on the very first day of the

71

voyage. My policy with men had always been to watch and wait, to speak only when I had something interesting to say and not to make myself the centre of attention. I let my eyes do the talking. They were very blue when I was young and quite my best feature. I found I could say a great deal without even opening my mouth. Only after the initial contact had been made, the first signal received, would I respond in kind. Men liked that, and Tony certainly seemed to. He said I was the most serious-looking woman he'd ever met, although he called me his 'will-o'-the-wisp'.

Our relationship was as passionate as it could be, given that we both had to share our cabins. It consisted of snatched moments here and there, stolen kisses, embraces and meaningful glances. We were unable to realize our passion fully until we reached dry land. Nevertheless, for a few happy weeks we both forgot that we were in the middle of a war, with the possibility of being attacked by the enemy at any minute. It is difficult to explain to people today but those extraordinary times made us seize every opportunity for happiness. All that we had known, all that was safe and secure, was gone. We were free to live for the moment.

It was Tony who first told me of our secret objective. 'We're heading for the naval base of Dakar on the Cape Verde peninsula of Senegal, held by militant forces of the Vichy French,' he said. 'It's strategically positioned within easy striking distance of the Atlantic shipping lanes and the Germans will do everything in their power to keep it in the control of their new allies.' He squeezed my hand reassuringly. 'Don't be afraid, Susan,' he told me. 'I'll look after you.'

But he'd misread my expression. Far from being alarmed, I was thrilled at the prospect: West Africa and an epic confrontation in the Senegalese capital certainly fulfilled all my criteria for adventure.

Having stopped at the British naval base of Freetown in Sierra Leone for a week, the convoy left for Dakar on

21 September. Two days later, at dawn and in the middle of an impenetrable fog, we found ourselves at anchor a quarter of a mile away from our target.

The events of the next three days are the stuff of history. Told to be ready to disembark at all times but ordered below with my fellow nurses for our own safety, I peered out of the portholes into the swirling mists. We could see nothing. All we could hear were the eerie blasts of the foghorns echoing across the bay. Tony had told me that Churchill's original brief had been that, on seeing the Franco-Allied fleet on the horizon, the uncertain Frenchmen of Dakar would capitulate and allow us entry, for fear of being crushed. The reality was that our sorry little flotilla – much smaller than had been envisaged – was completely invisible to the garrison because of the fog. The Vichy forces had been bolstered by the recent arrival of reinforcements. These men were still smarting from the loss of their navy at the hands of the English at Mers-el-Kébir and the close proximity of the *Ark Royal* and the *Resolution* only fuelled their anger.

Determined to press on with the plan, that evening de Gaulle broadcast a rallying call to the French-speaking people of Dakar from the bridge of the *Westernland*, as British and French planes swooped in overhead to drop propaganda leaflets. He then sent a delegation of three officers in two small unarmed planes. We waited for news, but none came. Ack-ack fire echoed across the bay as the guns of the Vichy-held battleship *Richelieu* and the cannons of the fortress gave us their answer. It later transpired that the aircraft had been seized on landing and the men arrested.

Undaunted, de Gaulle ordered that our ship and the *Pennland*, along with the Free French sloops, move closer to the port, approaching in the mist. A second delegation of five officers was dispatched, this time by motor launch, bearing the white flag of truce, with instructions to deliver a personal letter from de Gaulle to the new Governor-General of Dakar, a man called Boisson. But Boisson –

73

who'd been appointed by the Vichy French and given clear instructions not to capitulate – had no intention of rallying to the Free French cause and he made his feelings clear. On landing, the five officers were threatened with arrest for treason against the Vichy government, a crime punishable by death. Fired upon by machine-guns, they fled.

Two of the officers, Commander d'Argenlieu and Captain Perrin, returned to the *Westernland* seriously injured, and were carried, groaning, to the dining room that was our makeshift sick bay. As the water around our ship erupted into white spume, we set to work for the first time, bandaging and tending their wounds.

'What is your name?' Captain Perrin asked me, squeezing my hand, his face pale and waxy.

'Susan,' I replied, mopping his sweating brow and darting glances out of the porthole.

'Don't be afraid, Susan,' he said. 'They're just bluffing.'

The bluff seemed to go on for a very long time. Intermittent gunfire continued for several hours, but our guns never replied. The cruiser *Cumberland*, badly hit a few hundred yards forward from our position, ordered some of its men to abandon ship. The captain radioed to the Dakar authorities to question the attack.

'Retire to twenty miles' distance!' came the curt reply, accompanied by further shelling. The bluffing was over.

The Free French guns returned fire for the first time at around five o'clock that evening, and only after considerable duress. Some of the men on the gun deck apparently loaded their weapons with tears streaming down their faces.

De Gaulle and Admiral Cunningham both convinced themselves that, with the right persuasion, the Governor of Dakar might still be rallied. They sent the French sloop *Commandant Duboc*, with a detachment of marines on board, to make its way through the fog towards the small port of Rufisque, just out of range of the Dakar guns, to attempt to land and to persuade the natives at least to join forces with us. Weighing anchor, we set off to cover them. Feeling the ship moving and seeing us nearing the shore – and the guns – I reported our movements to Captain Perrin, now lying in the sick bay.

'What's happening?' he asked, trying to raise himself up.

'Things are getting warmer,' I replied, my heart in my mouth.

The next thing we heard was gunfire, this time from above. Vichy planes flew in and raked the sloop, killing several men and wounding many others. We watched helplessly from the ship.

'What's happening now?' Captain Perrin enquired.

'Looks like you're going to have some company,' I told him sadly. 'We'd better get those extra beds set up.'

The sloop limped back to our ship and once again we were put to work. The men who'd survived had mostly suffered flesh wounds and a blow to their dignity. Seeing their injuries, General de Gaulle had little choice but to make for the safety of the open sea. We spent the next night on tenterhooks, wondering what would happen.

The following day saw yet another stalemate as ultimata were exchanged once again. Firing continued, this time shooting blind through the fog. That night, the *Barham* came alongside and de Gaulle and Spears went across in a little rowing boat to see Admiral Cunningham. The rest of us watched and waited. My overriding emotion was not fear but bewilderment. It seemed utterly nonsensical, from my Anglo-French perspective, that the French were so bent on destroying one another and yet so reluctant to do anything at all about the Germans and Italians.

Urged by Churchill to press on with the original plan, de Gaulle and Cunningham did just that, for fear that the momentum of the entire Free French campaign could otherwise be lost. The next two days saw us bobbing around on the fringes of the firing line, watching as ship after ship closer to shore came under attack. It was like a giant game of chess, with pawns being snatched by the bishops. Only these pawns were flesh and blood, and the bishops were meant to be on the same side. Death and destruction ensued, with the torpedoing and near-sinking of the *Resolution*, the loss of four aircraft, a destroyer and two submarines. It was senseless carnage.

With heavy hearts, de Gaulle and his British advisers finally gave the order to abandon Dakar. Setting sail, we headed back to Freetown. Tony told me that the general had virtually locked himself in his small cabin. 'He's beside himself,' he said gloomily. Not surprisingly. The world's media had attacked him for his 'absurd adventure' and blamed him for its failure. They accused Churchill of being too easily led. There was even talk of de Gaulle being ousted and replaced by someone such as the veteran General Catroux.

But the response of the men in our fleet was remarkable. They decried the press reports and continued to offer de Gaulle their unconditional support. Back in Freetown, one legionnaire told me: 'He's the only real hope we have. We must stay with him, especially now we've seen what those Vichy bastards are prepared to do on behalf of the Germans.'

Freetown was a small town on a peninsula in the lee of a forest-clad mountain in the shape of a lion, after which the country of Sierra Leone was named. It had one dingy hotel where we ate rather poorly and everything came with rice. The climate was unbearably hot and steamy, and our only respite was a swim in the sea at one of the palm-fringed beaches of Freetown Bay.

The experience of those early days of the war was for me as much about daily privations as physical danger. Living in a cramped cabin with two other women in insufferable heat, wearing a simple uniform and with none of my little luxuries around me, I'd never known such discomfort. The town offered scant relief, and every time I stepped ashore I felt crushed by the oppressive heat, the flies and the people pressing all around me. For someone who'd grown up in Cannes and spent much of her life in the rarefied air of high society, this was really living on the edge.

The heavy atmosphere matched the mood. Kepi-wearing legionnaires huddled together in groups, talking endlessly of what might happen with de Gaulle and how it would affect France. I couldn't help noticing how very handsome our soldiers were. They had a way with them which was uniquely confident and attractive and each was his own man through and through. Legionnaires, I was to learn, were single-minded soldiers of fortune with a common bond of allegiance. I wandered among them, offering mangoes, listening to their earnest talk and determined attitudes and admiring them even more. These were not people who would allow one setback to deter them from their course. The future of France and the free world was at stake and their unerring patriotism in the face of failure was inspiring. For the first time in my life, I felt truly alive and part of something much bigger than my immediate horizons. My previous existence suddenly seemed shallow by comparison.

Fortunately for de Gaulle, Churchill continued to back him publicly. Plans were drawn up for our convoy to move on elsewhere and try to redeem our objective of rallying support for the Free French in Africa. Our cause was helped slightly by Marshal Pétain in Vichy, who'd agreed to ban Jews and women from working in public services, the media or industry. There was widespread shock at the realization that the Vichy government was not just allying itself with Nazi Germany for its own safety, but was actively endorsing its Aryan policies.

Our next destination was settled as the port of Douala in French Cameroon, where the British fleet would leave us to carry on alone. Never again would Churchill allow himself to share the blame for any failure of the Free French to accomplish their mission. He needn't have worried. We arrived on 8 October to a rapturous welcome from the French colonists, natives and troops. De Gaulle, delighted and bolstered by their enthusiasm, left immediately for Chad and the other friendly French territories.

At Douala, the country's chief port and trade centre on the Wauri estuary, new orders were received for those of us who'd come to serve. I very much hoped to be able to go wherever the legionnaires were sent. Sadly for me, they were to be dispatched to Yaoundé in Cameroon and Libreville in Gabon to finish off the Vichy forces still holding out there. It was a fratricidal engagement undertaken with a heavy heart, neither side wanting to kill their fellow Frenchmen. But after a few initially cautious exchanges of shots, there was some serious fighting. Tragically, twenty men were killed and many more wounded. A promising young French captain, Marie-Pierre Koenig, led the troops into the rubber-shipping port of Libreville and secured it within a few hours, winning the admiration of his men and the praise of his commanders.

It was an uncertain time for the French in those autumn months of 1940. Some of those who'd travelled so far with us returned to England, disillusioned. The rest of us waited to learn our fate. De Gaulle was to remain in Douala for a time before going back to England for talks with Churchill. Kelsey would stay in Douala too, to set up a hospital with some of the nurses, while the rest of the troops were to go to Pointe Noire, the chief Congo port. My destination, I was told, was Brazzaville in the Republic of Congo, where I was to be sent with five other nurses, along with General Spears and the British Liaison Mission, including Tony.

None of us was entirely happy about going to Brazzaville. I certainly wasn't; I knew that, as it was in undisputed territory, there'd be no action and I could see myself getting stuck in the middle of nowhere. Setting off on the *Westernland* for the journey to the Congo, I decided to cheer myself up by holding a cocktail party in the captain's cabin. General Spears and all the liaison officers came and it was a great success. For a moment, sipping champagne and eating canapés, I could almost forget that

I was heading into the back of beyond. A few days later, we crossed the Equator.

Brazzaville was a depressing town on a plateau, its white-painted bungalows and their gardens sadly neglected and forlorn. All the *colons* living in the old French Quarter seemed to dislike one another and, divided into rigid social cliques, were mainly pro-Vichy and anti-English. There were three restaurants and no shops except a native market, run by Portuguese and Syrians, who erected little wooden stalls from which they sold smoked catfish, lemons, oranges, coconuts, bananas and hundreds of other strange and exotic goods for the local Kongo and Vili tribes.

There were no roads anywhere. If you wanted to see anything of the country, you had to go by train or by motor boat up into the tributaries fringed by mangrove swamps and giant cotton trees. Invariably the vessel would run out of petrol, leaving you at the mercy of the whirl-pools and rapids until someone came and rescued you or the swift currents led you to the wide flat sandbanks covered with reed-grass.

To my dismay I found that the only work for me was in a humble dispensary for mothers and their babies in Poto-Poto, the poor quarter of the capital. The dispensary was far inferior to the one for white people and I was shocked to discover that, among the French colonials, this was con-sidered quite normal. My friends Nadine and Rosie shared a bungalow with me and we had our own houseboy, John; being together was the only thing that kept us all sane.

On our first night, with each of us lying awake in our respective rooms and all the doors and windows open in a vain attempt to keep cool, Rosie announced glumly from her pillow: 'I never thought I'd be doing the Lady of the Lamp in darkest Africa.'

Her words echoed our thoughts. We had each left England with high hopes of nursing wounded soldiers at the front. Instead, we found ourselves in a seedy colonial town far from any action. As we were not real nurses, we weren't much use at serving the local population.

Nadine and I were in our second day at the dispensary when an old woman, doubled over with arthritis and age, stripped off her brightly coloured cotton wraps to show us that she was covered in white marks. The brown skin on her entire body was mottled and blotchy. Through her watery eyes she stared up at us sadly with a look of enquiry and fear. Nadine and I didn't know what to do.

Madame Pichaud, the chief doctor at the clinic, stepped forward. Reaching for a pin, she pricked the marks and asked, in the local Bantu: 'Can you feel this?' The old woman replied that she could not. Nadine and I wondered if it was some hereditary complaint peculiar to the area, and we both leaned forward for a closer look. But Madame Pichaud soon put us straight.

'Well, ladies, this is probably the first case of leprosy you've ever seen,' she said with a wry smile. 'Learn to recognize the signs, you'll certainly see it again.'

We recoiled, horrified.

The stifling heat in the Congo was the worst I'd ever come across. Day or night, I was never dry. It was the beginning of the rainy season when we arrived and as the temperature soared, huge dark clouds would gather, invading the horizon as a storm brewed. I'd look up at the sky pleadingly, praying for rain, for anything to break the oppressive heat. The witch doctors would invoke the African spirits with the same request. Yet no respite came and the clouds would roll thunderously away again, causing angry electrical storms to rage through the dark skies overhead.

Sometimes, in the slanted evening light, Nadine, Rosie and I would go down to the Congo river to swim among the water hyacinths, carefully avoiding the hippopotami that sat blinking at us on a sandbank opposite our little beach, or half-submerged in the water. The river was vast, the colour of beer, with an extraordinary tide that kept ebbing and receding every five minutes. The swimming was good and helped to cool us down, but there was one major problem – every time we exposed even an inch of white flesh, we were eaten alive by the clouds of mosquitoes rising and falling above the water. Then, at night, we'd have to contend with the infernal itching as well as the heat. In the end, we decided it simply wasn't worth it.

When the rains did come, the water clattered on the corrugated-tin roofs of our buildings day and night. And still it was hot. It was impossible to sleep, impossible to work, impossible to think. Stray goats and damp chickens sought shelter under our eaves or in the lee of the mango and banana trees. The geckoes, also seeking refuge, formed intricate geometric patterns in the lamplight on the walls of our home; snakes and creepy-crawlies of every description became our roommates. At the dispensary, the children's infected insect bites wept and oozed.

Within two weeks, Nadine and Rosie had had enough. They were so disillusioned with the work that when a British consular official arrived asking for 'girls who could type', they jumped at the chance. They preferred to do clerical work in an office with a single fan whirring slowly overhead rather than carry on being little more than a nanny in the middle of the African jungle. I couldn't type – I'd never used a typewriter in my life – so I was left behind.

My only distractions were my pet African grey parrot – whom I called affectionately 'General Spears' – and the close proximity of Tony Drake, of whom I was still very fond. I'd been glad of his company at first; the girls each had their own boyfriends within the liaison mission and I'd have hated to be on my own. But the relentless tropical climate and the miserable working conditions did not help to nurture a budding relationship. We saw less and less of each other and, after a while, Tony told me that he was seeing someone else. I really shouldn't have been surprised or hurt, but I was.

Exasperated more with myself than with him, I knew I had to get away. So I took myself off to see the Inspector-General of Brazzaville, a Frenchman called General Sisse, to ask if there was any chance of my rejoining the Free French troops.

'I don't know where they'll be going or what they'll be doing, but I want to be with them, wherever the war is,' I told him emphatically.

He eventually agreed that I could travel with some supplies for the brigade on a boat that was shortly coming into Pointe Noire. 'I have no idea if they'll take you, or what may lie in store,' he told me gravely, 'but I can see that you are a determined woman. I won't stand in your way.'

He signed the relevant papers and waved me off with a smile. I think he was glad to see the back of me. Against the advice of Tony and to the horror of my fellow nurses, I'd managed to secure myself a place with the Free French en route to North Africa.

After a hazardous month-long journey on a filthy cargo ship with a dangerous list, I watched as the requisitioned troop ship *Neuralia* pulled into the port of Durban. The bulk of the Legion was on board, fresh from Gabon and Cameroon. I was given a permit to go aboard and travel with the men I'd come to know at Dakar and elsewhere. Best of all, Kelsey was on the ship, already in the operating theatre.

'Just getting everything shipshape,' she boomed, her sleeves rolled up to her elbows, her gap-toothed grin wide. 'You'll be in here with me, acting as a buffer and interpreter, Travers.'

My thoughts flashed back to my disastrous last performance in the operating theatre in Poitiers and I stared at the anaesthetic machine with the greatest trepidation.

To my delight, Simone, the Belgian nurse from the *Westernland*, was also on board, along with a British liaison officer called Henry Enriques, who I knew as a colleague of Tony Drake's from the *Westernland* and in Brazza. There was also a Madame Mescier, a charming and pretty woman whose husband was a planter in

Cameroon and who'd enlisted as an ambulance driver when de Gaulle called for help. Marie-Pierre Koenig – the man who had led them so well at Narvik and in the Gabon and who was now a colonel – was not on board. He'd gone down with a bad case of African flu and had been sent overland to Cairo to convalesce.

The *Neuralia* set sail on 29 January 1941. It was a crucial time. Tobruk had just been captured from the Italians by Australian and British forces after a spirited campaign which brought General Wavell's Army of the Nile right into Libya. Mussolini's beleaguered Italian forces, which had suffered a series of humiliating defeats at the hands of the British, surrendered in their droves. The question on everyone's lips was whether or not Wavell would push on to Benghazi.

But rumours abounded that the Germans were gathering together a considerable force to strengthen the Italian resolve. The advance guard of the German Afrika Korps was about to land in Tripoli. Specially trained for desert warfare and with a panzer division commanded by the legendary Major General Erwin Rommel, the elite corps would be supported by squadrons of Luftwaffe planes. It was a dramatic move that would change the course of the war.

7

AMONG STRANGERS

'No mortal eye could see
The intimate welding of their later history,
Or a sign that they were bent
By paths coincident
On being anon twin halves of one august event.'
THOMAS HARDY, 'THE CONVERGENCE OF THE TWAIN'

The first time I set eyes on Commandant Dimitri Amilakvari, pacing the deck of the *Neuralia* in full military uniform, I knew I was in trouble. A White Russian prince, tall, athletic and devastatingly handsome with a square jaw and strong features, he was adored by his men and irresistible to women. A revered member of the French Foreign Legion, in permanent exile from his homeland since fleeing the Bolshevik Revolution at the age of fourteen, Amilakvari was married to one of the three Princesses Dadiani, famed as the most beautiful sisters in Europe.

Having passed out of the Saint Cyr military academy with flying colours, he had served with distinction in Morocco and Norway and had rallied to de Gaulle in 1940, bringing many devoted men with him. Never without his trademark green cloak, purloined from Norway and shot through by shrapnel which narrowly missed his throat, he inspired courage, love and loyalty in equal measure. Now aged thirty-five and in charge of a battalion of 13DBLE, he was preparing his men to engage in what looked likely to be a long and bloody conflict against the Axis forces on North African soil.

I'd never met anyone as magnetic as Amilakvari, known affectionately as Amilak to all his friends. He oozed charisma. His crystal-blue eyes sparkled and when they locked onto mine, they seemed to peel away the layers of my soul. He was well practised in the art of seduction and his faint Russian accent only added to his attraction. When he first approached me, I was on deck looking out to sea, the wind blowing the hair from my face. He brushed my arm with his fingertips, a gesture so sensual it took my breath away. 'They say that if you look long enough at the ocean, its spirit will steal part of your soul,' he said.

Amilakvari was one of those men who believe that women are placed on this planet purely for their own pleasure. I was not the only woman on board – there were five others, four nurses and an officer's wife – but I was the one he chose. In truth I think he saw me as just another conquest, an amusing diversion during the six-week voyage. In my early thirties, I was not a *jeune fille*, nor was I a great beauty. In fact, since being in Africa I had abandoned all attempts to retain any femininity, my face clean of make-up and my khaki uniform barely setting me apart from the men.

But Amilakvari could sense a woman at several hundred paces. Although I didn't allow myself to fall in love with him, I knew that he was the sort of man I had been looking for all my life and I revelled in his company. He became my dashing personal escort to the Horn of Africa. His irresistible charms sealed a succession of intense sexual encounters and secret assignations along that ancient naval route. I tingled at his touch and ached for it when he wasn't there. I had never been so stimulated by a man or yearned more for one. He was married with two children and way above my head socially and intellectually, but none of that seemed to matter. Scarred by my lonely child-hood and abused emotionally by a succession of men over the years, I'd developed an intense fear of rejection. That was never more true than with Amilakvari. I wanted him, I needed him to want me and I was delighted that it was me he chose to be with.

Our voyage took us through the Mozambique Channel, into the Indian Ocean, round the Horn of Africa and into the Gulf of Aden and the Red Sea. The few patients we had to deal with were merely suffering from *mal de mer*. I began by sharing a cabin with Madame Mescier. It was appallingly hot because of the blackout rule, which meant that the porthole had to be closed and shuttered. After two weeks of similarly unbearable sleeping conditions on the cargo ship to Durban, I knew I couldn't stand another night soaking in my own sweat so I took to sleeping on deck, where it was lovely and cool, and where I could secretly meet my beau. Unfortunately, the decks were washed down every day at exactly 6.30 a.m. The clatter of buckets on wooden decking became my early morning alarm call, when I'd struggle to my feet, grab my bedding and head downstairs for a shower and breakfast.

The passengers comprised the 13th Demi-Brigade; the ACL field hospital with us, the Moroccan troops, Henry Enriques (the liaison officer and friend of Tony Drake) and a few other officers I knew, including Captain Paul Arnault, a thin but kindly father figure; the dashing Captain Gabriel de Sairigné, with his jovial sense of humour; Captain Jacques de Bollardière; a White Russian called Boris Nazaroff and a charming wireless officer called Renard.

Captain de Sairigné had an open, friendly face and kind eyes. Devoted to the Legion and to Amilakvari in par-ticular, Gabriel was gregarious, affectionate and very amusing company. 'I think you and Amilak deserve each other,' he told me once, his eyes twinkling. 'You're both equally pig-headed.' I liked him at once and felt in-stinctively that we would always be friends.

Captain de Bollardière was exactly one's idea of what a French officer should be – good looking, polite, amiable and always well turned out. I'd first met him on the *Westernland* where he'd made a great impression on me by always wearing his gloves. The rest of us were very slovenly by comparison.

Boris, too, was always immaculate, even in the hottest climates. Completely bald, he shaved his head every day. He was a man who could drink all night and rise next morning as pink and fresh as a rose, which was more than any of the rest of us could do. Renard was a different character altogether, known for his extraordinary tall stories. Simone had fallen head over heels in love with Renard on the *Westernland* and had been devoted to him ever since, wondering where he was and what he was doing. Now they'd been reunited, they were both very happy. It was the start of a relationship that would last many years and lead to marriage.

Kelsey was a remarkable woman, an excellent nurse, the mainstay of the operating theatre. Goodness knows what we would have done without her. She always knew what to do and never flapped. Under her strict rule, my routine was to work in the hospital morning and afternoon, with a break for lunch. Most days I'd have drinks with Henry and the Purser before dinner, which was a meal taken with the other nurses in a separate mess (we weren't allowed to dine with the men). Dinner would be followed by a drink or two in the lounge, where the men would play cards.

Amilakvari was a tremendous bridge player. With all the cunning, charm and skill necessary to outwit his opponents, he was a pleasure to watch. I once took a hand at bridge but had no idea until then quite how badly I played. Bridge had not been as popular as baccarat among my circle. 'I'm so sorry,' I told him apologetically one night after my worst ever performance. 'I'm much better at gambling.' After that, Amilakvari gave me money to play baccarat – I was too poor and too mean to play with my own – and he was surprised and delighted when I won.

One of my companions at the card table was a charming young American boy called John Hasey, who was only just out of his teens but who'd managed to fulfil a lifetime's ambition by joining the Foreign Legion as a second lieutenant. He was a cheerful, good-hearted lad, a former employee of Cartier in Paris, and everyone liked him. He'd fled from Paris when France fell and had joined up with de Gaulle's Free French in London, just as I had. One evening we played baccarat with some other officers and John kept on winning, much to his delight. But to my horror the officers continued playing and losing large sums of money into the bargain, a situation which, I feared, would not stand him in good stead. Leaning over to him as discreetly as I could, I whispered: 'You've got to lose now, John.'

He looked at me, confused.

'Lose!' I urged with a hiss before playing my hand. John did, in the end, get my drift and he lost the last game so that the officers were able to recover some of their money. Shortly afterwards, the playing of baccarat was banned.

Amilakvari was deputy to Lieutenant Colonel Magrin-Vernerey, who used 'Monclar' as his *nom de guerre*. Monclar was a stocky, grey-haired man with combed-back hair and a disconcerting, swashbuckling air, a Frenchman through and through. It was his job to instil in the men the great traditions of the Legion and to sustain its honour and that of the Free French, even if that meant fighting and killing their own countrymen. It was a prospect that filled all of them with foreboding but, with someone like Amilakvari leading them into battle, they would be better able to follow.

Monclar was a terrifying little man, someone people (especially women) tried to avoid wherever possible, not least because he was prone to persistent bouts of hiccoughing which made it difficult to keep a straight face when talking to him. Unfortunately for me, on our final night at sea he threw a cocktail party for all the officers and I was placed at his right hand to translate for him to the ship's captain, while everyone else was getting merry. My mood didn't improve when the colonel warned me that he'd been advised that I might not be allowed to continue on my journey with the legionnaires. I spent a restless night wondering how I would manage to sneak ashore.

We landed at Port Sudan, on the Red Sea, on 14 February 1941, and, to my delight, nobody challenged us at the harbour about women being on board. One of the nurses told me that Tony Drake was already there. I had lunch with him ashore, but our ardour had been cooled by the experiences we'd both enjoyed since we last met.

'I'll see you around,' he said, with an affectionate kiss, as we parted.

I nodded and wondered if we would.

Disembarking with all our luggage, we caught a train to Suakin, south of the port, a typical Arab village with a single Greek restaurant. Our camp was on the plateau above the settlement. There was an abandoned town nearby, on the harbour, entirely deserted apart from one reclusive Englishman who had a house by the sea. The rest of the houses, with their fretwork panels through which the Muslim women could gaze without being seen, were derelict, their shutters banging in the wind.

The days passed in a somnolent haze. There was no work to do, no-one was sick, and I spent my time with the Legion, or with Henry Enriques who had a little motorcycle on which we'd travel down to the Greek restaurant each day for lunch. Tony Drake was around for a while, as liaison officer for General Le Gentilhomme, but he then left with him for the neighbouring Italian colony of Eritrea. We lived in primitive conditions in tents, our toilet no more than a hole in the ground and our washing facilities the sea (sharks permitting). Amilakvari and I could meet in private only occasionally because of the constraints of our new situation. But whenever our paths crossed all he had to do was wink or smile at me and I no longer felt quite so lonely.

* * *

It was in Sudan that I first realized that the Legion had an unsavoury reputation among the Allied military commanders. The welcome we received from our British counterparts in Port Sudan was at best unenthusiastic and at worst openly hostile. Legionnaires seemed to have an almost mythical status as a mercenary force peopled by foreign men with false names, who had joined up for the minimum five years to flee troubled pasts. Despite the fact that the Legion was a French creation commanded by officers loyal to France, its members – many of them foreign – took their motto literally: their only allegiance was to their corps.

I remember the legionnaires being described as a collection of 'hot-tempered Cossack horsemen, German officers, ill-educated Turks, Russian counts and Hungarian lotharios'. They were certainly men who needed and were prepared to accept strict discipline and absolute obedience. But I had found them utterly charming and endearingly old-fashioned in their views of honour and valour. '*Honneur et fidélité*' is the rallying cry, and while that allegiance may have extended only to those within their particular band, it included those of us on its periphery. I'd been with them only a short while but whenever the great Legion march '*Le Boudin*' played, I always found my own feet twitching to the music.

Not that the British suspicions about the Legion were altogether unfounded. Legionnaires were undoubtedly expert thieves and specialists in 'appropriating' vehicles, ammunition and military equipment from those around them. Looting and pilfering were commonplace – survival had often depended on it. The British jealously guarded their own supplies and frowned heavily upon the black sheep in their midst. As a member of the French group, I was treated no differently. After all, I looked like a legionnaire, dressed like one and rarely spoke English, although it amused me greatly to think that, in different circumstances and at a different time, these pompous British officers who dismissed me out of hand might well have smiled at me over one of Gladys's famous candlelit dinners in her fine chateau near Poitiers.

Life in the camp soon became tedious and we itched to move on. But because of the hostility of the Allies, the Legion and the rest of the Free French were given little to do. The British had done very well in the region under General O'Connor, who had hit the Italians hard; it was their show and they wanted to control the action. There was also understandable nervousness about using an armed force whose countrymen had signed an armistice with the Axis forces.

When the British left Suakin and went on ahead to Eritrea, between Sudan and Abyssinia, we were ordered to wait behind for a Free French battalion from Chad coming up through Africa partly on foot. The Chadians duly arrived, a remarkable group of men from the Oubangui-Chari tribe who brought with them their own camp followers and even their own witch doctors. Their noisy, dusty arrival was like that of a warrior tribe descending on a fort. With them came Dr André Lotte, their divisional medical officer, the *commandant médecin*. Commandant Lotte was a French colonial, a little man, short and fat with a round face and round spectacles, a very merry person who found amusement in everything. He had fairish hair, twinkling eyes and a resilience about him, which was just as well because it was to be his thankless task to organize the evacuation of the most seriously injured from the front lines, and to get them to the advanced dressing stations or ADSs.

Lotte arrived overland from Chad accompanied by his orderly, a native 'boy' called Assab, who was in fact a large, elderly Negro. Assab was very gloomy and quite hideous looking, but completely devoted to his boss. Like most native 'boys', he travelled everywhere with his saucepans and frying pans hanging on string from his belt and clanging together to make an awful din. Lotte said that the journey by train from Chad had been an epic one, with Assab, wearing his *casseroles* strung round him, unable to get through the carriage door.

My luck changed the day Lotte arrived. He couldn't drive and all the male drivers were busy with lorries and trucks, so I was nominated as his chauffeur. I was delighted. It meant getting away from the horrors of nursing and doing what I'd always wanted to do. I was finally at the heart of the action. I was grateful to be doing valuable work in an important area of the war and the sense of satisfaction and pride kept me going. At last, I thought, I was doing something my father would have been proud of.

The men initially joked about the two of us being alone in the car together, but I took no notice and the good *commandant* showed no sign of minding at all. When I first saw the beaten-up old Humber I was to drive, however, my heart sank. It was quite the most exhausted-looking vehicle I had ever set eyes on, but the only one available, as the British had taken all the best. The self-starter had been lost, so I had to wind it up by hand which was extremely hard work and not always something I could manage on my own. I had hoped to use Assab as my orderly – all the other chauffeurs used their boss's orderlies – but the proud Negro wouldn't have it. He thoroughly disapproved of women, and refused point blank to act in any way on my behalf. It was simply beneath his dignity. He would occasionally bring me a cup of coffee in the mornings, but I could see that even that went against the grain. Usually Assab followed on behind us, perched atop Lotte's luggage in a lorry, but sometimes we squeezed him into the Humber, complete with frying pan, on top of the rest of our bags.

By the end of February, the Free French had left for Eritrea and it was the turn of the medical staff to follow them a few days later. We got up at four o'clock in the morning, ready to leave just after six, and my Humber was placed at the head of the convoy, which I found rather intimidating. But the day went well and we managed to cross half of the one hundred and fifty bumpy miles south-east to the border without major incident. Although some roads were surprisingly good, most were very bad, as if the money had run out suddenly and they'd gone back to little more than a dirt track.

The great advantage of being at the front of the convoy was that I didn't have to travel in anyone else's dust. Behind me, the vehicles tried to spread out as far as the trackway allowed so as to avoid travelling in ours. The Humber stalled twice en route and I had to ask someone else to wind it up. We eventually reached our stopping point after eight hours at the wheel and it was all I could do to erect my little tent, crawl inside and go to sleep.

The next day we were up at four thirty and on the road again by six. We'd all been threatened with the loss of four days' pay if we were late. The roads became fearfully stony and bumpy with tremendous dips and I found myself wrestling with the gears just to keep going. Then came the sand and I got stuck in it and had to be towed out. Another hundred yards further on, I got stuck again. I was mortified, but Lotte was very magnanimous. 'These aren't the most ideal conditions, my dear,' he reassured me from the front seat as I struggled once more to attach the tow rope. After that, I was terrified at the sight of sand and went to great lengths to avoid it.

We eventually reached the Eritrean frontier and the road became comparatively good. It was seven o'clock in the evening before we arrived at our destination – a straw-hut village in the middle of nowhere – by which time I was so tired I could hardly walk. 'Where's the well?' I asked someone wearily, brushing clouds of dust from my clothes. I needed more water for my canteen and the car radiator. 'Five miles further on,' came the reply. Reluctantly, I got back into the car, found the well, filled up, returned for dinner and went straight to bed.

The next day I took Lotte and others to the local hospital, manned by English-speaking staff, and inter-preted for them. Someone showed me the road to

Kub-Kub winding away in the distance, our remote destination for the following day. Kelsey set off ahead in two ambulances with Simone and a doctor called Fruchaud. I went to the well again, where I found some natives standing on one foot and staring at their bony cattle. They offered me a drink of camel's milk from a goatskin bag, which I accepted. But it tasted so warm and rancid that I nearly spat it out.

It took us six hours to get to Kub-Kub the next morning, travelling up to the high plateau via some dangerous mountain roads, watched over by troops of cackling baboons. Kub-Kub was a baptism of fire for many of the men, their first sight of action and a rude awakening to the horrors of war. There were several days of deadly exchanges. Hot and thirsty, pinned down by the Italians, they could not stay in position for longer than a few days because of the lack of water. Some even killed mountain goats, slitting their throats to drink the watery green liquid stored in their gullets. Wounded men from the front were brought to our hospital hut in camouflage trucks by boat, up the muddy brown river, just as we arrived. The Free French were further up the mountains with the Chad battalion, helping the British, Sikhs, Punjabis and Senegalese in the fight against the Italians, who were holding the riverbed. I stayed below with the car, feeling nervous. I could hear the gunfire and smell the cordite on the air and we were warned that there were several loose tanks in the area.

Whenever there was a lull, Lotte and his staff would climb the mountains on mules or camels to tend to the most seriously injured and dying, bringing those they could help back down with them to be treated in the field hospital, where the staff were often English and I had to interpret. It was hazardous; many of the injured had suffered serious flesh wounds from the Italian hand grenades – which continued to rain down on Lotte and his men as they worked. Most of the battlegrounds could be reached only on foot or by beast of burden, as they zigzagged their way through hills 4,000 feet high, on the top of which the fighting was often the fiercest.

To try to get extra supplies of food and ammunition to the men, one of the first airdrops of the Second World War was attempted: sandbags full of hardtack rations and boxes of small-arms ammunition were thrown out of two ancient Allied planes as they circled over the mountains. I watched them lumbering overhead and wondered what was going on. The attempt was not always successful: many of the sandbags fell into enemy hands. This method of supply was, however, put to great effect later in other theatres of war.

A few days after arriving, we were invited to lunch at brigade headquarters, where I met up again with Henry Enriques.

'Good God,' he said, on seeing me emerge from the car in a great cloud of dust, 'you look like you could use a bath.'

Very kindly, he arranged for me to use the colonel's canvas bath, lightly screened by a rug, and to rest on his proper bed.

I usually had to sleep wherever I could, but my regular roost at Kub-Kub was a little hut made of branches, with a stretcher for a bed. The nomadic tribesmen were wary of us at first, following each of our movements with curious eyes. One morning I approached a cowherd and tried to ask for some milk. The terrified boy ran off into the bush, taking his small herd with him, afraid I might steal one of his precious beasts. After a while, the locals grew accustomed to our presence and realized that they could make money from us. They then relaxed considerably and – through an interpreter who spoke the native Tigre tongue – they told us of their simple lives and how their biggest fear was not the war but the swarms of locusts which could devastate their crops far more quickly than any battle.

Locusts weren't my problem: wear and tear on the old Humber was. I spent much of my time trying to get spare parts from the mobile repair shop. It was such an old heap really, always breaking down. The timing advance was too slow; the handbrake didn't work so I had to put stones under the wheels if ever we stopped on a slope; the tyres were bald and the seats were the most uncomfortable I'd ever sat on. My father's old Cottin-Desgouttes seemed like a Rolls-Royce by comparison.

When the car was working, it was my job to ferry Commandant Lotte back and forth across Eritrea, through some fearful mountain passes, up rocky tracks and through vast plains to the various military camps. En route I'd bump into Tony Drake and Amilakvari, and also Kelsey and Nadine, who seemed to spend their entire time treating men suffering from dysentery. What luck that I was no longer a nurse! Only Fruchaud was seeing action – he was sent off with the troops to set up a forward operating theatre on the front line. He was no athlete, so it was a pretty good effort on his part.

Lotte loved the Chadians, so we'd often go and visit them, although their *commandant*, a man called Garbay, didn't like women and wouldn't have me in his mess. This meant that I had to eat alone in a corner, not daring to speak and feeling rather awkward. What I was able to overhear from their conversations appalled me. The gentle Chadians spoke of their role in the dreadful battle for Kub-Kub, when they'd no water to drink and the whole place stank of dead camels, killed in the shelling.

The Italians had lost more than a hundred miles of territory as the British and Commonwealth troops advanced, with the Free French following on behind. The British allowed our forces to take part in the series of bloody battles for Keren, a strong point in the shadow of the 7,000-foot-high Mount Engiahat which controlled the main road to the high plateau. Keren was surrounded by an Italian ring of steel, a barbed-wire perimeter fence which remained impenetrable for several weeks until the Free French and other reinforcements arrived. It was a test of sorts and the men did well, fighting with dash and courage. They helped sweep the Italians aside, even though, man to man, they were heavily outnumbered. They certainly improved their status in the eyes of the Allies.

As we pursued those who were pursuing the enemy, Lotte and I must have driven over a thousand miles on appalling tracks, criss-crossing deserts and precipitous escarpments. The driving was extremely hard going. The steering on the car was very heavy, even on the few metalled roads, and on rough terrain it was all I could do to lock my hands around the huge wheel and maintain control. Driving in sand was even worse. As the dunes shifted with the winds, so did the texture and shape of the terrain. Wheel ruts left by other vehicles made matters worse. Shell holes from previous air raids could rip a sump off in an instant, and the ever-present risk of mines meant I had to go very carefully to avoid tipping over, getting stuck or having us both blown to oblivion. Time and again, I had to get out and pile rocks and brushwood under the wheels for better traction.

It was my sole responsibility to keep the car safe and in working order so that the doctor could get to where the fighting was and tend to the wounded. Not only had I to keep it running for the great overland treks, but I also had to do my best to protect it from the constant risk of air raids or shelling, covering it with camouflage material, hiding it under trees or in the lee of a cliff and occasionally digging it in. There were consolations. As far as the men were concerned, the doctor and the cooks were the most vital staff of the whole brigade and I, as the *commandant*'s driver, had acquired the same level of importance.

The Humber was my home and it soon became my sanctuary. Sometimes I slept in it at night and often I rested in it during the day. Commandant Lotte knew absolutely nothing about cars and expected me to do everything. Fortunately, after many years' experience of driving and of watching others making repairs, I'd picked up quite a bit of knowledge and what I didn't know I improvised. I changed the tyres and learned how to mend a leaking radiator or fuel tank, replace a fan belt and repair a slow puncture. I managed to get hold of some basic tools and would just set to work. Lotte was mechanically inept and never helped, apart from one day when a tyre burst and I needed to change the wheel.

As I struggled to position some large boulders to act as a jack, the fat little doctor watched me from the passenger seat. 'Need a hand?' he called out finally.

Puffing and panting, I dropped the boulder at my feet and looked up at him through the sweat that was pouring into my eyes. 'Two would be better.'

Smiling, Lotte got out and humped the rocks for me so that I could drive back onto them.

We travelled companionably together, Lotte and I in that trusty old Humber, penetrating deep into the bush, looking for small villages in which to set up camp ahead of the battalion in readiness for casualties. I thought it a marvellous place, Eritrea, a beautiful country. It had a good climate, much drier than the Congo, and was a land of incredible contrasts. We would drive across the arid desert and then there would suddenly be mountains and greenery, lush with wild flowers, birds and animals.

The country was peopled by Arabs with ebony skin, who were always friendly and had wonderful smiles. They lived simply in their cluttered mud-hut villages, places I could never have imagined existed in my former life, and yet they kept clean and healthy. I often wondered what they must have thought as their biblical land was invaded by a series of foreign armies with their massive machines of war.

I remember stopping at one village with traditional straw-roofed huts. The people ran out to meet us, as they always did, their bony hands outstretched in welcome. The air was full of dust and flies, we had been driving for hours and it was very hot. The thick, sweet smell of dung fires filled the air and village cattle mingled lazily with half-naked children. I couldn't speak Arabic but Lotte could, and he asked the villagers for food and water. They were very kind and gave us some milk and unleavened bread as we crouched with them in the dust.

Through Lotte, the women – all of whom had gaily coloured cloths covering their heads and wrapped around their bodies – shyly asked me what I would most like. Without hesitating, I replied: 'A bath.' I had been in the bush for weeks, using holes in the ground as a toilet, with only my canteen of water for washing, and was desperate to be clean again. It was the aspect of my previous life that I missed the most: the luxury of having one or more bubble baths every day, the smell of scented soap and eau de Cologne.

Now, dirt-streaked and sticky, my uniform sweat-stained, I was led into a woman's hut and shown a kind of large washbasin which was filled for me with water from rustic earthenware pots. 'Thank you, *merci beaucoup, shukran, yekanyelah*,' I repeated, waiting for them to depart. Delighted at the prospect of a wash, I peeled off my filthy clothes and stepped naked into the bowl, splashing myself with my hands. I started to wash, but as my eyes grew accustomed to the dark, I realized that the hut was full of village women. They were whispering and trying not to giggle, as if they were watching a scene from a play. I felt embarrassed, but then realized that they'd probably never seen a white woman before. I continued unabashed, although I washed myself rather more hastily than I'd planned. Dressing myself again, I wandered back outside into the dazzling white heat only to be covered immediately in a sheen of sweat, but that brief, cool respite from the dirt bolstered me enormously.

Each night we'd stop at a new encampment, where I'd either try to find a hole in the ground in which to sleep, usually one recently vacated by one of the advancing soldiers, or – if there was time – erect my tent and have some privacy. One night I even slept in the hollow of an abandoned machine-gun emplacement.

It was always very cold at night, so I'd wear all my clothes to keep warm. I'd try to drift off despite the constant noise of distant shelling or the closer – and far more irritating – distraction of the camels' jangling harnesses. First thing in the morning, I'd take myself off to find a quiet bush, hoping that I wouldn't be mistaken for a gazelle or the enemy and swiftly dispatched, my knickers round my ankles. I walked miles sometimes just to find some privacy, but it wasn't always possible to wait that long, with the fearful diarrhoea that was sweeping through the camp, and through me. I was ill on several occasions, lying shivering, fully clothed, with a fever and excruciating pains raging through my belly. Then it was time to lie still and eat nothing but rice and potatoes.

On one such occasion when I was laid low, the *chef des ambulances*, Père Deon, took my Humber to go shooting with some NCOs. I was furious when I found out.

'It's my car, I'm responsible for it and I have a hard enough job as it is preventing it from falling apart,' I yelled at him angrily, when he returned with the carcasses of two deer and a large bird.

'I'm your superior officer and you can't talk to me like that,' he yelled back. Exasperated, he added, before storming off: 'My God, you're a nuisance.'

He was right, of course. But he never dared borrow the Humber again.

Word from the front was encouraging. There'd been several men wounded, and some deaths, but the Italians were – apart from the odd moment of bravado – on the retreat. Commandant Lotte set up advanced dressing stations and the men were ferried back to the field hospital when they could be moved. While he was busy, I divided my time between the Naafi, buying beer for the Chadians, or attempting to ride camels, which was very painful without a saddle. One night, some English officers took me out into the middle of the desert and we drank beer and threw hand grenades. Sometimes, if I was very bored, I'd go to work in the hospital, talking to the wounded, helping the

100

nurses where I could, but I never seemed to be of much assistance.

Whenever Lotte had to go to brigade headquarters, I'd happily drive him there for the breakfasts were always very good and – joy of joys – I could even have a fried egg. If Colonel Monclar invited us for a meal, we'd be even more delighted, for we'd be served fresh vegetables, tomatoes and, on one memorable occasion, hare – a dish I hadn't enjoyed since my chateau days.

The Humber continued to be my biggest problem. By this time it had no lights because the dynamo wasn't charging, and no brakes at all, which made coming down the winding mountain passes through the forest fairly alarming. One wheel was nearly off. The workshop managed to find me some new shock absorbers and – bliss – a self-starter, but they pinched everything out of my car in the process, and I had to make do without the brakes for ages.

But still the resilient old banger kept going. While the troops were fighting the Italians at nearby Mount Engiahat, which they eventually took, I drove the nurses up a terrifying pass to a little village called Nacfa, where they grew vegetables and flowers. In the middle of a game reserve supervised by an Englishman called Maxwell Darling, with whom we took tea, we saw three wild boars and a gazelle, who were so unafraid they just stood and stared at us. I was even able to pick some mountain daisies, burying my nose within the heavily scented blooms and remembering past flower-filled days. I wondered how long this haven would survive.

By April we were only fifteen kilometres from the front lines, and Lotte and I had arranged to meet at an advanced dressing station. Crossing a Bailey bridge over a dried-out wadi, I eventually found the ADS which was under a little bridge and just in front of the guns. It was so noisy, we had to shout to make ourselves heard. Lotte went off to see what he could do while I parked the car under a bush, alongside two artillery guns and a Humber.

Exhausted and hot, I flopped down onto a rock in the shade next to a small tent. Within seconds, a French cook came running across and shouted at me: 'Don't sit there! They always bombard there.'

I got up and dusted myself off. I'd taken only ten steps when I heard the unmistakable whistling of an incoming shell.

'Run to me, run to me!' the legionnaire yelled and I ran, like a rabbit, towards him.

He grabbed my arm and we both dived under a cannon. We covered our heads with our hands as a huge explosion blasted smoke, earth and fragments of rock all over us. Five further shells burst even closer.

When the dust had finally settled, I stood up somewhat shakily, my bare legs stinging, and looked back to where I had just been sitting. My boulder had been completely obliterated. Furthermore, a few feet to its left, the newly erected kitchen tent and the surrounding ground had completely disappeared into a series of large craters. I realized my left leg was badly gashed. While I tore a strip of cloth from an oily rag to stem the bleeding, the cook threw down his dishcloth and stamped his feet in sheer rage.

After that, shelling became a regular feature of my war. On numerous occasions Lotte and I scrambled for cover, the shells whistling over our heads. Some time later, my leg became infected and when I developed a fever, I went to see Dr Thébault at the hospital. He pulled out a piece of shrapnel I hadn't even known was there.

At the port of Massawa on the Red Sea – the largest port on the east coast of Africa, with the dubious distinction of having one of the highest average temperatures in the world – there was another big battle. Lotte and I watched from the safe distance of a nearby ridge, listening to the machine-guns and the artillery, seeing the men and the weaponry move forward, watching, waiting and praying for a speedy conclusion.

Massawa was taken after a massive bombardment on

9 April and the Italians surrendered, albeit without much grace. The Italian commander, Admiral Bonetti, threw his ceremonial sabre out of the window and into the sea rather than relinquish it to Monclar. But, in typically cheeky style, Gabriel de Sairigné, who'd watched where the heavy, ornate sword fell, waited until low tide and then retrieved it and presented it to the colonel.

'A fine blade with which to slice an Italian sausage,' he told me afterwards with a wink.

Almost five hundred Italian officers were taken prisoner, only to be given what remaining rooms there were in the devastated town on two separate islands across a causeway, while we had to sleep under bushes. But as people organized themselves, life slowly became more tolerable. Lotte was put up in a hotel and the Free French were eventually given an encampment of little mud huts on the outskirts of the city, at an oasis called Ghinda, from where they could see the great hulks of bombed warships slumped in the harbour.

I had the rare luxury of a room to myself in a house shared with English and French officers, including Amilakvari, Henry and the scruffy pet dog Henry had acquired, who used to howl at night on his chain outside and keep me awake. My bed had a rubber mattress, which was unbearably hot in a climate with no significant fluctuation between night-time and daytime temperatures, and the communal showers were filthy, but at least there was running water. More of a problem were the infernal mosquitoes, the cockroaches and the enormous spiders that seemed to take up permanent residence in my room.

While I waited for my new orders from the transport division, I spent my days drinking marsala wine and going fishing in the sea with the officers, using hand grenades. The beaches to the north of the town were excellent and the swimming good. There were turtles and dolphins and schools of sardines and anchovy. Pelicans, storks and herons were our regular companions and, occasionally, a few of the greatly feared Red Sea sharks. None of the sea life seemed to notice the detritus of war all around them in the harbour.

In the evenings, when I could acquire some gin or wine, I'd often hold a small drinks party after which poker would be played. Here too I spent my final secret nights with Amilakvari under a mosquito net. Shaven-headed because of the heat, but still just as handsome and passionate, he reminded me of gentler days. We'd grown inordinately fond of each other and throughout the Eritrean campaign he'd occasionally send me extra provisions or a bottle of whisky to keep me going. A kind look from him during a long and tiring day would be enough to boost my flagging spirits. He also made me realize once more that I was a woman. On a whim I went into the town and – speaking my pidgin Italian – bought myself an entirely useless pair of pink satin pants and some white silk pyjamas. I felt I simply had to have something feminine.

Up until then, I'd been wearing no make-up and had few accoutrements apart from a skirt, my folding camp bed and canvas bath from the Army and Navy, my tin helmet and a toothbrush. I'd figured out long ago that the way to avoid causing trouble with lots of men around was never to make a fuss or get oneself noticed. To that end, I'd almost become an honorary male. In a strange way, I enjoyed it. Being 'one of the boys' made life so much easier; I could shut down my heart and pretend that love and relationships and intimacy didn't matter. It was greatly preferable to all that painful emotional nonsense. But recently, with my unkempt hair and masculine clothes, I'd been getting so many strange looks from people that I thought I ought to tidy myself up a bit. I even tried to find a looking-glass.

If anyone had such a thing it would be an Italian, I thought. Even in the most primitive of conditions, they surrounded themselves with luxuries from home that apparently they couldn't live without. Whenever an Italian position was taken, especially in a town like Massawa, there was always a scramble to see what they had left behind. While we were surviving on bully beef and poor wine, they'd have sausages, cheese, pasta, bread and tinned delicacies such as sardines and beans. They even had champagne, Benedictine and every type of exotic liqueur.

In between driving Lotte wherever he needed to go, I would pillage whenever I could, rummaging through bombed-out houses or seeking out those who had acquired the best things and were willing to sell them. Having abandoned my search for a mirror, I decided that a sewing machine would be useful, God knows why. Food of any description was always a high priority and I'd happily part with my hard-earned wages for the luxury of a tin of asparagus or some succulent Italian salami. In my hours off, I'd bathe in the sea and marvel at the beautifully coloured zebra fish. Evenings were spent playing table tennis, going to the cinema to see incomprehensible Italian films, or getting drunk in the Bar Torino with the officers and sailors on leave from one of the many ships in the harbour.

I was never unduly pestered by any of the men. Fortunately Colonel Monclar had already established a Legion brothel – a BMC or *bordel mobile de campagne* – with native girls and the two remaining white women willing to encourage the soldiers to part with their cash. The British were most indignant about the BMC. They disapproved of it and did all they could to suppress it, but the colonel was unrepentant. He said that without it his men would storm the native quarter, from which they were banned, and there would be a riot.

The men went to the forbidden quarter as well, of course, especially after they'd had a drink or two. There was a huge fuss one evening when the town's mayor found some legionnaires there and tried to arrest them himself. In their drunkenness three of them pushed him over and trod on his face, and he fired his gun and wounded one. The next day he insisted on a parade of the Legion, so that he could recognize at least the wounded man. The offending soldiers were quietly spirited away and the poor mayor never found his assailant.

It was at Massawa that I first met a bright young officer in the Legion, a second lieutenant called Pierre Messmer. We ate together in the mess each evening, in a beautiful spot overlooking the sea. I liked him very much and we became firm friends. Seven years younger than me, he had joined the Legion in 1939 as a sub-lieutenant and a year later was so sickened by Marshal Pétain and the Vichy government that he had gone to Marseilles with a young captain called Jean Simon. The two of them had made off with an 8,200-ton Italian boat (and its valuable cargo), which they had somehow managed to sail to Liverpool under a Free French flag. From there they joined de Gaulle's forces under Amilakvari, paying for more recruits with the money they made from the cargo that they had sold. Pierre Messmer had been in the same convoy as me to Dakar, and had fought in Gabon and in Cameroon. I found him thoughtful, intelligent and *très gentil*; he seemed even then to be someone who was going to have a remarkable life. I was not unduly surprised when he eventually became prime minister of France.

By late spring, the weather had changed quite dramatically. Thunderstorms cooled the air. Sandstorms rolled in across the plain. We had power cuts all the time, and the rains brought the rats into the house, seeking shelter. The atmosphere was heavy with humidity as we prepared to embark on the next leg of our journey, north via the Red Sea to Cairo.

I very much hoped to be able to board the liner the *Président Doumerge*, along with Amilakvari, Gabriel, Henry, Messmer, Boris Nazaroff, de Bollardière, Arnault, Jean Simon and all my friends in the Foreign Legion. But the ship sailed without me and Commandant Lotte. The little black boy the orderlies had employed to do all their work for them was practically in tears, as they'd left without paying him. I promised that if he stayed until the day I left, I'd pay him what he was owed.

Having filled the car with petrol and found a new battery for it, I watched it and the ambulances being loaded onto the next ship to leave and managed to secure myself a nice large cabin. Better still, I persuaded the cook to make me an omelette from the captain's breakfast eggs. On 7 May we finally set sail, travelling north towards Suez, through a calm azure sea plied for generations by spice traders and pilgrims en route to Mecca. On this voyage, however, I spent much of my time in bed with another bout of dysentery, feeling wretched. We arrived in busy Suez five days later and waited a further two to disembark. During that time none of us was allowed below decks for fear of air raids, which only made me feel worse. There was a searing desert wind and it was too hot to touch anything. When the order came to disembark, the usual pandemonium began – quaysides littered with boxes and people running around screaming and shouting, making a fearful noise. I watched as my old Humber was heaved over the side and reached the safety of the ground, then I packed up my belongings and drove to the medieval walled town.

Suez, I discovered, was a delight, with its palm-lined streets, colonial buildings and churches. The sky was filled with huge eagles circling on the hot thermals and the light seemed to have a special quality to it. The next few days were some of my happiest in Africa, spent bathing in the sea and attending parties and dances. It was a brief but welcome return to the old days for me, a reminder of the gayest days of my past. I danced till I thought my legs would drop off.

But the news always found a way of filtering through. In Norway, British troops had sunk eleven German ships; in the Mediterranean, British warships had destroyed a large part of the Italian fleet; the United States, fearing a German threat to convoys, had occupied Greenland on behalf of the Danes. Yugoslavia and Athens had fallen to the Germans and on 13 April Rommel's Afrika Korps, newly arrived in North Africa, had taken back the initiative, capturing the town of Bardia in Libya and pushing onwards towards Benghazi and the Egyptian frontier. A fortnight later, three columns of the Afrika Korps crossed east into Egypt.

Just three weeks after that, on 17 May 1941, and less than four hundred miles away, I climbed into the Humber with Dr Lotte and set off north – the second vehicle in line – in a massive convoy across the Sinai Desert, towards Palestine and the Levant. We were heading for battle.

8

THE FINGER OF FATE

*'Love nothing but that which comes to you
woven in the pattern of your destiny . . .'*
MARCUS AURELIUS (121–80)

By the time we reached Gaza on the Mediterranean coast,
I was ready to drop. The camp was vast, with miles and
miles of white canvas tents all full of Australians. As usual,
I was tired, thirsty and hungry and there was nowhere for
me to sleep. A kind English major gave me a bottle of
lime juice and pointed me in the direction of the hospital.
There, to my great delight, I discovered Kelsey, sleeves
rolled up once more, attending to the usual matters of
hygiene late into the night.

'Come in, Travers,' she said, as if she'd seen me only five
minutes before, 'come in and give me a hand with this.'
Between us we pushed a newly erected and incredibly
heavy operating table into the middle of the operating
theatre. 'You look like you could do with a drink.'

She reached into the copious front pocket of her apron,
retrieved a small hip flask and handed it to me with a grin.
As I had nowhere else to sleep, the new operating table
became my bed for the night and, after a few slugs of
Kelsey's whisky, I went out like a light.

Over the next few days I was shunted from pillar to post
as a succession of tents became available. Sometimes I had

to share with other women, which I hated. I'd grown accustomed to a great deal of inconvenience and discomfort since the war began, but eating well, sleeping in private and keeping hold of my few possessions had become of paramount importance. I greatly resented any intrusion into my routines.

Promoted to *adjudant* (the French equivalent of warrant officer), my primary role, workwise, was shunting Lotte and his staff between the camp and the Spears hospital, which had been set up by Lady Spears and a team of 'Spears nurses', known affectionately as 'Spearettes'. I was also sometimes lent to the British liaison staff, including an imposing British major called Sneyd-Cox, who was very handsome and extremely charming, and on one memorable occasion ferried General Paul-Louis Le Gentilhomme (formerly in command of French troops in Somalia) between camps as he inspected the medical facilities. The day was memorable because the self-starter wouldn't work after the general had climbed into the back of the car, and I had to slip discreetly out of the driver's seat and ask some passing Senegalese soldiers to push us unceremoniously down a hill. The general sat ramrod straight, staring dead ahead throughout the process.

When his inspections were over, he lined us all up and told us we were to get a new matron and eight English women drivers. A woman called Mrs Fisher was to be put in charge. The news roused us to fury because although we squabbled among ourselves, we'd all been together for a long time and were united against anyone from the outside. I spoke to Henry and Sneyd-Cox about the problem; they were sympathetic but unable to help. I hoped to goodness Mrs Fisher wouldn't make my life complicated.

Feeling tired and unwell, I took eight days' leave at Haifa on the Mediterranean coast, having travelled by bus to Tel Aviv first. Once ensconced, I discovered why I was feeling so poorly; somewhere along the way I'd contracted enteritis (inflammation of the intestine). I was placed on a bland diet of porridge and tea. After a few days of rest, disgusting food and medication, I felt miles better and was able to get up and take a look around. Haifa was built on the lower slopes of Mount Carmel, its square white houses wedged side by side. It had the most wonderful souks and Arab cafés and I spent much of my time shopping and drinking sweet tea, retiring to my hotel at the top of Mount Carmel for as much rest as I liked.

But when I returned to Gaza after my break, I found that my tent had been slept in during my absence. Consequently I awoke the next morning in a bad temper, which was not improved by the appearance of Mrs Fisher, our new boss. Minutes after we'd parted rather awkwardly, Commandant Lotte arrived in a great flurry and took me to one side. 'You've missed all the excitement,' he said, beaming. '*Quelle agitation!* The general told me I was to have Mrs Fisher as my driver, but I stood up for you and refused to change. The general was most put out. It seems that Mrs Fisher is a friend of his.'

Staring into the face of the fat little Frenchman and realizing how close I had come *in absentia* to being demoted back to dysentery duty, I could have hugged him. Knowing that such a public show of affection would only embarrass him, I squeezed his arm instead, thanked him as warmly as I could and resolved to buy him a fine dinner somewhere, some time.

My day improved still further. Boris Nazaroff suddenly appeared at the flap of my tent to invite me to dinner with the Legion later that evening. 'We heard you were ill but that now you are better,' he said in his broken English. 'We want to see you tonight.'

I was delighted to accept. It was some time since I'd last seen all my friends from the *Neuralia* days. I put on my smartest khaki skirt and a clean shirt and combed my hair as best I could without a looking-glass. Putting on a fine trace of lipstick, almost as an afterthought, I wandered over to the Legion mess where I found Amilakvari, Boris, dear John Hasey (the American boy who had almost won too much at baccarat), several other familiar faces and five

Australian officers. Everyone seemed to be in good form and pleased to see me. We dined well and drank even better.

Halfway through the evening Amilakvari declared that from now on I was to have a Legion nickname, a great honour for someone from outside its hallowed ranks. 'We shall call Adjudant Travers "La Miss",' he announced drunkenly. 'She is, after all, the only mademoiselle among us.'

To uproarious applause and much banging of the tables with hands, elbows and even feet, a toast was called and everyone drank my health. Beaming at them all, and taking a manly swig from my glass, I basked in their kindness and thanked them all for my new title, a name which would stick for the duration of the war and beyond. Needless to say, we all had far too much to drink that night, but the Australians exceeded even the Legion and ended up smashing all the glasses before being carried, singing, back to their tents on stretchers. John Hasey kindly walked me home.

The next morning I had the most terrible hangover, made worse by the fact that I had to be up at five thirty, and it was cold and raining. It was 7 May and we were leaving in a vast convoy for Syria. Everything was in a fearful muddle but I managed to position myself behind the cars from the headquarters and stuck to them like glue. It was devilish hard driving and even harder to stay awake when I'd had so little sleep the night before. We arrived at our rendezvous point in the dark passing a vast company of men on horseback.

Next day we drove on along the coast towards Tel Aviv in the slowest time imaginable, leaving before light and stopping every half hour for the rest of the convoy to catch up. Climbing slowly up a winding mountain road, unable to overtake or get ahead, the old Humber overheated badly and I wondered if it would make it to the top. It did, with steam pouring from under its rattling bonnet, and I resolved to stop at the next available opportunity to fill up the radiator and allow the poor old heap to cool down.

We had just reached the summit and were looking for a spot to pull over, when we heard the unmistakable noise of aircraft. High above us in the western sky we could see German planes, with the distinctive Luftwaffe swastika, bearing down on our vulnerable line of vehicles.

'*Vite! Vite!*' someone shouted, as we all leaped from our cars and dived for cover. Running in every direction, we just managed to hit the ground before a bomb dropped a hundred yards from us, showering us in rubble. Scrabbling to my feet, I ran for the shelter of a rock wall and found a boulder at the side of the road around whose contours I tried to mould my body for protection. Others acted similarly or simply lay on the ground, their hands cupped over their heads.

Above the noise of the aeroplanes' engines came the sound of machine-gun fire, the *rat-tat-tat-tat-tat* that could only mean the air crew's gunners had us in their sights. The bullets skimmed the hard surface of the road and ricocheted off in every direction. I felt one whizz past my left ear. Injured men cried out, vehicles hissed and slumped as the bullets slammed into their tired old bodies, and still the *rat-tat-tat-tat-tat* continued. After a while there was silence, but not for long. Ten minutes later the planes returned, although this time their bombs dropped further away. By the time they finally wheeled away into the distance, they'd left four men dead, three seriously injured and five vehicles in flames.

Our destination was the north of Vichy-controlled Syria, near the Turkish border, the British and Australians having already taken control of the south. When we eventually crossed the border at Deraa and began to engage in fighting with the Vichy French, our commander-in-chief, Colonel Monclar, resigned his commission. De Gaulle replaced him with his second-in-command.

The new colonel was a tall, thin, sallow-faced forty-three-year-old officer of Alsatian stock named

Marie-Pierre Koenig. He'd joined us from Cairo and had already led his men successfully into battle against the Vichy 6th Regiment at a little outpost called Deir Ali. Colonel Koenig was much admired by the men and many thought his appointment a wise and diplomatic move. With the help of the Allied troops, Koenig and the Free French were gradually able to push the Vichy French back as far as Damascus, where they were to dig themselves in for a long siege.

Much of Syria is mountainous. Behind the narrow, fertile coastal plain the mountain ranges, scored by deep valleys, drop eastward to the Great Rift Valley which continues to the Red Sea and into Africa. Driving across rutted roads and through deserted villages, I was struck by an air of sadness which hung about the place. An important trading crossroads, the nation had paid a heavy price for its coveted position, and its people bore this latest invasion with the long-suffering expressions that I'd come to recognize wherever I went. How tired they seemed of war; how sickened by the constant raping and pillaging of their lands for greed or glory. Their eyes peered out of their heavily lined faces with a resignation bordering on despair.

We were entering fiercely contested territory and the next few days of that scorching June 1941 were marked with battle after battle as we inched our way towards Damascus, through small towns and villages. Graves lined the road from Beirut to Ras el Naquora, the frontier post. In one day alone, thirteen men died and many more were wounded. Air raids became a common experience, the flies and the heat made everything worse, and I spent my time ferrying Lotte and his staff back and forth between hastily erected camps at Derur, Deir Ali, Salemaine, Racaoub and Tcherkmesskine. En route I'd collect any wounded soldiers I came across, pick up any stranded villagers and constantly search for better and less hazardous routes through to the battlefields that didn't involve driving over huge boulders.

We travelled through sleepy villages, past silver olive groves and terraced vineyards and across sun-baked hills. If they saw me struggling over some bumpy field or stranded in a pothole made by a recent shell, villagers would come scurrying from their cracked mud-brick homes, waving a white flag and shouting '*marhaba*' (hello) before helping me to move the offending rocks so that I could be on my way. Their long robes caked with dust and dirt, the little children clinging to their mothers' black yashmaks, the villagers looked bedraggled and bereft. '*Shukran, shukran,*' was all I could say, smiling, and if I had any chocolate left I'd break it into small pieces and divide it between them.

Each night when I returned home to bed, wherever that might be, I'd be dog tired and almost too exhausted to eat. Then I'd have to be up in the grey dawn and off on some bumpy road once more, avoiding German aeroplanes, rocks and other hazards. Sometimes Commandant Lotte would be my passenger, sometimes it would be his grumpy deputy Vialard Godou, and if the car was empty I'd pick up Arab stragglers on the road for company. I felt safer in the car when I wasn't alone. The background noise was constant gunfire and shelling, as distant mountain tops and vantage points were fought for and won.

Each time I arrived at a new encampment there would be a great flurry of activity. There had always either just been an air raid or they were expecting one and were moving off. It was a wonder I found anyone where they were supposed to be. Having just missed a raid at Deir Ali, I returned to Racaoub and found them preparing for one. I'd just sat down in my little hut after lunch to read a book when six planes flew low overhead and bombed us, the last of them returning four times and strafing us with machine-gun fire, before letting off one big bomb about fifty yards from where I sat. Getting up off the floor, where I'd lain since the raid began, I emerged from my little hut. Two people had been badly injured, one ambulance and a motorcycle completely destroyed. My car, thank goodness, was untouched.

115

By this time, we were in a notoriously dangerous area known as the Garden of Damascus. Lotte had gone ahead with another driver in a Legion ambulance with a motor-cycle outrider to try to find a road along which an advance party could evacuate the wounded. He left me at the camp with a smile. 'You stay here. I've been warned that these roads are often mined and are far too dangerous, my dear.' For once, I didn't argue.

It was in fact our mines, not those of the enemy, that caused the most trouble. The leading sappers were sup-posed to surround them with wire and markers to let us know where they were, and the sappers at the rear were supposed to remove the markers so that the enemy wouldn't see them. But that didn't always happen. Sometimes the sappers were under bombardment when they laid the mines and didn't have time; more often they didn't realize that we'd be coming through straight after-wards. Either way, bringing vehicles through was a hazardous business. People could get out and walk – there were no anti-personnel mines – but cars had to be driven through, usually by the driver.

Sadly, Lotte was proved right. The first I knew was when his driver sped into the camp on a motorcycle shout-ing, 'My ambulance has hit a landmine twenty kilometres back. One man's dead and Dr Lotte's very badly injured.' I wanted to go to the doctor and help if I could, but Mrs Fisher forbade it. Instead, she told me to collect Dr Thébault and send him with some troops. I was in such a state, not knowing if Lotte was alive or dead, that when I got into the Humber to drive off to find Thébault, I ran straight into a wall.

Lotte was eventually ferried back to the camp. Only partially conscious, his face chalky white, he was in a great deal of pain. The landmine had almost blown his legs off and his driver was lucky to escape with his life. Their motorcycle outrider had been killed instantly. I helped tend to Lotte's shattered leg and foot, believing that he would almost certainly die from loss of blood.

Miraculously, he survived, but was sent to a base hospital for treatment. I couldn't sleep a wink that night.

The next morning, I learned that my new boss was the huge and imperious Dr Vialard Godou. Tall and thin, he was most indignant at having a woman as a driver. Realizing that there was no-one else available, Dr Godou retaliated by insisting on driving the Humber himself, with me sitting next to him in the passenger seat, absolutely terrified. He drove far too fast, had no respect for worn tyres and pushed the weary old car to the limits of its endurance. He crunched through the gears and hit every bump and stone but I put up with his appalling driving for two days, until he crashed the Humber into an anti-tank wall, almost killing us both and badly damaging the steering.

'You're a terrible driver,' I told him angrily as I arranged for a crew from the tank regiment's workshop to hoist up the crumpled car and tow it away. 'And this car is my responsibility. Kindly remember that.'

The next day I spent a miserable morning cleaning the battered Humber and waiting for the mechanics to arrive. Godou was impatient. Every five minutes he'd leap to his feet and curse. 'Aren't they coming? Why don't they come?'

I remained silent. There were very few of us left in camp; everyone else had packed up and gone on to Deir Ali.

After an hour the mechanic arrived, ashen-faced, his car full of wounded men. 'The road's been bombed. I couldn't get through,' he said. 'There's many more injured back there.'

Without a word to me, Godou commandeered the mechanic and his car and drove off at great speed, back to the scene of the air raid, leaving me with seven wounded men. I arranged them as best I could under the trees and made them comfortable. Fortunately, most were only slightly hurt, with flesh wounds from shrapnel, concussion or shock. Only one was serious, a young man with flaxen hair and pale blue eyes, whose abdominal injuries were so severe that I suspected he would not survive. Taking off my coat, I laid it over him to keep him from shivering.

It was several hours before the mechanic returned, his tunic covered in blood. His hands were still shaking as he fixed the steering on the Humber.

Godou came back in a foul mood and barked at me: 'Come on, we've got to get to the advanced dressing station before it gets dark.'

Slipping in front of him just as he was about to climb into the driver's seat, I stared up at him coolly. 'I'm driving from now on. At least until we get to Damascus, or this car won't make it.'

He was about to protest, but he could tell from my expression that I would brook no argument. Huffing and puffing, he reluctantly took his place in the passenger seat.

Over four thousand men were killed or wounded that dry, hot summer, some of whom I knew well. Captain Jean Simon, whom I'd first met on the *Neuralia*, was shot in the head in the Garden of Damascus, losing his right eye. As I drove him to the base hospital for treatment he said: 'Tell me honestly, La Miss, do I look very frightening?'

I smiled. 'Not at all. You'll look terribly dashing with an eye patch.'

Worse still, John Hasey was hit in the face and chest by four machine-gun rounds and had his jaw shot off, taking his larynx with it. He was the first American in the war to have been injured in the name of France and General de Gaulle made him a Companion of the Legion. His war was over and, as soon as he was well enough to travel, he was shipped home for plastic surgery in the US.

My ideas of high adventure and dashing heroics were usurped by the cold, harsh reality that I could easily be killed, along with any of those I knew and loved. Visions of Lotte, Simon and the men I'd seen maimed and dying assailed my senses. In the shifting sands of Syria, I finally grew up and came to realize that nothing mattered more than life itself.

Driving alone was particularly frightening. Bumping the old Humber along the appalling Syrian roads, it was almost impossible to hear when the bombers were approaching. Often I had to keep one eye on the road and the other on the sky. Bombarded almost every day, I soon learned to recognize the different planes from the sound of their engines. The heavy Vichy bombers and the big German Junkers had a deeper resonance, while the Stukas and the Messerschmitts gave a high-pitched whine. The fighters were a much more personal threat because of their speed and agility but all of them were terrifying. It was always much easier in a convoy because there were usually other people who could watch out for the planes and warn of their approach.

It didn't always work that way, though. I remember driving up through southern Syria with Dr Godou and a detachment of the Free French on a bright spring day in 1941. The first I realized that we were in the middle of an air raid was when a bomb landed fifty yards ahead of me, narrowly missing a troop truck and showering sand across the road. One second everything was normal, then the view in front of me changed completely as our car was rocked backwards. The explosion blew the side off the truck and toppled it over into a dune. Men and equipment spilled from the ruptured vehicle, many of the troops bleeding and dazed. We all had a single objective, however.

Where there is one bomb, there are almost certainly a dozen more and none of us wanted to be caught out again. 'Air raid!' someone yelled, albeit a little late, and his cry sparked us into action. Leaping from our respective vehicles and diving for cover as best we could in the middle of the sandy valley, we heard the droning overhead for the first time and immediately identified our low-flying predators as Messerschmitts.

I knew that the Humber was too low to crawl under, so, when I saw a second truck being hit further up the stalled column, I chose a supplies vehicle which had gone off the road and into some dunes behind me. Quickly, I wriggled underneath, finding a place in the soft sand alongside several others, including a British soldier. Trying to catch my breath, I lay face down in the dust, my hands clamped over my head as the bombs started to rain down around us. Machine-guns strafed the road, sending up little puffs of sand a few feet from my nose. More bombs fell: one, two, three, and then another wave: one, two. There was no third and I raised my head to listen.

The noise of the engines was fading. The bombing had stopped and the planes were moving on, evidently satisfied with the damage they had done. Shuffling forward on my hips and elbows, I picked myself up, dusted myself down and looked around hastily to check on the Humber. It appeared unscathed. Several trucks were on fire, though, and many men lay dead or injured on the road.

Trying to decide to whom I should offer my assistance first, I caught sight of the only other person on his feet – an imposingly tall, blond man who had emerged from under a nearby truck at the same time as me. He was standing ten feet away and was as dishevelled and dusty as I was, but I could still make out the distinctive embroidered stripes on the epaulettes of his khaki shirt.

It could only be *le colonel*, my new Chief of Staff, Marie-Pierre Koenig. I'd never met him before but even with his cap slightly askew he had the bearing of a man of command. Our eyes met – his were grey-blue – and in those few moments we acknowledged our mutual relief at our salvation. I was surprised to find myself reddening at his half-smile.

Straightening up, I brushed myself down further and flicked a strand of dark hair from my face before heading back towards the first truck that had been hit, to see what could be done. The colonel watched me go, then strode purposefully back to his car, fished out his chauffeur who was still cowering beneath it, and continued on his way.

The next few days were some of the toughest of my life. Dr Godou seemed to me to be quite the most infuriating man I'd ever known. Still sulking because I wouldn't let him drive, he worked me extremely hard, and it was all I could do to keep up. If I wasn't ferrying him to and fro on uncompromising roads, he would make me fetch and carry for him, giving me what I felt were completely unreasonable deadlines in which to make the journey, and then expect me to drive him long distances again immediately afterwards.

I was exhausted. Even the troops were allowed more rest periods than I was! All that kept me going was my fury. I feared that if I succumbed to exhaustion he would turn round and say: 'Well, what can you expect? That's what happens when a woman thinks she can do a man's job.' I was determined that I wasn't going to let that happen.

He would have me up early in the morning, out all day and coming home after dark, when he knew I'd have to drive at only five miles per hour without lights along difficult roads, avoiding craters, anti-tank walls or abandoned vehicles, my eyes stinging with tiredness. But despite my fatigue, I was as stubborn as he was. I never once complained which, of course, only served to irritate him more.

One day at the end of that summer, he finally snapped. Ordering me into the passenger seat early one morning, he drove me in silence to the main encampment ten miles from where we were based. I had no idea what was going on, and felt so depleted that I didn't care. Wiping the perspiration from my forehead with the back of my arm, I soon gave in and fell asleep.

We pulled to a jerky halt outside the command tent twenty minutes later.

'Wait here,' he ordered crisply.

I did as I was told. Sitting half in, half out of the car, the door open for some air, I wondered how much more of his driving the old Humber and I could take. I felt unusually unwell.

The doctor wasn't long. Within ten minutes he was out

121

of that tent like a bear from his lair. He looked at me with an angry glint in his eye.

'You have a new assignment,' he said. 'Take your things and report to HQ.'

Jumping to my feet, I asked him what he meant.

'Just get your things out of this car,' he snapped. 'From now on, I shall be driving myself. *Adieu*.'

He got back into the driver's seat and turned the key in the ignition, barely leaving me time to grab my tools, my suitcase, my guns and other belongings from the boot. Speeding off in a cloud of dust, Dr Godou and the lovely old Humber disappeared from view.

Stepping gingerly towards the HQ, all my worldly goods in my arms, I squinted into the sunlight as a tall figure emerged from the dark tent and came towards me. '*Bonjour*,' he said, politely extending a hand, 'Colonel Marie-Pierre Koenig.' I recognized him immediately. 'Adjudant Travers? You're to be my new driver.'

Dropping my things to the ground, I wiped my sweaty palm on my shorts before shaking his hand in bewilderment. The date was 17 June 1941.

It was several days before I discovered what had happened. Dr Godou had gone directly to the colonel to complain about me. 'She is completely unsuitable to the role,' he railed.

The colonel had listened in silence and then stood up, to indicate that the doctor's unscheduled audience with him was drawing to an end. 'Very well, if that's the way you feel,' he responded, 'she'll no longer work for you. I need a driver. Mine was killed yesterday. I'll take her off your hands.'

I'd never driven a colonel before. It was a big promotion. All the other senior officers' chauffeurs were men, and they were treated with the utmost respect because they had the top jobs. They were at the core of the action, responsible for the safety of their commanders. They had to keep their charges alive and mobile at all costs. I'd come to the Middle East for adventure and, as Colonel Koenig's new driver, I was most certainly going to get it. He had a reputation as a front-line soldier, the type of man who led his troops into battle personally. I was thrilled. I just wished my head wasn't pounding quite so much.

My first few days as the colonel's driver were spent getting used to his car, an old Humber 38 with very stiff acceleration and no brakes, but with a French tricolour proudly fluttering on its bonnet. Not that there weren't teething problems. The colonel's former driver had been hit by a shell as he unwisely picked vegetables in the Garden of Damascus, the keys to the car in his pocket. I enlisted the help of a mechanic to rig up a hot-wire system to start my new vehicle – rubbing two wires together under the steering column to start the engine – a system that was never superseded in the entire time I was to drive that car.

Once I'd got it working, I spent much of my time ferrying his staff to and from Nazareth, where the new headquarters had been set up. Sneyd-Cox, the colonel's new liaison officer, was my most frequent passenger. The ride to Nazareth was long and dusty. All I could hear was the blood thumping in my ears and I seemed to have an unquenchable thirst. The Lake of Tiberias looked beautifully blue and cool and all I wanted to do was leap into its waters. Nazareth itself was disappointing, I thought. Dirty and dusty, full of people and vehicles, it was little more than a ramshackle cluster of buildings and churches. The Turkish influence was still evident in some of the Moorish architecture and there were a few grand British edifices, but overall it felt and looked like a town that had changed hands many times.

In the bustling souk I bought some things for myself and some grapes and melons for the colonel. On the way back, we came to a bridge patrolled by some Australians.

'You're the first vehicle across since it's been mined,' an officer told me in his distinctive twang. 'You'll have to go very carefully. Would you like one of my men to drive the car across for you?'

I shook my head emphatically. 'No, thanks,' I replied, as cheerfully as I could. 'I've strict orders not to let anyone else drive this car. I'll manage.'

Sneyd-Cox was out like a shot, telling me jauntily that he'd join me on the other side. An Australian corporal walked slowly in front as I rolled across with barely enough room for my wheels to pass between the rows of sandbags. The sweat drenched my shirt and the unnatural beating of my heart left me in no doubt that I was far from the heroine they thought me to be.

The headquarters had been moved after the bombardments and by the time we returned the only sign of where it had been was several still-burning armoured cars. We eventually found the new HQ in one of the crusader castles. We reached it after dark, driving slowly and with no lights. I was dead tired and couldn't eat. The colonel took one look at me and offered me the use of his bed for the night.

I had been told that the colonel usually rose at five. The next morning, I was up at four thirty. Feeling lousy, I got the car ready and filled it with petrol. The front tyre was flat, so I persuaded some nice Englishmen to help me change it. I fell asleep in the car and was woken at nine and ordered to take two of the colonel's staff to Kissoue. Once there, I felt tired to death again. I couldn't manage any lunch and I hoped I wasn't going down with anything serious. Wiping the perspiration from my forehead, all I felt was an incredible urge to sleep.

Deciding to take a bath to make myself feel better, I fetched the canvas contraption from my luggage and got it ready. Along with the canvas bed from the Army and Navy, it had been a lifesaver over the previous eighteen months. They were my most prized possessions.

The bath was suspended from a simple A-frame. Once it was in position, I could fill it with water from a jerrycan, climb in and have a really good wash. All I needed was a bar of soap and some privacy. Looking around the castle, I unlocked a door to a half-ruined stable block in a small courtyard and peered inside. Blinking back at me were a dozen or so pairs of brown eyes, belonging to a group of men lying on the straw-covered floor. I assumed them to be Arab scouts or interpreters for the Legion, so I clapped my hands together and turfed them out into the courtyard. I fetched some water, bolted the door behind me and had a nice wash.

Clean and fresh and in a much better frame of mind, I unlocked the door and wandered out into the courtyard, my hair still damp, a towel around my neck.

'What on earth do you think you're doing?' an officer barked as he marched towards me, his expression thunderous. Behind him, sitting cross-legged on the ground, were the evicted former tenants of the stable block.

'Taking a bath,' I replied, brushing past him and heading for my car.

'You had no authority to release those men from the building,' the officer persisted, striding along beside me, hands on hips.

As I looked down at them, I suddenly realized who they were: Italian, French and Arab prisoners of war from the Vichy side, for whom the stables had been a makeshift prison. Fortunately for me, they'd been far too tired and hungry to run away.

By 21 June Damascus had been taken, and I had to drive the colonel across the Bekaa valley to take part in the 'triumphal' parade. It was one of the first times I'd ever driven him and I felt unusually nervous at the responsibility.

The largest city in Syria, the burial place of St John the Baptist and Saladin, Damascus lived up to its reputation for beauty: it was a green oasis rising from the desert. Even though I felt so unwell, driving through the dusty streets was a memorable experience. With the colonel sitting beside me in the front seat, I was trembling with anxiety and hardly dared look at him. We were the third car in the procession, behind General Catroux and his staff, sur-rounded by the Tcherkess cavalry, who practically had to gallop to keep up with us. Our rearguard was protected by armoured cars and our troops marched through the out-skirts of the city shouting: 'We come to wash away the shame of Vichy capitulation.'

But when we arrived in the city itself, we were received in stony silence. People took to the streets to watch us pass, but they did so with their arms crossed, faces long. The parade was not seen as a triumph by those who'd allied themselves with the Vichy French. On the contrary, many still saw us as the traitors. The colonel said nothing, but I saw the muscles in his jaw tighten as he realized that he and the general had been cheated of their grand spectacle.

Damascus became my home for several weeks as the colonel settled into his new role, organizing the troops still fighting the last of the Vichy French in Syria and liaising with their commanders, trying to persuade them to come over to our side. I had little to do except drive his staff around and tend to the car, which was just as well because as each day passed I felt worse and worse. My insides were burning, I had a pain deep within me, and a dreadful lethargy that overwhelmed me completely. Whenever possible I lay down and slept, sometimes on the floor of the garage where the car was parked. Eating was difficult and staying awake was more so. I got some sort of tonic from the chemist but it didn't do any good. My limbs felt so weak, it was all I could do to drive the car.

Finally admitting defeat after a dreadful night of stomach cramps, fever and headache, I took myself off to the hospital to get something stronger.

'I need a prescription for a bad stomach,' I told the doctor rather impatiently, having been made to wait for an hour.

Taking one look at me, he shook his head and laughed. 'You'll need more than that. Look at the colour of you!' Holding up a mirror, the first I'd seen in months, he showed me my yellow reflection. 'You've got jaundice, my dear. You'll have to be admitted to hospital straight away.'

Placed in a ward in a former Vichy hospital, I slumped into a bed with no intention of getting up again. Later I was transferred to the Spears' hospital – a lovely clean place with white walls and blue blankets – where I was diagnosed as having severe hepatitis. It was my first encounter with serious disease since I'd set foot in Africa, although hundreds of others with me had been stricken with malaria, dysentery and hepatitis through a combination of poor sanitation, bad water and tainted food.

Complete rest was prescribed, which I tried to resist, fearing for my new position. Lying in bed with my skin and the whites of my eyes bright yellow, I was un-doubtedly seriously ill, but my biggest concern was the colonel. I expected to hear any minute that he had taken on another driver, someone more reliable, probably a man. Whenever anyone came to see me, I asked for word of him. Boris Nazaroff was my first visitor, dropping in from an adjacent ward with a huge bandage on his head. He had been hit by flying shrapnel. I was very pleased to see him but the news he brought was not so comforting.

He told me that the Free French, led by Amilakvari and his men, had been involved in some heavy fighting at the front. The losses had been enormous on both sides and, despite the fall of Damascus, the Italians and Vichy French were showing no signs of surrender. Amilakvari had tried to negotiate, ordering ceasefires and sometimes going forward alone to attempt to reason with the Vichy com-manders. On one celebrated occasion, some Vichy soldiers had wandered into the Free French position and asked directions, thinking they were on the same side. Amilakvari chastised them severely for getting lost and told them: 'You'll land yourselves right in the shit if you go any further.' Stunned to realize they were face to face with a legendary Free French commander, they surrendered im-mediately and joined his company.

At one gun emplacement, he found a timid young French sergeant who told him he had orders to hold out until 1 a.m.

'Very well, then,' Amilakvari replied, with a smile. 'We shall return at two.'

The sergeant, relieved that he would not be disobeying orders and that he would have enough time to retreat with his men, thanked the gallant White Russian prince.

I also learned that General de Gaulle was in town, and had visited some of the wounded in the ward a few doors along from mine. Colonel Koenig must have accompanied him, and yet he hadn't bothered to come and see me. I feared that he was exasperated by my dereliction of duty in falling ill so soon after being taken on, and was too angry with me even to pop his head round my door.

The doctor came to see me twice a day and was most attentive. Other friends trickled in and out, bringing flowers, chocolates (which I was not allowed to eat) and the latest news. Lying in my bed, despondent and weak, I feared my front-line role was coming to an end. If the Free French, and with them the colonel, moved on to Russia as Boris told me they might, I'd probably be returned to the nursing staff and spend the rest of the war driving heavy ambulances through sand dunes.

Rolling over despairingly, I buried my face in my pillow and groaned.

9

DAYS OF WINE AND ROSES

'He who wants a rose must respect the thorn.'

PERSIAN PROVERB

It was a sunny morning at the end of June and I had been in hospital for a week. I was looking out of the little window in my room towards the purple mountains in the distance, and feeling rather sleepy, when there was a gentle knock at my door.

Turning, I was astonished to see Colonel Koenig enter my room. He looked dashing in his best khaki, and far from angry.

'May I come in?' He spoke in English with a marked French accent.

'Yes, yes, please, *entrez*,' I said, struggling to pull myself up to a sitting position. Seeing how weak I was, he rushed forward to plump up my pillows. Embarrassed, I pulled my blue blanket up to my neck and thanked him.

'How are you feeling?' he asked, pulling up a chair and sitting under the window. His blond hair looked like golden straw in the sunlight. On his lap lay an enormous box of chocolates, tied with a red velvet ribbon.

'I'm getting better every day,' I assured him, my gaunt features belying my words. 'I should be out of here any time now. I just need a few more days' rest.'

'Well, you're not to worry,' he replied. 'Take your time.

129

My orders are to stay in Damascus for a while and I've hired a civilian driver until you're better. We can't have you getting sick again, can we?'

I was encouraged by his words but could only lean back against the pillows in response, aware of my yellow skin against the white cotton. The conversation which followed was stilted. We hardly knew each other and I'd only driven him once or twice. We had little in common and I wasn't up to small talk. Realizing how much he was tiring me, he stood up and said goodbye, remembering the chocolates as he was leaving the room.

'Oh, these are for you,' he said, handing them to me rather hesitantly.

I thanked him again and he left. For several minutes afterwards, the room smelt of his aftershave and the leather of his well-polished shoes.

Sliding back down the bed, I wondered what his visit had meant. Was he just being kind? Perhaps now that he'd seen how unwell I was, he'd understand that I wasn't going to be fit for some time. He might even replace me.

But I needn't have worried. That evening, a huge bunch of flowers arrived at my bedside. The card read simply: 'Koenig.' Astonished and touched, I knew that my job was safe.

Over the next two weeks, the colonel sent a selection of books for me to read, clearly carefully chosen. Among them were books of poetry written by soldiers such as Wilfred Owen and Siegfried Sassoon in the First World War. I don't know if it was because I was feeling under the weather or because I had started to appreciate the stark realities of war, but their sad words often moved me to tears. I was touched to think that a man as apparently battle-hardened as the colonel could be so sensitive.

I knew I was getting better when my appetite returned. I felt ravenously hungry all the time and could think of nothing but food. I was, at last, allowed a small portion of meat once a day and that appeased my hunger a little, but not much. I couldn't wait to get out and find a restaurant somewhere for a really good meal. Hearing this, the colonel sent an enormous basket of fruit. It was delivered by his orderly who also gave me the message that the colonel would be coming in to see me later that afternoon.

I washed and put on a clean nightgown for the occasion, and waited about all day. By the time I heard a knock on the door, I'd virtually given up hope. It wasn't the colonel, but Rosie Curtis, the nurse who'd been on the *Westernland* and with Nadine and me in Brazzaville. She was now a Spearette and had popped in from another ward to say hello.

'I must say, I do envy you being Koenig's chauffeur.' Her eyes were wide as she perched on the end of my bed, gobbling my grapes. 'That's far more glamorous than being in here cleaning out bedpans.'

There was another knock. It was Simpson, a British officer I'd met in Brazzaville, with more flowers. 'Roses for a rose,' he crooned, and Rosie and I nearly burst out laughing. I rather uncharitably hoped that both of them would leave before the colonel arrived. I didn't want Koenig to think that the Englishman was a suitor or that I had more than my fair share of visitors already. But Simpson seemed depressed. He told me a good friend of his had been killed in the latest fighting and I didn't have the heart to turn him away.

The colonel arrived at eight, long after Simpson had left. He came with more books and flowers and our conversation flowed far more easily this time. I guessed he was probably rather lonely and was glad of the chance to chat to someone outside the military and not of the same sex. The longer he stayed, the more he relaxed. He smiled from time to time and his eyes sparkled. He was attentive and kind, and I decided that he had a most attractive manner when he wished. There was much about him which reminded me of my father.

Stung by the thought that I hadn't had any contact with my parents for a while, I wrote Father a letter later that night, telling him my news. 'I've been very ill, but am on the mend,' I said cheerfully. 'I now have a job as the colonel's chauffeur, and when I'm discharged from hospital, I hope to be of more use to those on the front lines.' Enquiring after him and my mother, I signed off and sealed the envelope. Now all I needed was a stamp.

Over the next week I was allowed out of bed more and more, first for an hour, then two, and at last for half a day. I put my release period to good use: I took a cab to HQ to find out when I was going to be paid (being an invalid had somehow meant a suspension of my pay), and had an enormous lunch out with Henry and Sneyd-Cox, my first proper meal in weeks. But my eyes were far bigger than my stomach and the food only made me ill and sent me back to bed for two days.

Some more beautiful flowers arrived from the colonel, this time with a note. 'Wishing you good health and a speedy return to work. Koenig,' he wrote. He came round later that evening and was very charming, sitting on the edge of my bed with the relaxed air of an old friend.

'You look so much better,' he told me, smiling. 'Your eyes are much improved with white around them instead of yellow.'

I giggled at his backhanded compliment and blushed slightly. It felt almost as if I was being wooed, and I was enjoying the attention.

'Perhaps when you're feeling up to it,' he added softly, 'we could have dinner?'

Touched and more than a little flattered, I agreed immediately.

After three more weeks confined to the wards, I was allowed out of hospital almost daily for a period of eight days' convalescence, after which I was told I could resume light duties. I couldn't wait to get back to work. The colonel seemed so much nicer than I'd ever imagined him to be and I was very much looking forward to working with him.

My first task was to make sure the car was still in one piece. To my horror, I found that although the Humber was fine, my tools – begged, borrowed and stolen over the years – were missing. In great indignation, I went to HQ and tried to see the colonel to complain about it, but was told that he was engaged. Storming back to the workshop, I found the corporal in charge and demanded that my tools be returned immediately.

'Certainly, madame,' he said courteously, reaching into a padlocked cupboard. 'I put them to one side for you to prevent them from being stolen.' My head thumping and the shame evident on my face, I thanked him and crept back to my hospital bed.

The next day I went to the souk and found a tailor, ordering myself a new uniform, two skirts and three shirts in unbecoming khaki, for the grand total of £4 10s, which felt like a fortune (I earned just short of five shillings a day). I couldn't find a beret anywhere. Instead, I went to the hairdresser's and had my by now rather unkempt hair cut into its traditional bob. Feeling much better and able to face the colonel when I resumed work, I returned to the hospital to rest. A letter from my parents was waiting for me, dated four months earlier.

The news from England made me realize how things were changing. Father wrote that Ernest Bevin, the Minister of Labour, had called for at least 100,000 women to come to work in the factories while the men were on active service. Compulsory registration of women in their twenties had begun, in a massive mobilization drive. Armaments factories were working round the clock and women were needed on the production line to fill shells and take on the jobs vacated by the men. 'They still won't let me go to the front,' my father complained. 'They've upped the age for enlistment for men to forty-two, but I'm apparently way over the hill.' Mother scribbled a few lines in her frail, spidery handwriting, saying that Laurence was busy and she hoped I was getting enough to eat. Some things never changed.

It was 7 July before I was finally discharged from the hospital. As I packed my belongings into a suitcase, the most enormous bunch of white roses arrived from the colonel. Once again, the note said simply: 'Koenig.'

Lady Spears had come to say goodbye and was in my room when the flowers arrived. She expressed her astonishment.

'My, oh my,' she said in her slow American drawl, her snub nose twitching above a mouth which bore the hint of a smile. 'I'd say this bouquet looks more like a gift from an attentive husband to his wife on their wedding day than from an employer to his chauffeur.' She looked at me askance, her kind eyes smiling.

I liked Lady Spears enormously.

The colonel himself then arrived in an enormous black taxi. Having dropped off my luggage at my new quarters, the Orient Palace Hotel, he took me to lunch at the local club. We had a lovely meal; he was completely charming and, I couldn't help but notice once more, really rather attractive.

'Thank you for the roses,' I said. 'They're beautiful. I adore flowers.'

'Then you should always be surrounded by them, my dear,' he said, reaching across the table to squeeze my hand. We went for a stroll together afterwards, chatting about the weather and our likes and dislikes. By the time I went home to bed, I felt physically exhausted by my first full day on my feet, but my head and my heart were pounding with a schoolgirl excitement, the like of which I'd never felt before.

The next few days were filled mainly with car duties (the colonel had driven the Humber in my absence and it was now not working), interspersed with the occasional evening out with friends. Simpson did his damnedest to court me, but I shed him whenever I could. I still wasn't feeling very well and was unable to drink, so I felt rather depressed and depleted much of the time. I was better off resting quietly.

I went to the souk to collect my uniform, but the market had been shut after a fracas involving some drunken Australians. Taking a cab to the mosque instead, I was impressed at how lovely it was with its ornate stonework and turquoise tiling. Collecting my shotgun (which I'd been given on a crocodile hunt near Brazzaville), I took it to the armourer and asked him to clean it and get some ammunition for me. He also promised to make me a leather case for it. By the time I returned to the souk it was open again and I had a lovely afternoon admiring the luxurious silks. I bought a dark red beret for £1, nearly fell for some expensive green brocade, and ordered two pairs of silk pyjamas. My uniform was ready. It was well made and becoming, despite the colour. I'd lost a great deal of weight during my illness and I thought it suited me.

A few days later, the colonel received new orders. The HQ was being moved to Beirut and so was he. There were hopes of an armistice with the Vichy French and he was to be the Free French delegate and one of the chief negotiators. To celebrate his good news, he took me to lunch with the Legion, accompanied by Henry and Sneyd-Cox. It was good to see the Legion again, although Amilakvari was in a very bad temper. I wondered idly if it had anything to do with the colonel being so attentive.

On my way home, I stopped at the souk and impulsively ordered the green brocade, asking for it to be made up into a gallabiyah, an Arab-style dress. Chastising myself for my extravagance, I wondered when on earth I would find an occasion to wear it.

By mid-July a ceasefire had been announced between the warring Frenchmen, and Colonel Koenig had been posted to the Armistice Commission at Acre in Syria to liaise with General Georges Catroux, our Chief of Staff. I took him there proudly in the Humber, delighted with the turn of events. Driving him around Damascus had been a privilege, but accompanying him on such historic business was truly exciting. I was also pleased to be given a chance to show off my driving skills. I'd been practising with the unfamiliar car and had even mastered the stiff accelerator pedal and the poor brakes. But the colonel was far too pre-occupied with his ever-present bundle of documents even to notice. It was a long time before I found out that he didn't need to be impressed.

Ferrying him around in those first few days, I began to watch him out of the corner of my eye and tried to assess what sort of a man he really was. Tall and straight-backed with blue-grey eyes and a moustache, he was more authoritative-looking than handsome. In his early forties, he was eleven years older than me and his hair at close quarters was greying slightly. Now that I was out of my hospital bed his manner towards me was much more soldierly, even rather stiff and formal on occasion, but then, I thought wryly, he was busy with matters of diplomacy and weighed down with responsibility. Even when he had been at his most attentive, sending me flowers, he'd never signed himself anything more than 'Koenig'. The colonel, I decided, wasn't a man who gave much away.

Less than a week after I'd left my sickbed, I collected him from his hotel and he sat beside me as usual, with barely a grunt, immersed in his documents. There was a long silence as I drove him up the mountain road to Beirut. I watched the spectacular scenery speeding past and privately congratulated myself on landing such a plum job.

The colonel broke the silence. 'What do people call you?' he asked finally, without even bothering to look up from his papers. 'Those who know you, I mean.'

Staring straight at the road ahead, I said: 'Those who don't know me very well call me Adjudant Travers, sir.' Glancing sideways at him, I added with a smile: 'But those who know me better call me La Miss.'

The colonel raised his head and looked at me, his expression level. I wondered if I'd said too much.

'Very well, Adjudant Travers,' he said at length. 'As I shall undoubtedly get to know you very well indeed in the long months ahead, La Miss it is.'

He returned to the documents on his lap. From then on, La Miss was the name he used to address me.

Later that night, we checked into a hotel near Acre and I retired early. I was exhausted from the long drive but unable to sleep. Not for the first time, I reflected on how destiny hung by an alarmingly slender thread. If Dr Lotte hadn't been injured, if Dr Godou hadn't disliked me quite so much, if Koenig hadn't been promoted, then I might never have found myself upon this unusual career path and in the company of a man who inspired me completely. I fell asleep with a smile on my face.

The following morning I drove the colonel to the Armistice Commission and waited outside all day, taking the opportunity to clean the spark plugs on the car and check the self-starter. On the way back to Beirut that evening, he seemed very quiet and thoughtful. I wondered if his meetings had gone badly. After several minutes of silence, however, I realized that he was watching me. Sitting upright and feeling tremendously self-conscious, I concentrated on changing gears smoothly and avoiding any holes in the road.

'Would you care to join me for dinner tonight, La Miss?' the colonel asked suddenly, his tone softer than I'd ever heard it. 'Just the two of us?'

I looked across at him to make sure that he was serious. 'Yes, sir,' I replied, without hesitation. '*Merci, mon colonel.*'

Nothing more was said and I drove on, delighted. I'd been very much hoping for another chance to reacquaint myself with the softer side of the man, the one who'd first sat on the edge of my bed and read me poetry, as opposed to the statesman and soldier so often bogged down with affairs of war. I wanted to be his friend, his confidante. I'd sensed from the start that here was a commander who needed an ally and I hoped that I might be the one he'd turn to.

We checked into a little hotel on the seafront at Beirut and I went straight to my room. After a long soak in a hot tub, I changed, swapping my shorts for my new khaki skirt, combed my hair and joined the colonel in the dining room. He welcomed me warmly, rising from his table to greet me with a firm handshake. Over wine and an excellent meal of fresh crab, he asked me about my life up until the war, and about my time in Finland and the Congo. He listened to tales of my childhood, my father's military career, our move to France and my life of tennis, socializing and travelling.

When I dared to ask a few questions of my own, however, he was less open. He had been sixteen when the First World War broke out, he told me. Leaving college, he had served with the infantry and been awarded the military medal. Spurning further study, he had stayed on with the army after the war, and seen duty in the Alps and in Morocco. When the Second World War was declared, he had led the 13DBLE as a captain in the battle of Narvik in Norway, not very far from where I had spent the early months. His success there had guaranteed him promotion, a fact which made his wife very happy. But once France had fallen, he had fled to Britain with six friends, catching a fishing boat to Jersey in order to join de Gaulle's forces. He'd sailed with the 13DBLE for French Africa on the *Pennland*, the sister ship to the *Westernland*, on the same day as I did. His 'defection' to the Free French was a move which upset Madame Koenig greatly, not least because it meant that her husband was officially branded a traitor.

'Have you any children?' I asked politely, at the mention of his wife.

'No,' he replied, after a short hesitation. 'None of my own, anyway; my wife has children from her previous marriage.'

'And what is your wife like?' I asked, realizing from his quick frown that I might have overstepped the mark. I played with my glass as I waited for his response.

There was an uneasy silence between us for a while. When he spoke, his tone was measured.

'Wealthy, well connected. An aristocrat,' he said, his

138

eyes far away. 'Sometimes overprotective and over-ambitious for me.'

Whenever he spoke of his wife, I noticed that his face clouded over slightly. But he was too professional a soldier to let me know too much. Choosing his words carefully, ever the politician, he directed the conversation away from personal matters each time I tried to pry. Painfully aware that he was my employer, not my friend, I didn't press him further.

We finished our dessert and wine, drank the rest of our coffee and said goodnight in the lobby, shaking hands and going our separate ways at the top of the stairs. As I closed my bedroom door behind me, I felt more content than I had for a long time. The more I got to know Koenig, I decided, the more I liked him. Beneath that well-bred, sophisticated and somewhat remote exterior, I glimpsed a man who was perhaps a little sad and lonely, and who wasn't accustomed to expressing his innermost feelings.

I'd seen him lose his temper once or twice with his subordinates and I knew that he could be sharp and even quite cruel at times, but I didn't believe it to be deliberate. It was more the result of frustration and an inner unhappiness, I felt. He was undoubtedly weighed down with the business of war, keen to play his part and to seek glory for the Free French and the Legion. But there was also another side to him, a gentler side which appealed to me on a very different level.

I was just about to undress when I heard a gentle tapping at my door. I opened it and, to my surprise, found the colonel standing in the doorway, with an expression on his face I knew only too well. My mind flashed back to the hotel room in Rome fifteen years earlier, when Hannibal had appeared with his bottle of champagne and two glasses. The colonel was empty-handed but his intention was clearly the same.

Stepping into the room, he pulled me towards him as he closed the door and kissed me hard on the lips. I was more than a little taken aback and, pushing him away, I told him so.

'I'm afraid I – I wasn't expecting this,' I said falteringly. 'You've rather caught me on the hop – sir.'

My disappointment must have been written all over my face. I think I'd hoped for better from him. I so wanted him to be different from those who'd gone before.

Seeing my hesitation, the colonel took my hand and apologized. 'I'm so very sorry, my dear,' he said. 'I thought we understood each other. I thought this was what you wanted too.' Moving towards me again, he began to kiss and caress me gently.

Trying hard to think what this would mean to my job, I took a deep breath and pushed him away once more. 'Colonel, I – I don't think it would be right if this went any further. I – I mean, if that's all right, I'd like some time to think about this.'

Koenig stopped. His face was a picture of confusion and I chastised myself inwardly for my unintentional forwardness. Yes, I found him attractive and I'd certainly allowed myself to entertain wild notions of our professional relationship developing into something deeper. But it would complicate matters enormously if we became lovers. I wanted the colonel to like me primarily for my companionship and my driving skills, not for anything else. I'd thought that was why he'd hired me in the first place. Now I wondered if I had been naive.

Taking my hand, he reached forward to nuzzle my neck. Again and again he tried to make advances which I resisted. It wasn't that I didn't want him to seduce me. I just felt that this wasn't something I should rush into as I'd always done before, usually with disastrous results.

Defeated at last, the colonel stopped, sighed, picked up his hat and left the room, closing the door quietly behind him. He left me dishevelled and shaken in the middle of my bedroom. What on earth was I going to do next?

The next few days were, I think, among the longest of my life. The colonel made no mention of the events of that fateful evening, and neither did I. It was strictly business as usual, with few niceties and no more kind gestures. He continued with his meetings and I carried out my duties as carefully and professionally as I could, all the while wondering when he might make his next move.

I had been placed in a very difficult position. It was not that I didn't find him attractive – the opposite was true – it just hadn't been what I'd expected when I was given the job. He seemed so far above me. He was my colonel and, although I was of much the same class and background, I was his chauffeur. My time in the army had served me well. I knew my place and, after the shallow years of my youth when I never really felt at home anywhere, I'd come to enjoy knowing exactly where I stood. Now here was the colonel upsetting the apple cart.

I was also being pushed into a relationship which I knew could only lead to heartache. Not only was he my boss, he was married. For the first time in my adult life, I'd become accustomed to being alone and was no longer prepared to jump into bed with anyone. The next time I slept with a man, I wanted it to be for real. I wanted to love and be loved in a way I never had before. Something inside had already told me that the colonel was someone special; that he above all others had the qualities and ingredients to make my dreams come true. But if he was to be the one, I wanted to choose him in my own time and in my own way, and not be rushed into it in such a perfunctory manner.

As I was to discover later, the colonel's way of handling disappointment was to become introverted and rather gruff. He'd always been very direct with me, and I'd come to accept that he could sometimes be harsh and a little self-centred. In public he behaved very much as the colonel and treated me as his chauffeur. In private he'd been much softer, but he never allowed me to think that I was any-thing but his inferior. We both knew that if I defied him, I would lose not only him but the job I loved so much.

On the fifth day after he had come to my room, he asked me to drive him to Beirut to attend more meetings. We journeyed along with a chasm of silence between us.

141

He pretended to read his papers but kept looking up and across at me, a fact which made me increasingly nervous. When we reached our destination he got out of the car with a sigh, slamming the door behind him.

I waited outside as usual, using a stick to fend off the filthy street children who wanted to pull bits from the car. When the colonel emerged from the building several hours later, he looked tired and fed up.

'To the hotel,' he snapped, climbing in beside me.

I started the engine but didn't move off. Swallowing hard, I asked timorously, 'Which hotel, sir?' He'd forgotten to tell me.

His eyes softened as he studied my anxious face. 'We're staying at the Sash d'Orange tonight.' There was a pause. 'It's very beautiful and overlooks the sea. I think you'll like it.'

I looked across at him and sighed, hoping that this meant an end to the awkwardness between us. I so wanted to be in his good books. 'Thank you, sir,' I said with a smile. 'I'm sure I shall.'

He was right. The hotel was beautiful and I stood on the verandah, watching streaks of red and gold light up the sky as the sun set across the sea, while he checked us into our separate rooms. Turning back towards the lobby, I studied him in his crisp khaki uniform at the desk, signing the register. He cut an impressive figure, I thought. A colonel was undoubtedly a catch, and he was attractive. Perhaps I'd been too hasty in turning him away.

After bidding me goodnight in the lobby, he climbed the stairs to his room. I watched him go, feeling a strange aching sensation inside. How good it would be to lie in his arms tonight. Not since Amilakvari had I felt such longing. Collecting my key with a heavy heart, I made my way to my room alone.

Waiting for me on a small centre table was a huge bouquet of white roses. The card read simply: 'Koenig.'

Within the hour he was at my door.

'This has gone on long enough,' was all he said as he

142

stepped inside and bolted it behind him. His eyes were bright and he reached up and ran his long fingers through my hair. Allowing my fingers to do the same to his, inhaling his special scent, I knew I could no longer hold out against him. When our lips met, I felt a pang of remorse that I hadn't let this happen sooner.

As if he was reading my thoughts, he kissed me on the forehead and held my face in his hands. 'You have nothing to fear,' he told me, his voice warm.

I reached up and brushed his lips with my fingertips.

Nothing further was said, and that night we slept together for the first time. His lovemaking was gentle and kind, apologetic almost. He seemed aware of my reticence, sensing my nervousness and referring back to my eyes time and again to make sure that I was comfortable with what was happening. I was, but I also felt strangely emotional. Blinking away my tears, I succumbed to his caresses and allowed myself to relax. After several hours, we fell asleep in each other's arms, his heavy limbs entwined around me. At dawn I felt him stir. Kissing my bare shoulder softly, he slipped out of my bed, dressed and crept from my room, without saying a word. I lay back, staring at the ceiling, trying not to cry.

Later that day, an armistice was signed between the Vichy French and the Free French in Syria. Under the terms of the agreement, the remaining Vichy legionnaires of the Syrian garrison – those who had not been killed or wounded or had not already defected to the Free French from POW camps – were to be offered a choice between repatriation to France or secondment to the 13DBLE.

This *séance d'option* was held a month later in the large square in the middle of T2, the Free French camp just outside Beirut. In suffocating heat, the colonel, in the presence of the dashing de Sairigné and others, told the Vichyists that they should file through a door, turning right if they chose to stay with the 13th and left if they chose to go home and wait out the war. Such was the feeling against

143

the Free French that all but one chose to go home. Those diehard supporters of Vichy France said that to go with the 13th would be to 'trample on the corpses' of their comrades in arms. The colonel was bitterly disappointed.

But there were no disappointments in my relationship with him, which became increasingly rewarding over the next few months. It was wonderful to share a bed each night as we travelled together throughout Syria, Palestine and Lebanon. Despite myself, I grew increasingly fond of him, and he of me. I think we surprised each other by our compatibility. Gone were his gruffness and sour temper. In their place were kindness and a surprising amount of sentimentality. In those early days he made me feel cherished and loved, despite the fact that our affair had to be conducted in the utmost secrecy.

'I'm a very jealous man, La Miss,' he told me from the outset, as we lay together one night in Beirut. 'I'm also a very private man. I know that I can trust you in both regards.'

I'll never forget his steady gaze.

'Of course, *mon colonel*,' I reassured him, choosing my words carefully. 'I promise I shall do nothing to disappoint you.'

He was a reasonable driver and often took the wheel to give me a break as we shunted back and forth along the Lebanese coast. I liked it when he drove me, and would sit in the passenger seat watching him endlessly. I never seemed to tire of the sight of him. Sometimes he would let me hold his hand, our fingers intertwined in a simple but deeply erotic gesture.

Once, when we reached the town of Haifa, he startled me from my afternoon nap in the passenger seat by screeching to a halt in the middle of a busy thoroughfare. Looking up, I wondered what he'd stopped for. Leaping from the car without a word, he ran to a flower stall and bought up every bloom the delighted girl had to sell. Filling my arms with the bouquets, he beamed at me, pleased at my surprise.

144

Me aged five with one of my
grandmother's bows in my hair.

Aged seven
with my mother,
brother Laurence,
and Duchess,
our labrador.

My father in the
Home Guard
when he was in
his seventies.

Grown up at last: on the steps of my parents' house in Cannes.

In the 1930s I embarked on a round of socializing across Europe, cross-country skiing in Austria and playing tennis. I never liked my white stockings and was delighted when Suzanne Lenglen had them banned.

My military identity card.

A proud member of the
France–Finland corps with my
ambulance in Norrmark.

Portrait of a lady ready for adventure.

Standing by my car in the El Tahag encampment in Egypt.

Bir Hakeim:
Lieutenant General
Willoughby Norrie
with two Spearettes.
*Imperial War Museum
(E13320)*

Dimitri Amilakvari
(*left*) and fellow
officers of the
French Foreign
Legion.
*Imperial War Museum
(E13274)*

Seasoned veterans enjoy a well-deserved break.
Imperial War Museum
(E13314)

Raising a cheer under the desert sun. A group of Free French Legionnaires and their dogs.
Imperial War Museum
(E13273)

Bloody but unbowed: the banner of the Foreign Legion
flies defiantly above Bir Hakeim.

Imperial War Museum (E13300)

'What's this for?' I asked incredulously.

'For looking so adorable when you're asleep,' he declared, and climbed back in.

With our car smelling like an English garden, he drove us on to our hotel and made love to me all afternoon. I was happier than I'd been in years.

Beirut in 1941 was the capital of the state of Greater Lebanon and was known as the Paris of the Middle East. Bustling and vibrant, it was endowed with cosmopolitan charm and glorious beaches. The overwhelming impression during the war, however, was of noise and traffic. It was full of generals, troops (mainly Australian) and vehicles, with convoys constantly passing through. The Australians were often rowdy, but they were fearless soldiers and much respected by their allies in the field.

The city was full of familiar faces: Kelsey, as busy as ever and ready with all the latest gossip; Nadine, who'd arrived with hopes of becoming a chauffeur too but instead became involved with a rather doubtful rich civilian; Sneyd-Cox, yellow from jaundice, along with Lady Spears and many of the British liaison staff, although not Tony Drake, who'd developed diabetes and been sent home to England. Friends frequently invited me to dinner but I usually declined, remembering my promise to the colonel and fearing that I might spark his jealousy. 'Thanks, but I've got a long day tomorrow,' I'd say and head for home.

Our days were divided largely between the various splendid hotels – St Georges, the Normandie, the Hammama with its water cascade – and the numerous conferences and meetings that were going on in the city night and day for the Armistice Commission, mostly at the offices known as the Grand Sérail. The men who tried to hammer out an agreement within those four walls had a tough job on their hands – the divisions were deep and everyone wanted a piece of the pie. The Arabs were demanding independence, the Turks wanted Aleppo, the Free French

145

hoped to maintain control and the Vichy French wanted a mandate. The colonel had never been busier.

Most of my time was taken up with menial tasks, chiefly ferrying the Humber to and from the workshop, trying to sort out problems with the brakes, tyres, steering and lights. It leaked oil permanently, guzzled petrol and bumped and crunched along with a terrible grinding noise. When it broke down completely, I was given an old Lincoln or an open-topped Hotchkiss to drive instead, vehicles which were just as bad and twice as heavy on the steering. Time and again I'd try for a superior car, pleading with the transport department for something less unwieldy.

'There are only old ambulances left,' the surly old *commandant* would bark at me. 'The British have taken all the best cars yet again.' Spitting forcefully onto the floor, he added: 'Even the Vichy French have better vehicles than ours.'

I'd retreat hastily, sorry I'd asked.

Like a true legionnaire, the colonel acquired a dog, a thin white saluki (who looked like a greyhound with fur) given to him by a friend, Germain, who'd bought it from an Arab. The colonel loved salukis or *sloughis persans* as he called them, and he and his wife had bred them in Morocco. Amused by my obvious devotion to animals, having seen me stroke just about every stray dog or cat that wandered into my path, he thought a pet would please me. He was right. Our 'family' felt complete.

Germain had given the dog the completely unsuitable name of Georges, so the colonel renamed it Arad (which means thunder) after a similar dog he'd owned in Marrakech. Arad had long white hair, almost down to the ground, and his startling appearance in the half-light would herald our arrival anywhere. I loved Arad and I so wanted him to love me back, but he was an Arab beast through and through: independent, remote and offhand. Even though I bought him a comfortable basket, his

146

preferred sleeping place was in the shade under the car. This meant that whenever he emerged, his soft white fur was covered in black oil, and I'd have the painstaking task of cleaning it off. Arad preferred men to women and would come only to the colonel at first, fretting every minute he was away. But in time he grew to trust me too and occasionally allowed me to stroke his soft silky ears, closing his eyes like a cat. Now I had two demanding men to worry about.

When the colonel and I had time, in the early evening we'd walk Arad on the beach and try to snatch a quiet meal somewhere together, staying in some of the charming smaller hotels and dining out under the stars. Only then could we truly relax and be comfortable in each other's company. Away from prying eyes, we were at our best – giggling together, holding hands, cuddling and kissing like young lovers. I'd forgotten how rewarding love could be.

Occasionally we'd drive to Damascus, where I'd get a chance to see some of my old Legion friends. Amilakvari (still bald), Gabriel de Sairigné, Simon (now with a glass eye), the white-gloved de Bollardière and Messmer were all billeted together and only too happy for an excuse to celebrate. We'd usually go for a meal or a drink at the Lido, an event which always bolstered my spirits, even if the colonel sometimes showed his resentment at how well I fitted in.

'Do you have to appear quite so relaxed in their company?' he scolded me once. 'It's not terribly flattering.'

He simply didn't understand that whenever I was with the Legion, it felt like I'd come home.

One night a group of us went to eat at a Hungarian pub, with traditional Hungarian music, food and waitresses. I loved it; all the costumes and the beer and the smell of candle grease reminded me of my happy days in Budapest. After a few drinks too many with the men, I leaned over to de Sairigné, sitting to my left, squeezed his arm to get his attention and told him, above the music: 'Hungarian men make the most marvellous lovers, you know. It's all that bull's blood and beetroot.'

Laughing, he threw an arm around my shoulders and swayed with me in time to the rousing accordion music.

The colonel's mood changed instantly. He stood up. 'Take me home,' he ordered gruffly and, leaving my beer glass half full, I grabbed my bag and coat and followed him to the door.

'What's the matter? Weren't you enjoying yourself?' It had seemed like such a jolly evening, with all our friends. Gabriel was an old and platonic acquaintance and I knew the colonel admired him. I didn't think I'd overstepped the mark.

The colonel scowled at me. 'I don't like to think of your life before me,' he said. 'And I don't ever want to hear of your Hungarian past again.'

Climbing into the driver's seat, he drove us home at a terrific speed. I sat beside him, my fingers gripping the seat, wondering quietly if his jealousy might be indicative of deeper feelings. I was excited by his anger and couldn't remember the last time a man had shown such possessiveness over me.

His bad mood continued when we got back to our hotel. He thrashed around his room in a tantrum, leaving me to wonder what lay in store. But, within the space of ten minutes, his entire manner had changed and he was fine again, even suggesting gently that we go to the Normandie for a late-night drink.

The next day he shocked me enormously. 'I'm to be given a house, somewhere outside Beirut,' he said. 'The hotels are too expensive. Would you help me find the right place?' His eyes were kind once more.

'Of course,' I replied, wondering sadly if this meant an end to our late-night hotel trysts. It would be far more difficult to sneak out of my hotel at night, or for him to sneak in.

'And then, when you've found the right spot, I see no reason why you couldn't come and share it with me. All

148

the other chauffeurs live in,' the colonel added nonchalantly.

Overjoyed, I took his hand and kissed it. 'Yes, Pierre,' I said, using the name he'd only recently allowed me to use in private. 'I'd love to.' I could hardly believe the news; we were to live together, like a proper couple. Once any guests had gone and the doors were closed, we'd be sharing our first home together. I felt so very happy. There wasn't the shadow of a doubt that this was what I wanted, more than anything in the world, and it was so rare that I could say that about my life. I felt as if I were in love for the very first time.

Until we could find such a house, Pierre and I lived in a beautiful hotel in Sofar, on the road to Damascus. It was near a waterfall and I had the best room – the most delightful one could imagine, which he filled daily with carnations, roses and other heavily scented flowers. The room had in fact been reserved for General Sir Henry Maitland Wilson, known universally as 'Jumbo', who commanded the British troops in the region, but Pierre insisted it was mine until the general arrived. It had an en-suite bathroom and the nicest views. Pierre had a smaller room not far from mine and would pad softly down the hall to see me in the middle of the night. They were happy days.

Our evening strolls with the dog would take us past the waterfall, through vines and olive groves, usually at sunset. Dinner was always on the balcony or in the garden. We talked a great deal, laughed a lot together and felt as if there was no-one else in the world. It didn't even seem like there was a war on any more, safeguarded as we were from all the action and the politics. We felt young at heart and deeply in love. We both knew it couldn't last, but we blocked our hearts and minds to the future, and took greater and greater risks to snatch every moment together.

In between the colonel's meetings and matters of administration, we'd sneak to the shops to buy sweets or flowers or books, or we'd take tea in a favourite tea shop. It was bliss. If ever we were spotted, we'd pretend we were just taking a routine break; but few who saw us together in those golden months in Beirut can have been in any doubt about how we really felt.

When General Wilson arrived, we had to move out of our lovely suites and into smaller rooms on the floor above him. (It always amazed and slightly embarrassed me how the British seemed to get the best of everything – the best rooms, the best cars, the best arms. The Free French were very poor relations by comparison.) The general's arrival and our ignominious transfer spurred us on to find a little house of our own somewhere, far away from prying eyes.

The colonel was given a list of requisitioned villas from which to choose a temporary home. Exorbitant rents were being asked by the owners, who had been given little choice about moving out and letting their homes to the military. I'm afraid I didn't care about their unceremonious displacement. I was just so excited, like a young bride embarking on a quest for her first home. I only wished we could have something as grand as the old villa General Catroux used, a splendid venue for parties and dinners (not to mention his army of Siamese cats), but it had apparently already been earmarked for General Spears. Poor old Catroux. Along with his beautiful but formidable wife, he too would have to find himself another home.

The colonel became busier by the day. Engrossed in high-level talks with Generals de Gaulle, Crystal, Wilson, de Larminat and Catroux, he left the choice of villa to me, although as usual he expressed a few strong opinions on the matter.

'I've heard there may be some small palaces available so go and look at those first, princess,' he said, with a twinkle in his eye. 'And if any of them are already occupied by the Vichy generals, let me know and I'll have them ousted immediately.'

For ten days I drove round and round Beirut, finding agents without offices and villas which had no official addresses or keys. It was a thankless task, but in the end I found the perfect place, an enchanting farmhouse covered in vines in the little hillside village of Aley. It had a balcony, a small garden and a separate flat downstairs for staff. There was a huge living room, very light and airy, a nice bathroom and kitchen and two bedrooms. Excited, I rushed to find the colonel to tell him all about it, and was a little peeved to discover that he was in a meeting all day and would be dining with the generals (and therefore not with me) later that night. The British had all gone on to Libya, leaving the French to concentrate on trying to settle their deep divisions and agree an uneasy peace. It was only at times such as these that I was reminded that there was still a war on.

When I eventually caught up with him and told him of the house I'd found, he seemed distracted and un-impressed. 'Oh, well, if you're not interested,' I said, pouting, 'I'll let one of the Vichy colonels take it.'

Putting down his documents, he pulled me towards him impulsively and kissed my forehead. 'I'm sorry. I'm sure the house will be fine. Why don't you arrange everything for me? I know you're disappointed that we haven't been able to see so much of each other recently,' he added, sens-ing my unhappiness. 'But because of my increased workload, I hardly have time to think, let alone play the gallant knight.' Seeing that I was still sulking, he became quite pensive and – holding my face in his hands – he returned to a recent theme of conversation, his fear that we were becoming too involved too quickly. 'Whatever happens between us, La Miss,' he told me ominously, 'I do hope that you will be happy.'

Gulping hard and quelling the butterflies in my stomach, I asked him what he meant.

'I mean, it may not always be possible for us to be together,' he said, speaking with slow deliberation. 'When I get back to the front and am commanding a regiment, you know, don't you, that you may not be allowed to come with me. The British might disapprove of a woman chauffeur at the front and in any event I'm not sure I'd want to take you to war.'

He was only speaking the truth, I knew, and was voicing fears I'd harboured secretly for some time. But his words stung me. Jumping up and grabbing the car keys, I went for a long drive up into the hills outside Beirut. Watching the lights of the city twinkling below me, I sat in the car, crying and crying until my tears were all spent. Returning to our hotel just before dawn, I slipped into my own bed and lay awake for hours, trying to sort everything out in my mind. There was no fighting it – I was in love. My feelings for the colonel were unlike anything I'd ever known before. All my life I'd been searching for a relationship of this kind with a man of this calibre, and now that I'd found it I had to accept that it could be snatched away from me very easily.

It was midmorning before I came to an abrupt conclusion. Stop feeling sorry for yourself, I told myself crossly, blowing my nose. This was no time to be sad. On the contrary, there would be plenty of time for tears in the future. I resolved to make the most of what I had with Pierre, to live for the moment – as we all had to do in the midst of a war – and see where it led us.

As if he, too, was racked with the same fears, the colonel became increasingly moody with me in public and I sometimes felt as if he were trying to push me away for my own good. He'd been angered by my running away that night; he feared that I might cause a scene and he worried for me.

'If you had to work for someone else, I'd have to stop all contact with you,' he reminded me. 'The only thing that allows us to see each other is that you're my driver.'

I found that I had to walk a very fine line between being his lover and being his employee. Sometimes I forgot my place and when I did, he could be really difficult, touchy and petulant for days afterwards. The worst incident was when I brought the car round to the front of the hotel to collect him one morning as usual, only to find him standing there with Arad. Cross that he should have brought the dog, who'd had an upset stomach in my room in the night and had kept me awake, I chastised him. 'What have you brought him for? He'll probably be sick in the car. Go and take him back to his room.' I knew the moment I'd spoken that I'd made a terrible mistake. With a face like thunder, the colonel marched off with the dog, returning a few minutes later and stepping forcefully into the car.

'How dare you talk to me like that in public!' His eyes were on fire as he rounded on me in the front seat. 'Anyone would think you were giving the orders around here, not me. I shan't allow you to speak to me like that ever again.'

He sulked for a full two days, refusing to dine with me and putting me in my place whenever the opportunity arose. I learned my lesson the hard way, adopting the most obsequious manner I could. Appeased at last, he relented and invited me to walk Arad with him one evening on the beach. I fell in step at his side with an enormous sense of relief.

In July 1941, my colonel – from whom the weight of command had never completely lifted – was promoted to *général de brigade*. Although I was enormously proud and sewed the stars onto his uniform personally, I worried that his promotion might mark a turning point in our lives. Now that he had a higher profile, I feared that he would be expected to have a male chauffeur, like all the other generals.

'Now that I'm a general, you'll have to wear your *adjudant*'s stripes on your shirt,' he told me, trying to jolly me along. 'Go and get some. I'd like to see you in them.'

I did as I was told, and attached them proudly to my shirt. Now that my rank had come into the conversation, I dared to tackle him on a subject that had been bothering me since I'd been on the *Westernland*.

'Pierre,' I began, speaking carefully. 'As you're now a

153

general couldn't you do something about my pay? You know I'm only paid two thirds of what a male *adjudant* gets. Surely you have the power to change that? It doesn't seem fair.'

His forehead creased into a frown and I wondered if I'd said too much again. But he nodded after a while. 'I don't see why not. I'll look into it.'

And, indeed, he did. My pay was duly increased along with that of the two other women *adjudants* working in the hospital. It wasn't anything very much, but I felt I had notched up at least a small victory for womankind. The general said later that he only hoped the rest of his new duties would be met with such a warm response. I was delighted and took a new pride in my stripes, only to meet Amilakvari in the street a few days later and be ribbed mercilessly.

'What on earth are those?' He pointed at me, his eyes twinkling with mirth.

Apparently I'd bought the wrong stripes – those for a policeman's uniform, not someone affiliated to the Legion. I ripped them off there and then, red-faced.

By August, our house was ready and we moved in with the greatest joy, accepting the keys gratefully from the Maltese owners. I had such fun going round the souks and shops to find furnishings and bits and pieces for our new home. I wanted nothing more than a few quiet weeks, with no parties or dinners, just the two of us in our little cottage. But it was not to be. The night we moved in, there was a huge party for General Lyttleton, the new Minister of State for the Middle East, at the official residency, the only consolation of which was that I was allowed to eat an excellent meal of chicken washed down with champagne under the stairs with the other chauffeurs, who were most envious of my employer's new status and his Aley house.

'Will you be living in, then?' asked one, chewing on a great drumstick, his eyes inquisitive. 'With your general, I mean?'

Picking at a wishbone, I looked him straight in the eye. 'Of course,' I replied steadily. 'In a room in the staff quarters. How else would the general get into town from way out in the sticks?'

The man and his colleagues eyed one another, and me, but said nothing more.

I drove the general home later that night, and he was in an excellent mood. He said the reception had been a success and he was pleased with the way things were going. 'Did you manage to find something to eat?' he asked sleepily, his head resting on my shoulder.

'Oh, the odd morsel,' I said, thinking of the very fine food and wines I'd enjoyed below stairs.

We arrived home late, to discover a grumpy Arad surrounded by mess, having eaten the bell and an electric light.

Staffing our new home, I engaged a gardener, two Lebanese soldiers as orderlies, a maid and a *marmiton* or kitchen boy. My quest for a cook took several days, however. I wanted a really good one, someone who would prepare the finest dinners for the general and his guests and would be the talk of the whole circuit. I so wanted Pierre to be pleased with my choice. I asked the head chef at the Grand Sérail if he could recommend someone, and after a search round the countryside above Beirut, I discovered the man I was after at a village called Dfun, which was apparently where all the cooks lived. The chef was called Selim and I had to offer him much more money than the general had wanted to pay to prise him away from the hotel where he was working, but in the end he agreed and said he would start work the following week.

Buoyant from my success, I drove back to Beirut to find the general and tell him the good news. We had lunch at the Legion mess, the Vichyists sitting on one side of the room and us on the other, neither side talking. Just as I was about to drive the general off after lunch, we bumped into Gabriel de Sairigné and had a pleasant chat. It was the first time we'd seen him since the Hungarian evening and

I was glad there was no bad feeling between the two men. But then, just as he was leaving, Gabriel squeezed my arm. '*Au revoir*, Susan,' he said, using my first name in a way he had never done before. The moment I saw the general's face, it was clear that he was furious. He refused to speak to me for the rest of the journey. The joy of my success with Selim left me completely.

I was reminded once again of the unreasonable moodiness of my father and how uncomfortable his unpredictability had made me feel as a child. Not surprisingly, in my distress I accidentally ran into a tram, which meant that the car had to be towed all the way home. The general, still fuming, had to find other transport. As I watched him go, his expression thunderous, I realized that his jealousy only made me love him more because it showed how much he cared.

In spite of our occasional spats, we were truly happy in our little cottage on the outskirts of Beirut. There, in the mountains, surrounded by orchards and olive groves, we lived as man and wife, with no-one but the servants knowing of our curious relationship. I shared Pierre's bed and woke next to him each morning. With each day that passed I became increasingly infatuated.

Together, Pierre and I bought some antique tables, beds, an ornate wooden chest and a divan, along with some Persian rugs. My favourite acquisition was a beautiful chest of drawers with mother-of-pearl inlay and china handles, which Pierre bought for me. I also found some lamps, had some pretty rosebud-chintz furnishings sewn for the chairs and beds, and made the cottage as homely as I could, with – of course – bowls of flowers in every room. The Lebanese orderlies were imbeciles, the gardener couldn't garden and killed half the goldfish I'd put in the little fountain, but thanks to Selim everything ran smoothly and we ate extremely well and far too much.

Slowly, in the idyllic setting I would remember fondly all my life, Pierre touched my soul in a way no other man had previously done. He was sophisticated and intelligent; his leadership skills and statesmanship attracted me more powerfully than looks or youth ever could have done. It was a love affair that allowed me to explore a place I'd never known before – the very depths of my heart. I gave myself to him completely, in every way – physically, emotionally, morally and intellectually.

My devotion to him was unlike anything I'd ever experienced. With my previous lovers I'd always remained aloof and cool, inwardly vulnerable but outwardly non-committal, for fear of rejection and betrayal. But because of the master–servant nature of my relationship with Pierre, I allowed myself to do everything I could to please him, without expecting much in return.

Occasionally the unfairness of my position stung me a little. After one particularly demanding day, when I'd been ferrying him everywhere, carrying his papers and doing his bidding, only to get home and discover he expected me to co-host a Legion dinner, I was at my wits' end. As we dressed for dinner together, I turned to him and said wryly: 'I sometimes think I've become little more than a devoted puppy in your company. You know, always following you around and waiting for a kind word.'

He stopped adjusting his tie and looked across at me. 'Yes, I know, *chérie*,' he said. 'And one shouldn't get too attached to little puppies, should one?'

Pierre was adamant that no-one should know of our secret relationship. Not only could it cost us both our jobs and him his reputation, but quite possibly his marriage too. If anyone asked, I was instructed to repeat what I had told the other chauffeurs, that I lived in the staff flat only because of the convenience of getting him to and from his meetings. In fact he panicked and nearly made me move out when he heard some tittle-tattle in town about how everyone thought it terrible that a general was sharing his house with a woman.

'It's made me wonder about the wisdom of what we're doing,' he warned me afterwards. 'You may have to leave here if people start to talk.'

I was very cross at his words and wished people would mind their own business.

We invited de Sairigné and Amilakvari, who had become one of the general's closest friends and most trusted commanders, to one of the dinner parties we hosted together at the house. Naturally, I had to revert to being the general's obedient servant, sitting at the opposite end of the table to him, while the most important person, Amilakvari, sat to his right. The long-planned evening was almost a disaster. My new dining chairs arrived that morning with the blue paint still wet on them so we all had to sit on newspapers; I was obliged to use Arad's food bowl as a vase for extra carnations, and he kept threatening to knock it off the table with his inquisitive wet nose; and I was sewing the curtains right up to the last second. Then, just when everything was ready and people started to arrive, the lights fused. Fortunately I'd bought eight candles and we stuck them in vinegar bottles.

Selim cooked as best he could with little light, and the meal was delicious, with traditional Middle Eastern hors d'oeuvres or *mezze*, followed by baked fish, lamb and sweetbreads. But the general was cross about the lights, which caused a slight cloud, and Amilakvari teased me mercilessly, as he always did, which I couldn't bear.

'Seen any policemen around here lately?' he asked the others, grinning at me. 'Only La Miss here quite fancies herself as one.'

Reddening, and hoping the general didn't take offence, I tried to change the subject.

Fortunately, Gabriel de Sairigné was there to keep everything jolly and he told Amilak to leave me alone. 'Better to be a sergeant with the wrong stripes than a prince with no kingdom,' he ribbed.

The evening improved after that and the men left at midnight, singing, to find their chauffeur drunk but dignified.

I was only ever allowed to dine with the general, instead of alone in the kitchen, during visits by his closest friends and those who already knew me. But even then I was forbidden to show any hint of affection for him. He made it clear that he would hold me personally responsible if the true nature of our relationship ever became public knowledge. It was a ploy that worked. So much so that on another occasion when Amilakvari came for dinner and to stay – the general giving up his bed and sleeping on the daybed in the dining room while I retired to 'my room' – I awoke in the middle of the night to feel a man sliding into bed next to me. Surprised that the general would risk being caught *in flagrante delicto* with a guest in the house, I succumbed to his advances and we began to make love.

It was only when I reached up to run my fingers through his familiar blond hair that I realized my mistake. My night-time visitor was shaven-headed. It was Amilakvari, who had assumed that he'd be welcome in my bed, as he always had been in the past. I was horrified.

'Amilak, my dear, I can't,' I said, my voice tremulous with fear. 'The general and I are lovers. You mustn't tell a soul – I thought you were him.'

Amilakvari, even more appalled at the thought of being caught sleeping with his brigade commander's lover, beat a hasty retreat, slipping out through the door to the connecting bathroom, which was the way he'd come in. At breakfast neither one of us said a word, and we were both hugely relieved that the general appeared to suspect nothing.

They were halcyon days in Aley and sometimes I felt as if my heart would burst with happiness. All my life I'd avoided permanent intimacy, inadvertently pushing lovers away, making them leave me. Now that I'd embraced togetherness in a way I never had before, I couldn't imagine life without it. Wherever we were – in the car, on the beach, out in a boat or on day trips into the biblical hills around Beirut – Pierre and I were as one.

As the nights grew colder, we bought a little stove. We lit it – at first nearly smoking ourselves out – and snuggled together keeping warm until Selim produced a delicious supper like fish with hollandaise sauce and chocolate bavarois, washed down with fine wines. Selim was more than a pearl; he was an entire oyster bed full of them.

The general became relaxed and romantic, showering me with flowers and small presents such as a bracelet with painted scenes of the Middle East on it (which I still have) and a lovely bag for my birthday, after I'd bought him a *trousseau de toilette*. We'd spend many pleasant evenings together, eating dinner, reading magazines or listening to the wireless. He loved poetry and wrote some himself, although he'd rarely let me see any of it. It was two years since I'd joined the Free French in Carlton Gardens, and in that relatively short time I'd achieved my lifetime ambition of living in a foreign land with a man of destiny. I never wanted it to end.

Our Aley idyll was to be short-lived, however. After three months, the currents of war began to tug at us once again, calling us back to our duty. The fighting between the Germans and the Russians had taken on a new intensity, with a jubilant Hitler nearing the gates of Moscow. In France, thousands of civilians suspected of resistance had been arrested by the Vichyists, in collaboration with the Gestapo, and hundreds executed. In North Africa, the British and Commonwealth forces under General Richard O'Connor were continuing to fight off the Italians in Libya, chasing them along the coast, while our Free French colleagues were waiting impatiently in the wings.

The general became a radio fiend, rushing to the wireless the minute he got in and fiddling with it all night long to hear the latest news. One evening when I'd asked Selim to cook a special meal to celebrate our three-month anniversary, I was unreasonably upset because I'd put on my green brocade gallabiyah for the first time and Pierre was so glued to the wireless he didn't even notice.

I'd listen reluctantly, wanting to block my ears and shut out the war that threatened to shatter our perfect world. I'd only stop to listen when the haunting song 'Lily

Marlene' came on. It struck a chord, not only with me, but with virtually every soldier on either side. It became a sort of theme song, and later an emotive symbol of desert war.

Like the general, the rest of the Free French were champing at the bit. There were endless marches and parades and medals were given out for service in Syria and Eritrea, but no amount of pomp and glory could compensate for the lack of action. They were soldiers first and foremost and they craved to be part of the show. De Gaulle and his staff knew they had to get their men to the front and soon, or they might even lose them. My general informed me excitedly that he'd been promised the Atrep division with two Legion battalions when the French were given their chance. My heart sank.

Then came the news I'd been secretly dreading. 'I've been appointed Governor of Aleppo and Syria,' he told me proudly. 'Naturally, I'll be moving there with immediate effect.' I knew then that we'd have to move out of our lovely little house in the vineyards.

It was several days before the general's excitement died down.

'It's been rather like a dream,' he told me wistfully on one of our final nights together at Aley. 'And now, *chérie*, the dream is over.'

I knew he was speaking the truth. There was nothing I could have done to cling on to what we'd had. Orders were orders. He was as reluctant to leave as I, but neither of us had any choice.

With the greatest of sadness, I called in the packers to hand-wrap every precious piece of glass and china in paper and straw, each item reminding me of some of the happiest days of my life – the flower bowls, the wine glasses, the rugs and chintz furnishings that had helped make up our happy home. Thanking a tearful Selim for all he had done for us, I let him and the other staff go. I packed up the rest of our furniture and belongings myself, arranging for some of it to be sent on with us, but the majority to be put in store in the wild hope that one day, maybe, Pierre and I might unpack it together. By the time the house was completely empty, it looked as desolate as I felt.

Putting Arad on his lead, I locked the door behind me and walked away from the vine-covered cottage, unable to look back, knowing it was a place to which I would never return. There were never to be such times again.

10

INTO THE CAULDRON

'This land was made for War.
As glass resists the bite of vitriol
So this hard and calcinated earth
Rejects the battle's hot corrosive impact.'

JOCELYN BROOKE, RAMC, NORTH AFRICA

FROM *THE VOICE OF WAR*

Built at the junction of two ancient caravan routes, Aleppo was a melting pot of faiths, languages and customs, a mecca for merchants, shoppers and pilgrims. Our long journey there on a road winding between the sea and the rough cedar-clad hills took several days, this time in the old Lincoln. The road eventually opened onto a fertile plain dotted with beehive-shaped houses between the Euphrates and Orontes rivers. We stopped at the town of Homs en route, where I was invited to have coffee with General Catroux's formidable wife, my first outing in 'society' for some time. I wondered at her motive. Perhaps she had wanted a closer look at the woman living with the new general.

'What is General Koenig like as a boss?' Madame Catroux asked, unable to hide her curiosity.

'Average,' I replied. Sitting on the edge of my seat, sipping from a bone china cup and eating little dainties while trying to make small talk with that fierce woman, I had never felt more intimidated. No wonder her husband always looked so tired, I thought.

Homs, an industrial town on the Orontes river and an important road and rail centre, bore the scars of some fierce fighting between the Italians and Vichy French and our forces; the walls of many of its buildings were peppered with bullet holes and the roads were pock-marked with shell craters. It looked a sad and sorry sight.

A Free French parade had been arranged for the general, at which he was required to hand out some medals and decorations to those who had served so well. There was the usual pomp and ceremony, with the Legion band belting out '*Le Boudin*' and the men lined up in their shorts and dust-covered boots. I was delighted to find John Hasey among the recipients, and I watched proudly from the wings as he stepped forward to be awarded the Croix de Guerre and the Liberation medal. I managed to see him briefly afterwards, and in the rasping whisper that was now his voice since he had lost his larynx to a bullet, he told me he was going home to Massachusetts.

'My family want me home, but I'm hoping to come back out to where all the action is just as soon as I'm better,' he said, his young eyes still bright with enthusiasm. 'I know I can still be of some use.'

'*Bonne chance, mon brave.*' I squeezed his hand, giving the unblemished side of his mutilated face a kiss.

I was never to see him again although he did, in fact, return to the front to become an aide to the general in the final years of the war. He then served in the CIA for nearly thirty years before returning to France in 1996, aged seventy-nine, to receive the Légion d'honneur from President Jacques Chirac.

In Aleppo, Syria's second city, our new home was much grander than our last. Ringed with ramparts and in the shadow of the moated Citadel, it had been the Governor's house. But although I was allowed to have a room not far from the general's and we were still able to meet secretly at night, we had to be far more circumspect and were never able to recapture the romantic intimacies of Aley. The staff weren't a patch on Selim and his team, the food was disgusting and Pierre and I seemed to have very little time together as he was always being invited out to dinner with important people. I made our quarters as homely as I could, buying curtains and unpacking some of the furniture I'd had sent on from our little cottage, but there was none of the atmosphere of our last home. On the few nights when we were alone we'd have dinner and he'd play the piano for me, or we'd sit listening to his big old Bakelite radio.

The Legion were my saviours. Old friends like Amilakvari, Boris Nazaroff and others would take me out for meals and the occasional adventure. There were even some would-be suitors but I was true to my general and spurned all advances, even if that meant I was often on my own. I had Arad for company, of course, but he'd never been an affectionate dog and sat whining for his master most of the time. Sensing my loneliness, the Legion presented me with a little deer, similar to the one I'd nick-named Duchess in Eritrea. It ate tobacco and lived in an enclosure in our garden right up until we left, when it escaped and returned to the desert.

As always, the general had meetings with local Arabs, the Vichy French and the Allies, and my chief task was to make sure he was in the right place at the right time for his many conferences. They weren't just in Aleppo, either; sometimes I'd have to drive him through Syria and across to Greater Lebanon. We'd go to the ancient town of Baalbek, an area littered with Roman ruins; through vine-yards, olive groves, narrow streets and palace courtyards. It was breathtaking scenery, but there was rarely any time to enjoy it or spend an intimate interlude.

By now my role was clear. First and foremost, I was the general's driver and subordinate. Gone were the romantic days of Aley, the strolls on the beach with Arad, the dinners under the stars and the times when we curled up together in front of our little wood-burning stove. These days I ate alone in the servants' quarters with the other chauffeurs, or at home on my own. Most nights too I slept alone, as Pierre came in late and dared not risk being caught in my bed. I mourned the loss of the life we'd led, and wished more than anything that we could go back. But Pierre was a general, we were in the middle of a war and I knew I should be grateful for the special times we'd had.

Our first chance to be together properly came that December when we left Aleppo for Egypt. At last the Free French had been ordered to prepare for a front-line role and to move towards the increasingly hostile theatre of war.

'How do you like the idea of Christmas in Cairo?' the general asked unexpectedly one morning after breakfast, when I presented myself for duty as usual.

I studied his smiling face. 'Really?' I said, afraid to believe what he was telling me.

He nodded. 'I'm sorry we haven't had much time on our own these last two months, but at least now we can spend Christmas together. Just the two of us.'

My face broke into a grin and it was hard to resist the urge to hug him.

The general was delighted at the move to Egypt and very pleased with the way things were going. General de Gaulle was clearly happy with him and had told him that he had been earmarked for greater things after the war. Now Pierre was going to be allowed to lead the Free French into battle once more, an ambition he'd been nurturing ever since I'd first met him.

We spent that Christmas, our first together, in the glamorous surroundings of the legendary nineteenth-century Shepheard's Hotel on the Midan Opera overlooking the Nile, with its fading colonial atmosphere, comfortable furniture, chandeliers and beautiful antiques. Large fans whirred overhead, rich Persian rugs lined the marble floors and the staff dressed in dazzlingly white gallabiyahs tied with crimson sashes. Each morning we'd be woken by the lilting prayer songs of the muezzins echoing across the misty city from the minarets, and slip back into a cosy slumber once the calls to prayer had ended. In the evenings we'd dine at Groppi's Corner House under a stained-glass rotunda or eat in an Arab club, watching belly dancers take the floor and fat pashas wheeler-dealing at the tables. On Christmas morning we found a Coptic church for Pierre so that he could attend Mass.

Sitting at the back of the church while he knelt and prayed near the altar, I inhaled the incense and watched the light from the candles flicker across the dozens of gold icons adorning the walls. I'd never been much of a churchgoer, my parents had little faith, and yet there was something comforting about the peace and serenity of our surroundings. Bowing my head and closing my eyes, I clasped my hands together.

'Dear God, if you're there, please keep Pierre safe from harm in the battles to come,' I whispered softly.

Later, we drove out to Giza, site of the pyramids, and strolled alone in silence around their historic perimeters. Gone were the tourists and beggars; war had put paid to all that. Abandoned by all but those who'd stayed for battle, the proud monuments to death and a distant past stood defiantly in the Giza plain, completely unmoved by time or war or man's stupidity. Wandering in the little town lying in the shadow of the pyramids, we found a restaurant that served us a simple but delicious meal of fava beans and minced lamb, salad, bread and hummus, all washed down with bottles of cold beer. It was the best Christmas meal I'd ever had. I thought of my parents eking out their meagre rations in England, probably with my brother Laurence sitting in silence with them at the dining table, and I thanked my lucky stars for war and for Pierre.

'It's been a magical Christmas,' I told him, raising my bottle in fond salute. 'It's wonderful to have some time together again. Thank you.'

'Yes,' he concurred, swigging from his bottle, his eyes

bright. 'And 1942 will bring even better times, with the defeat of the enemy and a return to glory for France.' He lifted his bottle to clink against mine, and I knew that he was already lost to me.

Walking the dusty streets of Cairo alone while the general went back to work in the first few days of that new year, I sought solace in this city of wonders, described as the 'Mother of the World' in the *Arabian Nights*, one of the favourite books of my childhood. The streets were thronged with people and loud with clanging trams. It was a place people either loved or hated, an intriguing mixture of old and new, east and west. I loved it.

The seedier side of the city held its own fascination, as I explored the *ghoraz* or hash dens of old Cairo and the City of the Dead, where poor families lived among the tombs. Directly opposite the entrance to Shepheard's, I could see the Sharia il Berka, the famous street of the brothels. I was mesmerized by the '*femmes de mauvaise vie*' in tawdry rags who staggered dishevelled into the street after a hard night's sex with innumerable Allied soldiers as well as their more regular customers.

My father had warned me against becoming '*une femme facile*', I recalled, in the carefree days of my youth. I thought back to those tipsy nights in Cannes when I came home after dawn, and I felt a little ashamed. Poor Father, how he must have despaired of my future. If he could see me now, older and so much wiser, the consort to a respected French general, doing a responsible job, I hoped he would be reassured. But then, I reminded myself, my general was married, and not to me. Father would not approve.

Thinking of my father made me write to my parents again, something I did sporadically throughout the war. I told them little. My letters home were short and un-informative. 'Cairo, January '42. Still with the Legion, working hard. Hot and dusty, but keeping well. Have seen the Pyramids. Can get the BBC on the wireless so keep

168

in touch with the news. Hope all is well. Love, Susan.'

For those first few peaceful weeks of 1942, the general and I remained sheltered from the war which raged in Europe and around the world. London was still being subjected to night raids after the Blitz and the Nazis were in the suburbs of Moscow, inspiring General de Gaulle to offer the services of his armed forces to the Russians instead, hoping that they might appreciate him more than the British appeared to. In the Far East, Pearl Harbor had been attacked – bringing America into the war at last – and the Japanese were advancing deep into south-east Asia.

I knew that in the Western Desert the news was not good either. Infuriated by the undignified retreat of the Italians in the face of the Allied forces, the Axis High Command had reinforced the Afrika Korps. Their commander, Major General Erwin Rommel, a renowned tactician familiar to all as 'the Desert Fox', ordered his panzer tanks to advance two hundred kilometres east towards Egypt, placing the Libyan coastal town of Benghazi once more under threat. The British army, holding out at Halfaya, was perilously overstretched.

Yet, despite all this, de Gaulle's insistent pleas for an immediate place in what he called 'the vital game' being played out between the Axis forces and the Allies appeared to go unheard. My general and his men listened to the news and remained on tenterhooks, while the British and Commonwealth forces tried to push back the enemy virtually single-handed. But events were about to take a remarkable turn. Neither the general nor I knew it then, but our greatest opportunity to prove ourselves was imminent. The British finally decided that they needed help and, for once, they didn't care where it came from.

The Première Brigade Française Libre or 1st Free French Brigade, comprising 9,57 legionnaires with a polyglot force of French colonials from Chadians to Moroccans to Tahitians plus two Spearettes and some Quaker medics, were finally ordered to mobilize and leave Cairo and Syria

169

to help in the fight for the Western Desert. They were to be attached to a division of the newly named British Eighth Army (formerly the Imperial Army of the Nile), and equipped as mechanized infantry to become the most modern French force. Best of all, thanks to the intervention of the general, I was to be going with them as his driver.

'They wanted me to have a male chauffeur, but I said no,' the general told me the day before we were due to leave. 'If you want to come, you can. There'll be no dishonour if you want to stay behind, La Miss,' he added, softening a little. 'Life in the desert is no picnic, you know, and there'll be few opportunities for us to be together.'

'Wherever you go, I will go too,' I replied, holding his gaze. 'That's all I ask.'

Nodding, he signed the relevant papers and handed them to me.

'Good luck,' he said and, to my very great surprise, he saluted me.

I shall never forget that massive convoy west. Men and machinery were spread out before and behind us as far as the eye could see, like a vast khaki-coloured snake twisting its way through the dust. Once we'd left the outskirts of Alexandria, with its gum trees and jacaranda, the long straight road went on and on into the distance; the clear turquoise sea on one side, the greyish-beige desert on the other, just dust and stones, all the same colour. A day into our journey, we came across a hand-painted sign in the middle of nowhere. 'To the Western Desert' it said and we laughed out loud. At least we knew we were heading in the right direction.

My car was now an old Ford Utility shooting brake, its side and rear windows almost completely painted in so as not to cause a glaring reflection that might be spotted from a German plane. It went reasonably well compared to my previous Humbers and the Lincoln and it was much more comfortable. Generals, it seemed, qualified for a better class of vehicle than colonels, which was just as well because the Ford rapidly became my home. I slept, washed and dressed in it. As the side windows were covered in brown paint, I could hang a rag over the windscreen and have almost complete privacy, something I'd come to appreciate above almost anything else in that all-male preserve.

The general had a caravan, a *camionnette*, made out of an old Renault delivery van, in which there was a bed, a table, seating and a little basin. The men of the Aleppo workshop had done him proud. It even had wood panelling inside, a little like the Orient Express. It was a proper wagon-lit and much coveted. As soon as the British generals saw it, they wanted one for themselves and asked their own workshops to come up with something similar, but none ever matched the general's for comfort and style.

The general's orderly was a young Indo-Chinese called My Fen, whom we nicknamed *mie de pain* or 'bread-crumb' because he was so tiny. Generally speaking, the commanding officer's orderly also acted as an orderly for his chauffeur, but that had its problems. The general knew that no legionnaire would be an orderly to a woman so he had arranged for My Fen to be taken on, knowing that he wouldn't be so prickly. My Fen knew very little French and was absolutely terrified of the general and he became my orderly without further ado. Arad came too but he and the general soon grew weary of each other in such close quarters and whenever we stopped to make camp Arad would leave the caravan and join the men, sleeping next to whoever he chose.

Having come the closest I had ever come to being a 'wife' in the previous six months, with a man to lie with each night, a roof over my head, food on the table and a means of keeping clean and cool, I was catapulted back to sand and sun and all the miserable privations of the desert There was no room here for romance or companionship; no ancient souks or little coffee shops in which to linger over a glistening pastry and a cup of thick, sweet black

171

coffee; just revolting bully beef and rice, tea in enamel mugs which always tasted metallic and was topped up with sticky condensed milk, and dry tack biscuits.

More unbearable still were the swarms of flies, which grew fat on the carrion of the desert and clustered around one's eyes and mouth and on food. The constant heat and the infernal stickiness it caused were also debilitating. To get sunburnt was a military crime. Considered a self-inflicted wound, it was punishable by court martial, but it was very hard for us not to burn on our necks, hands and any exposed areas of skin. Red, raw and in pain, the men would sometimes roll sweatily in the sand, in order to obtain some sort of barrier.

Worst of all was the dust which found its way into every pore and crevice, forming little ridges in folds of skin and matting hair so tightly that no comb would pass through it. I longed for hot water and shampoo, for the luxury of scented skin and glossy hair. Instead every surface was covered in a thin layer of dust – tables, beds, water. Food was always gritty to eat, sand had to be skimmed off every drink, shoes always had to be shaken out each morning, and clothes beaten.

When the rains came in sudden driving squalls of sleet, men leaped about in it, pleased at first to be rid of the sand. But then the temperature plummeted, the sleet turned to hail, and the heavy grey storm clouds looked as if they threatened snow. Driving torrents of water turned the ground to marsh as sand and debris were carried into every tent. Boots leaked, roofs poured water, cold, wet summer clothing stuck to the skin and everyone shivered under greatcoats and tarpaulins, praying for the sun again. Watched over by the vulture-like kites who landed on our tent roofs to wash their feathers and spy out any scraps in the passing torrents, we waited for the storm to pass.

The Western Desert was a severe shock to our systems. Not only were the conditions physically draining, but the vast empty landscape that stretched to the horizon imposed its own psychological strain. Just finding one's way around was exhausting. We had to navigate using sun compasses, and often got lost. The few linen maps we had of the area had so few bearings marked that they looked more like naval charts. In the harsh climate, I had to check the car over every hour or so, monitoring the oil, fuel and water, as well as feeling for overheated tyres which might burst, and air filters which regularly clogged with sand.

And then there were the sandstorms which made life impossible. When one came rolling in across the desert like a great black wall of cloud, blocking out the sun, everything stopped: battles, convoys, meals, even sleep. There would be a low, rumbling sound like a distant train and we would see the dark mass on the horizon. We would all dive for cover, in sealed vehicles, under blankets, wherever any protection could be found. Hitting speeds of sixty kilometres per hour, a sandstorm sucks all the oxygen out of the air ahead of it and drives each tiny insect in its path crazy, making them swarm. The heat becomes unbearable, the light goes, and whirling grains of sand stick to one's sweat, caking themselves onto every exposed area of skin. I saw men maddened by the thought of being buried alive under the sand pressing down on them; they would struggle to stand up, only to be knocked sideways by the force of the wind and whipped by the sand until their skin bled. Only when the storm had passed would we all emerge, blinking and grey, to see what damage had been done.

My general hardly seemed to notice the conditions, or mind about his sudden transition from metropolitan diplomat to desert army commander. In his blue and red kepi, he was at his most militaristic, barking orders and directions in a show of stiff professionalism. He became reserved and moody, often shouting at me when I was driving for going over a bump or missing a vital track.

'Mon Dieu!' he'd cry. 'Why don't you look where you're going? I could do a far better job myself.'

The trouble was that if I went round all the bumps and the scrub, I'd no longer be driving in the straight line dictated by the sun compass and I'd risk getting lost. I was constantly having to weigh up the two alternatives in my mind. Usually the bumps were the lesser evil, even if this meant incurring the general's wrath and breaking yet another pair of springs on the car.

Our first few months in the lunar landscape of the Western Desert in the spring of 1942 marked the beginning of the most dramatic phase of Pierre's military career. Since Narvik he'd been involved in no great battles and although there had been several skirmishes in Eritrea and Syria, they paled in comparison to events elsewhere. A soldier through and through, he wanted to serve his country and the Allies by taking part in battles that would mean something in the history books.

As enjoyable as his time with me in Aley and Aleppo had been, I think he must have felt as if he were in a waiting room. Now, with such a formidable foe as Rommel to contend with and the appeals of the mighty Eighth Army in his ears, the general and his men knew that their time had come.

For me, on the other hand, these months were the loneliest of my life. Without the distractions of the city or the intimate company of the man I had come to adore, I seemed destined to have a very private sort of war. I had to put my feelings to one side, block my emotions and try not to think about the future. There was no other work for me: in the army each man had his own designated job and would have been upset if I had started to interfere or offered my services elsewhere. As we trundled slowly across the desert plains towards Libya, a journey of some seven hundred kilometres, I found I had little to do for weeks on end and no-one for company. One day melted into the next.

Consigned to the kitchen with the men, I no longer ate with the general or even with the officers I knew and loved. Arad, being a clever dog, quickly learned that if he headed for the orderlies' and the legionnaires' tents each time we stopped to camp he stood a much greater chance of being fed, so I saw him only if I tied him up in my tent for company or protection. He still had lovely soft ears and I found it a great comfort sometimes just to sit and stroke them, talking to him gently all the while. But as soon as I let him go, he would run off to play with the other dogs or to find the mess tent and then I might not see him for days. '*Avez-vous vu mon chien?*' was probably the most common question anyone there heard me ask. Like all the men in my life, he was fiercely independent and did exactly as he pleased.

At night I slept alone in the car, a thick sheepskin coat I'd bought in the Aleppo souk tucked up around my ears to keep me warm during the bitterly cold desert nights. The front seats, which were attached by hooks, could be folded back to join the back seat and make a comfortable bed. It was a long way from the hotel suites I'd enjoyed in Beirut. One day, I was driving my general and a British four-star general, Willoughby Norrie, to a meeting – they were both in the back – when, to my great embarrassment, my seat collapsed. With an almighty bang I suddenly found myself horizontal, my head on the general's knees. The car nearly went off the road.

'For God's sake, woman, get up!' the general yelled, as if I'd done it on purpose.

I managed to scramble into an upright position just in time to prevent the car from going into the sand. As soon as we stopped, I asked the mechanics to find something better than hooks to hold the front seats in place.

At some of our encampments, such as El Tahag, near Cairo, I was allowed the luxury of a small tent in which I could erect my little canvas camp bed and have complete privacy. My only other belongings were my bath, my tools, my small suitcase stuffed with a few items of khaki uniform, a spare beret and a pistol. My sole concession to womanhood was a hairbrush, some sanitary towels and a couple of pairs of underpants. (I couldn't wear the men's underpants because they were too long.) I didn't wear a bra – I'd never really needed one – and I washed my own underwear separately while My Fen did the rest of my washing. It was a spartan existence and a million miles from my former way of life with all its fripperies and frills.

Camping at night under the winter stars, we made our way in a slow convoy across miles of burning desert towards Halfaya. I had never seen night skies like the ones we saw in the open desert. It was as if the world had been turned on its head and the stars were reflections of some vast blinking metropolis, illuminating the flat earth below. The splendour of the night skies was enhanced by the silence which pressed in, enveloping everything, stilling tongues and unnecessary movement.

By day we could see nothing but endless plain, divided by a series of low rocky ridges or cliffs. The only vegetation was patches of thorny scrub, and the soil was an arid mix of sand and rock. All my expectations of desert life were dashed. There were no rolling *Beau Geste* sand dunes, no palm-fringed oases and no tented Bedouin encampments – the Bedouin knew better than to venture into this harsh wasteland unless they had to.

Mealtimes were the highlights of our day. The British generals would often come to my general's tent to discuss tactics with him and it was not by chance that their visits usually coincided with supper. The British had exactly the same rations as us – bully beef, rice and thin army biscuits, hard yellow cheese, tinned herring, prunes, beer if you could get it from the Naafi, wine occasionally, tea or 'char' every day. But whereas their cooks just heated up the tinned beef or served it cold, our French or Indo-Chinese cooks would make a delicious stew of what they had, putting in anything they could get their hands on – wine, beer, garlic and sometimes even an onion.

Eventually we reached Halfaya, a razor-edged escarpment on which a narrow road twisted precipitously around the edge, and immediately understood why it was known as the Eighth Army's 'gateway into Libya'. From the top one could see right across to the Egyptian coastline, and the endless thick barbed-wire fence constructed by Mussolini years before to stop Libyans escaping his Fascist regime. The British had been ahead of us and had already routed the Italian Savona Division and a battalion of Panzer Grenadiers; it was our task to mop up and then occupy the position for a while to make sure the Germans didn't get their hands on it again.

'The British called this place Hellfire Pass,' Gabriel de Sairigné told me one freezing night when we sat huddled together, drinking coffee. 'It makes it sound warm, doesn't it?'

I was too cold to answer.

There were a few skirmishes when we first arrived, but it became relatively peaceful once Amilakvari and his men had gone in and the Germans had moved on. Sent on to the inland position of El Mechili in February, we discovered that the Germans had got there first, so we had to retreat in the darkness, a thousand vehicles spread out in four columns, fighting a rearguard action as we went.

At each point we reached, we could tell that there had been some serious fighting between Axis and Allied forces ahead of us. Burnt-out tanks and vehicles still littered the roads. Like the bleached bones of vast prehistoric monsters, the metal carcasses had been picked clean of every valuable component by the various mobile workshops from each side as they passed through. In the desert, nothing went to waste.

Our overall objective was to prevent the Axis forces reaching Cairo and gaining control of the Suez Canal. So far Hitler's armies had seemed invincible as they advanced across Europe and now across North Africa. We were all determined that this should stop. There were reports of almost constant fighting on the road between Alexandria and Tobruk, the vital route for Allied supplies. Much to our annoyance, however, we were initially employed solely in minor mopping-up operations further south. Sent on to Duba camp, fifty kilometres west of a place called Mersa Matruh (where Antony and Cleopatra were said to have bathed), we saw little action, despite raised hopes. We spent our time waiting, just waiting for something to happen. And then, quite unexpectedly, it did.

After several weeks of relative inactivity, Rommel suddenly switched tactics. On 21 January he had ordered his Panzerarmee to undertake a volte-face in the desert, and seize the upper hand. In response, the British commanders had hastily regrouped and ordered our heavily armoured Free French forces, including nearly a thousand men of 13DBLE, plus British, African and Indian brigades, to go to the abandoned Italian fort of Bir Hakeim in the barren wilderness of Cyrenaica, eighty kilometres south of Tobruk. It was the last piece of useful terrain before the desolate area known as the Great Libyan Sand Sea. The 3,723 men (including 957 legionnaires), plus me, Fruchaud, Simone and an Australian nurse known as Miss Smith, were to relieve the British 150th Infantry Brigade, made up of men from Yorkshire and Durham, who had been holding the forlorn outpost for several weeks.

I drove the general towards Bir Hakeim across miles of ragged desert in the old Ford Utility, as part of a motley convoy of commandeered vehicles, rusty old trucks, ancient cars and buses, all rattling across the desert to their remote destination. It was a region which was only vaguely mapped, with stony tracks and few signposts. Compasses were the only means of finding one's way between one little fort and another. To get lost would have meant almost certain death in such constantly shifting terrain.

When we reached Bir Hakeim on St Valentine's Day 1942, we discovered it was less of a fort and more of a road junction, an ancient crossroads for the nomadic Bedouin caravans that plied their trade before the war. No more than a flat, slightly raised area of sand and stone, twelve kilometres square, it housed a pre-war Italian fort whose small stone buildings had long since crumbled. There was little there, and nothing but windblown desert for miles around. The ground was hard rubble, and the sunken stone cisterns known as *birs* which collected what little rainwater there was and which had once supplied the colonial fort were cracked, covered with drifting sand and half-empty. The legionnaires jokingly called them *les mamelles* (the breasts).

We stared incredulously at our new home. I could hardly believe my eyes. Only a war could have brought people here, I thought. There was nothing but dust under Libya's molten sky. The word *bir*, I'd been told, meant water in Arabic and I'd wrongly assumed it to be some sort of oasis. But instead of swaying palms reflected in a lake, there was flat rock and a few tumble-down cement shacks with a small hill at one end known as the Observatoire. As we approached, several dusty heads popped out of the ground to greet us, and when we got closer we spotted half-buried vehicles in the sand. To our surprise, the British regiment had dug themselves into trenches and small dugouts, a veritable warren of rabbit holes, one for each person and a few larger ones for mess and communal areas.

'Is this all there is?' I asked an officer, caked in dust, who was walking by.

'Aye, lass,' came the reply in a thick Yorkshire accent. 'The men here call it "hell on earth", and I'd not argue with them.'

From the Allied point of view, Bir Hakeim was the least important and bleakest outpost of the Libyan campaign. It formed the southernmost point in what became known as the Gazala Line, a vast V-shaped barrier of resistance the British forces had managed to create running sixty kilometres south from the coastal hamlet of El Gazala near Tobruk. I was told that every outpost dotted along the spine of the Gazala Line was to be surrounded by its own 'box', a vast minefield laid transparent by sappers, with secret routes through known only to them. Each box was to be given enough provisions to withstand a siege and various nationalities were to divide their time between the

179

various points. Gazala was to be held by South Africans, the box known as 'Knightsbridge' by the British, El Adem by the Indians, Tobruk by the South Africans and the English jointly, and Bir Hakeim by the French. Bir Hakeim was to be the fulcrum of the plan.

South of us was nothing but the cruel dunes of the Sahara. North and east were the massed forces of the Eighth Army, dug in behind 500,000 British anti-tank mines. If Rommel – a hundred kilometres west – wanted to keep mobile and reach Egypt, he'd have to either punch a way through the formidable Allied defences further north or try to round the most southerly point, in which case Bir Hakeim would suddenly become pivotal.

The French brigade had clear orders – to hold onto our desert citadel at whatever cost so as to give the Allied command further north time to regroup and mount a counter-attack. For me and my unhappy comrades, the idea of spending several weeks in Bir Hakeim waiting for just such a moment held minimal appeal.

Trying to get my bearings, and to reconcile myself to the fact that we had arrived at last, I began to inspect my new surroundings. Each dugout was covered with a makeshift roof formed of planks of wood, strips of tarpaulin and netting, even debris from aeroplane wings or engine cowlings. It was like an underground shanty town. Remarkably well built, the trench system even had lavatories or latrines in the middle, six all in a row, each one little more than a piece of wood with a hole in it, above a bucket. One of the doors carried the sign 'Brigadier'. Getting his priorities right, the general immediately chose his own lavatory and put the 'Brigadier' sign on it. In the great tradition of driver's perks, I was the only other person allowed to use it. There were no underground washing facilities; the men were told they would have to erect their own ablutions tent and wash outside. I would have to make my own arrangements.

Within a few hours of arriving at this dreadful oven of a place, the handover had been completed and the 150th

Infantry Brigade had disappeared over the limitless horizon. They were to man a similar post ten miles further north but would get a break in Tobruk first, a chance for a wash and a swim in the sea, before transferring to their new posting. We were on our own. The HQ was set up in the middle of the plateau and surrounded by great coils of barbed wire as a last defence should the enemy break through. That wire was to become a comfort to me later on – no matter how poor the visibility, through darkness or the unreal yellow light of a sandstorm, if I found my way to the wire, I knew I was home and safe.

The general's *camionnette* was set up at the centre of the HQ, the tent flaps which emerged from either side of it forming a small area of shade in which he could sit, receive orders and visitors, and, occasionally, invite some of his senior officers for drinks. Officers like Amilakvari, de Sairigné and Simon were scattered to the periphery of the vast encampment with their men and were rarely allowed away from their posts. Immediately next to the general's caravan was his own dugout, and those for his chief of staff, Colonel Pierre Masson, and for his British liaison officers, Captain Tomkins (who was also commander of the anti-aircraft section), Donnelly, Edwards and Major Sneyd-Cox.

After settling the general into his new quarters and emptying the car of all his private papers and personal belongings, I had time on my hands. Looking around and wondering where I would end up sleeping, suspecting it would be the car again, I realized that the plateau was already a hive of activity, with men bronzed and stripped to their waists, wearing just shorts and sandals, all digging like moles. They set to, creating even more slit trenches, circular holes for equipment and gun pits and larger dugouts for command posts. Before long, the surface of the plateau was literally honeycombed with holes. Large tents were also erected, housing a hospital and the HQ and various messes for the officers and men and communications.

181

Someone tapped me lightly on the arm and I turned to see a young sapper from the engineer corps of the Legion with a pickaxe in his hand.

'Adjudant Travers, we've prepared a dugout for you. Would you care to come and inspect it?' he said.

The general or Amilakvari had undoubtedly had a quiet word and organized a digging party on my behalf.

My new home, just a few yards from the general's *camionnette*, was a palace compared to the cramped conditions of the car. Waist deep, about four feet wide and ten feet long, it was piled up at the sides with four deep walls of sandbags. One of the legionnaires helped me step down into it and showed me how to roll across the canvas top.

'This is to protect you from the sun in the day and the cold at night,' he explained shyly.

I nodded my understanding. The men stood around at the edge, watching as I inspected it carefully and waiting for my verdict. It was like nowhere I'd ever lived before, but it was mine alone and I was very grateful for their kindness. I flashed them my most winning smile and thanked them warmly.

'*Bienvenu au Château Travers!*' I announced with a flourish of my hand as they bowed in mock deference.

I arranged my few belongings in the dugout as best I could. There was enough room for my camp bed, a little folding chair-cum-table, and my suitcase, which doubled as another seat or table. My folding bath stayed in the boot of the car along with my tools. The general was just a few yards away, but he might as well have been in another country for the amount of time I expected to see him.

When I'd finished settling in, I looked around for somewhere to conceal the car and found several large sloping pits which had been dug especially for vehicles. Choosing the one closest to my dugout for the safekeeping of the Ford, I nosed it carefully down the steep slope into the hole, piling the engine end of it with a wall of sandbags and covering the rear with a frayed piece of camouflage material. For the moment, my work was done.

With nothing to protect us, the blistering heat of the days gave way to chilling cold nights. In the summer the temperature would rise to 51°C (120°F). Our only slight advantage was that Bir Hakeim provided an oblong observation point twenty or so feet above the rest of the desert floor. Water was the most vital commodity and convoys of tanker lorries brought foul-tasting distilled sea water from Tobruk, after the men quickly drank *les mamelles* dry. Each unit had its own water tank on wheels and we'd fill our canteens as regularly as we were allowed.

Having finished the trenches, the troops set about improving the defences, laying the barbed wire and vast minefields they hoped would protect us against any attack, digging in their 75mm field guns, anti-tank weapons and newly acquired British Bofors anti-aircraft guns, and setting up observation points in key areas at the periphery of the six-sided compound. Every sort of mine, from anti-tank to anti-personnel devices – 50,000 in all – was laid.

The soldiers were of vastly different backgrounds and experience, but they all pitched in together. There were Africans, Tahitians, Bretons, Moroccans, Algerians, Lebanese, Mauritians, Madagascans, Germans and Spanish. They ranged from dedicated career soldiers and hardened legionnaires to civil servants and settlers from the colonies who had risen to de Gaulle's call to arms. French was the universal language, although there were men of every nationality there, including a small British detachment manning some of the mighty Bofors guns.

Once the work was done, and the three narrow access routes plotted through the mine marsh into no-man's-land, there was little to do but wait. Day after day, the men sat gazing into the shimmering heat haze until their eyeballs burned. Only the light breeze which occasionally whipped the sand into mini-tornados stirred the white-hot stillness of the atmosphere.

Cut off from Pierre and the other men in the furnace heat, I sometimes felt overwhelmed by loneliness. Simone and Miss Smith, on the other hand, were envious that I had a dugout to myself.

'We have to share,' they complained. 'Our camp beds are just a few inches apart, and in this heat it's quite insufferable.'

'The grass is always greener,' I told them wryly. 'Personally, I'd be jolly glad of the company.' For once, I meant it. My only roommates were the ever-present flies and ants, or an occasional scorpion.

Meals, heralded by a bugle call, continued to be a highlight, although they often held little appeal. I ate in the kitchen to begin with, supplementing my meagre meals with tins of sardines and asparagus which the general or Amilakvari occasionally sent over to my dugout from the officers' mess. But it was a lonely place with all the men scattered to the corners of the encampment and after a while I asked tentatively if I might eat with the NCOs, who dined in a strange pyramid-shaped store tent which must have come from Syria, for no British tent ever looked like that.

'Do you think anyone would mind if I joined your table for meals?' I asked Rosenzweig, the kindly *adjudant* who looked after the sick troops. Sensing his hesitation, I added, 'I wouldn't be any trouble, and you could have my rations of whisky and cigarettes in return.'

After private deliberations, the men agreed and thereafter I ate with them twice a day, swapping their company for my monthly rations. It was a fair trade. I no longer drank or smoked, and it was wonderful to look forward to some occasional conversation. Without them, I would often have gone several days without speaking to a soul. There were only three of them – Rosenzweig, who smoked heavily, Schmidt, the Alsatian paymaster with a wicked sense of humour, and a young corporal from the workshop whose real name I never knew, but whom I nicknamed 'Lofty' because he was shorter than me.

The four of us struck up quite a friendship during the next few months, finding out one another's likes and dislikes, sharing stories and memories. I didn't see the point in telling them too much about my past, so I spoke instead of my love for tennis and animals, all the while asking them questions. Lofty was especially sweet. Young and inexperienced in love, he was never quite sure how to handle me, the woman in their midst, standing whenever I entered the tent and holding my chair for me. He'd always pass the food to me first and was clearly embarrassed if either of his comrades swore or made lewd remarks in my company.

'Don't worry, dear boy,' I'd whisper into his reddening ear. 'I've heard it all before.'

We remained in the dead land of Bir Hakeim without incident for three months. It was truly the most boring place anyone had ever been in, with nothing to do but sleep or read. Major Sneyd-Cox had lent me a book he'd taken from the Beirut library called *Said the Fisherman*, all about an Arab. I read it so many times, its pages came loose. There was little change in the seasons apart from a steady increase in the heat, and little for me to do but lie in my dugout and reflect on my life. I ached for the general and found it hard to bear that he was so close by and yet so unattainable. I was rarely given a chance to be in his company, to smell his scent, touch his skin or hear his voice. Instead, I relived every moment of my time with him in Beirut and Aley in my head and fed on the memories to sustain me through the long, cold nights.

Once every few weeks, the compound would be struck by one of the terrible sandstorms, sweeping in from the Sahara on a gale-force wind called the khamsin and lasting for up to five days. Sometimes the wind had such biting ferocity that it would set off some of the mines surrounding our desolate posting. The storms brought unbearable heat and carried a mist of dust as fine as talcum powder, which turned every fair grey, filled the eyes, lungs, nose and throat, and tainted the food and water.

Worse were the still days, those without a whisper of

breeze when legionnaires, their faces hidden in the deep shade of their peaked kepis as they sat on sentry at the furthest outposts, talked fearfully of 'the cockroach', the name for a desert madness which supposedly comes to men in such conditions. Shielding my eyes from the incessant white glare as I watched them, I imagined the little cockroach crawling round and round inside a man's brain and entirely empathized.

The best days for the men came once a fortnight when they were transported by truck the eighty kilometres north to Tobruk and allowed to swim in the Mediterranean at a point that became known as 'Koenig's beach'. Leaping naked into the waves to wash the sand and grime from their bodies revived their spirits enormously. Permanently on standby in case the general suddenly needed to go somewhere, I was afforded no such luxury.

For me, the waiting game continued relentlessly. I never left the precincts of the HQ except for the occasional trip to the Naafi, the workshop or to visit the other troops such as the Bataillon du Pacifique, who were very pleasant men, or to the British brigades such as the Royal Engineers. With little else to do, I developed an uncanny knack for finding my way and retracing my steps; it was a skill which would stand me in good stead.

My happiest days were when the general invited me out with him to lead the Jock Columns (named after the British general Jock Campbell), secret two- or three-day reconnaissance missions with troops and cannon, wireless truck and armoured cars, to map out the desert and see where the enemy was. Usually we'd head along a route known only as 'Route F', in the direction of El Mechili, and if we saw anything we'd open fire. If we were pursued, we'd run. It was a kind of game.

It was highly dangerous undercover work, but it relieved the monotony and was welcomed by all who were invited to take part. Best of all, I got to sit next to the general for the duration of the sortie. More than once we nearly got caught and I had to drive the general to safety, fleeing from enemy fire at great speed or hiding in a dried-out wadi as the German or Italian tanks rolled by. It was akin to a battle at sea – no land was taken or positions held, everything shifted like the sand; we were two sets of professionals, hunting each other out, opening fire and running away. As long as you didn't get hit, it was very exciting and pretty good fun.

The Jock Columns were a delight for other reasons, too: they felt like picnics in the country. We even had our own chef who accompanied us and we sometimes slept out under the stars. I remember one delicious meal of white desert snails with garlic that the chef prepared for me and the general in the middle of nowhere. He even brought some wine to wash it down with. The chef was delighted that the general had eaten the meal.

'These little snails are everywhere and now that the general has tasted them, I can serve them to the rest of the men,' he said proudly.

In the few instances that the general and I were alone, he would always ask me how I was. 'Is everything all right?' he'd say. 'Do you still want to stay? I can send you somewhere else if you'd prefer. This isn't much of a place for a woman.'

'No, General,' I'd insist. 'I'm fine, really. Where you go, I go, remember?'

On one Jock Column the general and I became separated from the rest of the group in the immense billowing clouds of dust their vehicles threw up. Unable to see them, I drove in a different direction, just as a sandstorm broke.

'Where are the others?' the general asked, panicking, as we tried to peer through the grey gloom.

'I don't know,' I replied, in all honesty. 'I think they're just ahead, but I'll have to stop the car now.'

The sandstorm became particularly vicious, battering the doors and windows, rocking the car and swirling sand all around us. Trapped together in the car, frightened and alone, we slid towards each other, flesh touching flesh for the first time in weeks. It felt wonderful to hold his hand again and to feel his lips against mine. The sandstorm raged on all around us but, for a while, we were completely oblivious to it. We resigned ourselves to having to sleep in the car together overnight. I didn't mind at all. I longed to be able to lie alongside him once more.

But, just as darkness was falling, there came a tapping at the driver's window. Through the angry grains of sand, I saw the face of the young soldier who'd been acting as our motorcycle outrider. Lost like us, he'd stumbled across us and was seeking shelter. Holding the handle with both hands so as not to lose the door in the ferocious winds, we opened it to allow him, and half of the desert, it seemed, inside. When he took off his goggles, his face was stained grey above and below where they'd been, leaving white owl-like skin around his eyes. Squashing up together on the sand-covered seats, we tried to get some sleep.

I don't know who was more surprised when we woke up in the morning, the general or the soldier, when they discovered that they'd inadvertently snuggled up to each other, snoring in unison. Mortified, the soldier leaped from the car as fast as he could open the door, dusting off the fine white sand that had crept up through the floorboards, and spent a vigorous two hours digging us out.

Generally, however, we managed to stay together on the Jock Columns and our moment of solitude was never repeated. Once encamped for the night, we weren't allowed fires or lights in case we were spotted, so it was always bitterly cold and tremendously silent. Only the general could use oil lamps in his caravan, and then only with the blackout curtains tightly drawn. As soon as darkness fell, the rest of us would go to sleep, waking only when first light began to tinge the sky pink.

Whenever we saw the enemy, the adrenaline rush was phenomenal. Crouching in the dust on the ridge of a dune, we would watch the Germans or Italians a few hundred yards away through binoculars, checking their strengths and weaknesses, and knowing that if we were spotted we

188

could be killed. After such encounters, I felt safe only when driving back towards Bir Hakeim and seeing, from the post of El Adem, the funny pointed store tent where I ate my meals every day. Then I knew I was home and dry.

Very occasionally when we were out in the desert it would rain, and though there was never enough water to fill the little streams or *wadis*, beds of wild grasses with scented flowers would shoot up immediately. They were all colours – mauve and yellow and blue – and you could almost watch them grow. I would marvel at the sight of the hundreds of desert blooms that sprang from the dust within an hour of the rain. Dry and dusty, I would lie among them, inhaling their scent and remembering happier days in Aley and rooms filled with bowls of roses. Before long, flocks of wild Bedouin sheep would arrive from nowhere to gobble up the lot. The sheep were protected by a shepherd and fierce dogs, so no-one could go near them, not even the chef, who told me how his mouth used to water at the thought of what a beautiful *gigot d'agneau* he could make.

In mid-April, word came from the British that we were to be relieved after our long and unremarkable sojourn at Bir Hakeim. A South African force was due to take over from us and its senior officers came to the desolate spot to look it over and assess what they needed to bring with them. Our joint reaction was one of relief.

'Maybe now we'll be sent back to Cairo for a rest,' I said to Rosenzweig hopefully over supper the night we received the news.

'Or somewhere far more exciting,' he replied, his soldier's eyes bright. Swallowing a mouthful of stew, he added: 'Maybe even somewhere like South-East Asia. The Japs are bound to come a cropper now Mountbatten's in charge. I'd love to have a piece of that action.'

I thought of the latest grim news from Singapore, Java and Burma as the Japanese forces continued their apparently unstoppable advance and wondered if we might be called upon to travel so far.

But events in the Western Desert took a dramatic turn. In May, with the Italians continuing to fail miserably, word came that Rommel, instead of advancing towards Halfaya as we'd expected, had switched a number of tanks from his panzer division in the north to the south in an attempt to turn the British flank in an area that became known as the Devil's Cauldron. We soon realized that they were heading straight for Bir Hakeim. All I and my four thousand fellow soldiers of fortune could do was to dig ourselves in deeper and await the arrival of the other players on the stage.

Much later, we learned that Rommel had told the Italian Ariete Armoured and the Trieste Motorized Divisions that it should take them 'only fifteen minutes' to crush us. When this didn't happen and the minutes dragged on into hours and the hours into days, he was furious and resolved to do the job himself, leading a shock force straight towards us. On hearing this, the Allied radios buzzed with activity. As we awaited the Desert Fox's arrival, the British signalled to us that they thought we could last eight days, just enough time for the Eighth Army to regain lost ground. In the event, despite being outnumbered ten to one, we held out for nearly twice that time. Fifteen days! And what days they were.

11

A PYRRHIC VICTORY

'I laugh at death, accuse her whore,
For she seduced, while in the mirth of life
My comrades, when she tore their fragile plants
From out the earth.'

DENIS SAUNDERS, WHO SERVED IN EGYPT,
'ALMENDRO', FROM *THE VOICE OF WAR*

Our ordeal began on a moonlit night in May, when loud firing was heard in the distance just before dawn. In the north, the sky was suddenly ablaze and there were bright flashes of gunfire and explosions. An Anglo-Indian Hindu Brigade outside the wire had been overcome by a heavy tank attack and far superior numbers while guarding the periphery. Half an hour later, the first of the enemy tanks rolled into view – eighty of them all advancing together, firing indiscriminately as they came, the squeaking of their tracks adding to the fearful cacophony now surrounding Bir Hakeim. They were immediately followed by an impressive number of trucks carrying infantry and artillery.

I retreated to my dugout, ramming my tin helmet onto my head, listening to the sound of distant landmines exploding under the caterpillar tracks of the huge metal monsters attempting to scythe their way towards us. Shells pounded as they landed nearby. Minutes before the main attack had begun, Amilakvari had appeared at the entrance to my little rabbit hole.

'This is for you,' he said, handing me his rifle and grinning broadly. 'I don't suppose you'll need to use it, but I thought it might make you feel better.'

I took it gratefully and flashed him a look of such gratitude and affection that he blushed. Sitting with it across my knee in my dugout for the next few hours, I did indeed feel much better.

At ten o'clock the little Indo-Chinese orderly we'd nick-named Trompette sounded his polished brass bugle for the all-clear, and those of us who had taken cover emerged blinking into the daylight to see what damage had been done. Despite the evidence of several large craters in the sand and rock all around us, the news was good.

Gabriel de Sairigné came to the HQ to report to the general, a smile on his dirt-stained face. 'The Italians have retreated, sir, with the loss of thirty-five of their tanks. Almost a hundred enemy prisoners have been taken and many have been killed, while on our side there are just two casualties and one gun destroyed. Sir.'

The general was delighted and so were we. On receipt of the news via the radio at British headquarters, a missive came from above that we were no longer to be known as the Free French, but as La France Combattante, the Fighting French. It was a name that never really stuck, but the honour was appreciated.

The Italians could barely believe what had happened. In fact, a few hours later, several soldiers, seeing their own (abandoned) vehicles and thinking the position must have been taken, approached Bir Hakeim in error. They were promptly captured and their carriers destroyed. It was a remarkable first day.

Over the next few days, we watched an endless convoy of enemy lorries and tanks circling Bir Hakeim out of range to the south before heading north, sloping round behind Allied lines. If any vehicles were careless enough to come within range, they were fired upon. The Free French troops, under Amilakvari and others, mounted several daring hit-and-run attacks on the convoys, capturing men, vehicles and ammunition and destroying tanks, stopping only at the sight of a huge dust cloud on the horizon one morning.

'Go and see what the hell that is,' the general barked down the telephone link to the commander of the handful of British tanks closest to the front.

Crawling on his stomach to the top of a small stony ridge, the astonished officer telephoned back his news. 'Looks like a brigade of Jerry tanks coming,' he reported. Then as the haze cleared slightly and he saw what was actually causing it, he grabbed the telephone once more and wound the handle frantically. 'It's more than a brigade, sir,' he exclaimed. 'It's the whole of the Afrika Korps drawn up in front of us like a bloody review!'

The dreaded Panzer Mark IV tanks and their Italian counterparts attacked in waves of fifty. Six of the first wave survived the minefield and lurched into the garrison, coming within twenty yards of the forward command post in which a frightened captain was frantically burning his orders. Luckily for him, tenacious legionnaires scrambled up over the tanks and fired their revolvers through the observation slits. It was an audacious move, but the sheer numbers making up the advancing Axis tide meant that it might be the last.

That night, the general came to my dugout for the first time, accompanied by Colonel Pierre Masson. 'A convoy is coming in tomorrow with water and ammunition and will take out the wounded,' he said stiffly. 'I thought you might like to go with it.' His face was pinched with tiredness.

'If you stay, sir, I stay,' I told him resolutely. 'That's all I aolt.'

The general half-smiled and looked across at Masson, who nodded reluctantly. I felt instinctively that the general regretted that he hadn't been able to spend much time with

193

me, and that he was comforted by my loyalty. It was just as well. The convoy he wished me to join was attacked by the enemy the following day and all the wounded were captured or killed.

Despite the constant threat of the enemy tanks, an Allied supply convoy did manage to sneak into Bir Hakeim under cover of darkness on the second night. Much to my disappointment, it carried with it a missive from the British high command, insisting that all female personnel – referring chiefly to the two nurses in the hospital tent – be removed from the theatre of war. 'No women on the front line,' was the order. The Spears hospital was to be replaced and I too would have to go.

The general summoned me to his *camionnette*. 'There's no point in arguing, La Miss,' he said, trying to pre-empt my predictable response. 'I simply can't refuse their order this time. They've been quite specific and your name is on the list.'

I bowed my head and sighed, swallowing my anger as best I could. I knew the general was waiting for me to pick a fight. Instead, I looked up at him. 'Can I try and come back when the danger's passed?'

'We-ell,' he hesitated. 'There's a new staff car ready at the workshop for Colonel Masson. If you were to collect that when you get to Tobruk and then wait until it's safe to return, I'm sure the British couldn't possibly object to the delivery of an important liaison vehicle.'

My fury tempered, I bid him farewell. After packing my few belongings, I tried to find Arad. But the dog had firmly ensconced himself with the Chadian legionnaires somewhere at the front and was nowhere to be seen. I left alone in an old canvas-topped Ford ambulance with Simone and Miss Smith following on in another.

We drove across the desert for a few hours and stopped at the next point up the Gazala Line, a place known as B Echelon, where we waited until morning. I slept that night in the ambulance, still wishing that I could have stayed at Bir Hakeim. I didn't like to leave the general or the Legion

194

and resolved to come straight back with Masson's car, regardless of the orders.

I was woken before dawn by a tremendous panic in the camp. Everyone seemed to be rushing about. 'The Germans are coming! The Germans are coming!' they were crying. 'Get away! Get away!' Scouts had seen a column of approaching enemy vehicles on the horizon. Placing two Indo-Chinese orderlies on each mudguard to check for enemy bombers, I started the engine and opened the rear doors of my ambulance to anyone who wanted a lift to Tobruk. It was soon completely full with about thirty British soldiers, all eager to flee from the advancing Germans.

'Come on, luv,' one of them shouted, hitting the side of the ambulance impatiently with the flat of his hand as I revved the engine and waited for any stragglers. 'We're the last bloody ones left. What're yer waiting for? Christmas?'

Setting off shortly after dawn and travelling with only a compass and my wits, I plotted a rough course north to the sea, hoping to God that there would be no marauding Germans in the way. Only a few of us were armed and I knew we'd easily be overpowered and captured if we encountered any hostile forces.

'Do you have any idea where you're going?' one of the English officers yelled at me from the back of the ambulance halfway across the barren desert, as I swerved to avoid yet another dried-out riverbed.

'Haven't a clue,' I replied cheerily, manoeuvring the giant steering wheel with the ease of a veteran truck driver. 'But if this British-issue compass is right, we should be paddling our toes in the Mediterranean by supper time.'

More by luck than judgement the compass did work, and we didn't encounter any enemy tanks on the way. Arriving at the coast road to Alexandria, we turned left and made our way bumpily to Tobruk. The badly battered port whose name became fabled in Second World War history had taken even more of a hammering since I was last there. The inside of the garrison was teeming with men and vehicles. Instead of the tremendous sense of detachment I'd experienced at Bir Hakeim, here I really felt as though I was in the middle of a war. Now that the Germans were just a day's ride away, all was chaos and nobody seemed to know what anyone else was doing.

I dropped my passengers off and found my way to General de Larminat's headquarters where I discovered that there was nothing for me to do. The only people who took an interest in me were men who hadn't seen a woman in months.

'Good-day, ma'am,' a sparkly-eyed Australian corporal yelled across the street with an appreciative whistle. 'Fancy a cold beer?' The men sitting with him, smoking, sniggered.

Suddenly aware of my Legion shorts, which showed far too much of my tanned legs, I hurried past with my head down and my eyes firmly on the ground. Feeling dirty and self-conscious for the first time in weeks, I thought how wonderful a hot bath and a hairwash would be.

Wherever I could, I asked for news of Bir Hakeim and the response filled me with trepidation.

'Bir Hakeim is surrounded and has been cut off,' one of the officers in the mess told me over lunch, his expression grim. 'Nobody's holding out much hope for them now.'

I shivered at the thought and lost my appetite for my first decent meal in weeks.

Having enquired after Colonel Masson's car, I was told it was ready and waiting at the workshop. Making my way there, I discovered everyone in great distress.

'The news from Bir Hakeim is very bad,' a captain told me gloomily. 'The Germans are at the door. Listen to the radio.'

He turned up the volume on his grease-stained wireless and we all stood around listening to Lord Haw-Haw, the English-speaking German propagandist, as he summoned us with his traditional 'Germany calling, Germany calling' and told us that it was only a matter of time before 'the miserable desert rats of Bir Hakeim are routed'. Armed with this information, I became ever more determined to get back into the desert and as close to Bir Hakeim as I could.

Discovering that a supply convoy was heading for B Echelon the following morning, I decided to go with it. Nobody appeared to care if I stayed or went, so – at the wheel of the colonel's smart new Ford – I drove back across the desert, passing a never-ending stream of vehicles and men fleeing in the opposite direction. No-one was at all pleased to see me at B Echelon (which had moved its position further north to avoid the Germans).

'You can't possibly go back to Bir Hakeim now,' a commander told me firmly. 'It's all but over there.'

He reluctantly agreed to allow me to stay, as long as I slept in the car.

I remained at B Echelon for three days, and was put to work driving an old Greek brigadier around the place. I hoped to come across the Spears hospital and find some familiar faces, but the brigadier just wanted to see the sights, such as they were, and the men wanted to be rid of him. He was a terrible old bore, and by the third day I was more than ready to move on.

To my great relief, when we returned to B Echelon that evening we found everyone in high spirits. 'The French have repulsed the enemy and the Germans have fled,' a man I'd never met before told me with a hug. I felt as if a great weight had been lifted off my shoulders.

When I found out that a food and munitions convoy was leaving for Bir Hakeim that night, I scrawled a hasty note to the general to go with it. 'I'm at B Echelon with Masson's car. Permission to return? Adjutant Travers.'

The following day a message came back, via Captain Thoreau, head of the transport division. The general's note said simply: 'Koenig.' I was going home.

With Captain Cance, head of logistics in the Fourth Bureau, leading in a pick-up truck and me in my new car with a pleasant young journalist from Cairo called Besnard, who'd asked if I would take him to Bir Hakeim, we headed south. Everyone else was going the other way.

Cance seemed very nervous and often stopped to look around with his binoculars to see if he could see anything. I just wanted to push on. Luckily there were no Germans to be seen and we arrived at last at Bir Hakeim, a place I never thought I'd be relieved to see. Nothing would have kept me away.

Having turned away the Germans and the Italian Ariete division and watched them flee, everyone was tremendously pleased with themselves. Amilakvari, Messmer and the others were already in hot pursuit. It had been a great triumph. Reporting personally to the general, I congratulated him on his success.

'*Merci*, La Miss,' he said, using my pet name for only the second time in as many months.

That very same evening, however, the tide turned. The Bataillon du Pacifique went out in a Jock Column to watch the fleeing enemy only to be attacked in strength by the Germans, who had regrouped. Luckily, most of the men managed to escape back to Bir Hakeim and told us that the Germans had returned in much greater numbers and we were now completely surrounded. Armed with that knowledge, the sappers spent the night relaying mines in the minefield as we all prepared for a further attack.

That night the general came to my dugout. 'I can't order you to leave because there is no way you can get out now, but will you please at least go to the hospital for your own safety?' he asked, his forehead furrowed. 'We think that this time the Germans won't be so easily pushed back. They might even use gas.'

I looked up into his tired eyes and thought of all the ghastly First World War stories I'd heard and of the poems of Wilfred Owen – '*he plunges at me, guttering, choking, drowning*' – which I had read in the books the general had sent me in hospital. I remembered, too, the joint declaration of the British and the French at the beginning of the war that they did not intend to use poison gas or germ warfare.

Agreeing that perhaps the best place for me would be the

hospital, I grabbed my tin helmet and, without thinking, held out my hand for the general's as I prepared to climb up and out of my narrow hole. But he looked so cross I withdrew my hand quickly.

'You fool,' he said. 'You've forgotten your gas mask.'

The hospital was the only tent left above ground – the rest had been taken down as obvious targets – and it bore the mark of the Red Cross as a warning to the German pilots. I arrived at its door in my unbearably uncomfortable gas mask, only to discover Dr Vialard Godou, my boss in Syria, in charge of the 'human repair shop'. There were also some American Quakers and a jolly Scottish doctor who, having given his own blood to some of the more seriously injured men, told them they were about to develop a 'mean and stingy' streak. Despite my nursing qualification, or perhaps because of it, I was allowed to do nothing but move from bed to bed trying to boost the spirits of the most seriously ill.

The patients were suffering from every kind of complaint – malaria, sand fly fever, yellow fever, as well as the various desert sores, prickly heat and weeping skin conditions caused by the dirt and dust and flies. Some were doubled up with the corkscrew pain of dysentery twisting their guts; others lay listless and weak from lack of salt and water. Heat exhaustion was very common (it killed some), and all that was before they'd been shot or shelled or burnt or lacerated by flying shrapnel. The beds were full of gas-masked men.

Fighting resumed at once and carried on all day, debris and shrapnel spraying the tented walls of the hospital, the distant rumble of guns acting as a permanent backdrop. It stopped only when a thick sandstorm – exacerbated by the hundreds of vehicles loosening the desert crust – rolled in from the desert, reducing visibility to zero and badly hampering my later attempts to find my way back to my dugout in the half-light. Bumping into some English anti-aircraft operators and asking them if they had any idea which direction the HQ was, I got the inevitable answer.

'Sorry, luv, no, we're new around here,' they said in their broad cockney accents.

Each of us stumbled off into the blinding dust, one of them demanding loudly what on earth a 'plum-in-the-mouth Englishwoman' was doing in this hell-hole.

I eventually walked straight into the barbed-wire fence coiled around the HQ and, although I nicked my hand, it was a huge relief. For a moment I remembered my childhood days in London, feeling my way through the pea-souper fogs by holding onto the Georgian railings behind Laurence and my indomitable grandmother. I made it home just as the shelling began again.

The following day, 1 June, the enemy offensive resumed in earnest, with Stuka dive-bombers, and Rommel's Panzer Mark IVs bearing down on Bir Hakeim from the north-west. We gave as good as we got, firing back with our 75 mm guns and our anti-aircraft weapons. Even the mighty Bofors guns were put to good use, despite the fact that the poor English operators were still waiting for official instructions on how to use them. I shall never forget the insistent roll of gunfire on the horizon as I dug the general's car out of the sand with my hands and started it to make sure it still worked after so many days of standing idle. It did and I was hugely relieved. My small role in the daily madness had been fulfilled.

The German and Italian losses were great in those early days, with legionnaires and colonials attacking their tanks with grenades and Molotov cocktails. Men would stumble from their burning vehicles in flames, desperately rolling in the sand. The suffering was appalling, and as all of us had the most enormous respect for those we were fighting we found it very difficult to watch helplessly. Rommel was legend enough; his Afrika Korps had an almost mythical status. The Italians, too, were considered fearless and energetic although they had the poorest equipment. There was never any sense of satisfaction in watching others die; just sadness at the lunacy which had brought us all to this oven of a place.

Whenever a position was taken or a crippled vehicle saved, the legionnaires would triumphantly bring home their spoils – weapons, ammunition, even entire vehicles sometimes, although the Italian Lancia trucks with their solid tyres were not much favoured. On the corrugated lunar landscape, the tyres shook the trucks to pieces. But what was inside them was coveted – hams, wines, sweet-meats, preserves and cheese. As in Syria, the Italians seemed particularly well stocked with provisions. I even got to eat some, although not in the NCOs' tent, which had been taken down as an obvious target, but back in the kitchen, which was half dug in and underground.

A large cage was erected near the HQ to house the grow-ing number of enemy prisoners and we now had to feed and water them too, which grated amongst some of the orderlies who couldn't understand why we didn't kill them. We were largely an honourable camp, however, peopled by proud soldiers and legionnaires, and the general went personally to the cage to apologize for being unable to provide the enemy officers with more comfortable quarters. '*Je suis désolé*,' he told them and I knew he meant it.

Still I had nothing to do and the bombardments only made me sleepy and hungry. When they began, I used to sit on the floor of my dugout with my tin hat on, and when they'd stopped, I'd peer to see where the bombs had fallen. Each time I emerged unscathed I'd think, well, it's not my turn this time. Others would emerge from their respective dugouts all around me with the same thought. Our second thought would be food. Soon, as the bombardments became more and more severe, the kitchen closed in the daylight hours and no more lunches were prepared, only suppers. After that, we had to live on tinned rations alone. Just when I thought I'd go mad if I saw another tin of bully beef stamped 'Smithfield Selected', the general sent me one of the food caches we used to take on Jock Columns, keep-ing the other for himself. Opening this treasure chest, I discovered all sorts of Naafi delights such as asparagus, sardines and salmon. There was even a can of beer. It seemed a pity to leave it to the Germans, so I scoffed the lot.

By 2 June, we were almost completely encircled. Still fighting, we were surprised to see a vehicle carrying a white flag approaching. Gabriel de Sairigné accompanied the two Italian officers to the HQ. They didn't speak French or English, but there were those in the Legion who knew enough Italian to understand their few words. The officers said that General Rommel, 'the great victor of Libya', demanded the unconditional surrender of our garrison, or we would all be killed. *Sterminare* was the word they used. They suggested that it might be better to surrender to the Italians, who'd look after us, rather than the harsher German troops.

General Koenig told them that it was not in the military tradition of the Legion for his men to surrender. 'My troops have arms and ammunition and are prepared to fight,' he said.

The officers saluted. He was a *'grande soldato'*, they announced, as they withdrew and were escorted beyond the Allied line.

At 8 a.m. on 3 June, shortly after I'd dug the general's car from the sand yet again, two captured British orderlies crawled on their stomachs into the encampment – they were being fired upon – with an ultimatum signed personally by Rommel. The Desert Fox's surrender demand, handwritten on a piece of yellow lined paper, read:

> To the troops of Bir Hakeim. Further resistance will only lead to pointless loss of life. You will suffer the same fate as the two Brigades which were at Got el Ualeb and which were exterminated the day before yesterday – we will cease fighting as soon as you show the white flag and come towards us unarmed. Signed: Rommel, General Oberst.

General Koenig, by then affectionately known among his men as *'le vieux lapin'*, the old rabbit, sent a little note to his officers. 'I'm in contact with Rommel. He says if we don't surrender, he'll make mincemeat of us. I told him to take a running jump.' He signed off with '*bon vent à tous*', 'God speed'. He then replied by opening fire on all the enemy vehicles within range.

Like the general, we were all flattered to have been given a second ultimatum, particularly by Rommel himself. It made us feel very special indeed.

In a hurry to press on to Egypt and infuriated by our resistance, Rommel used every weapon at his disposal to rain firepower down on Bir Hakeim. The world watched and waited – all eyes were upon us. He had made our destruction a personal objective, defying the High Command in Berlin. 'I'll get the French, I'll get them,' he vowed.

In the dreadful first week of attack that followed, one of our ammunition dumps was hit, exploding over a hundred shells. Fires raged everywhere in the compound, and many dead and wounded lay unattended. The Germans' large 88 mm guns which dominated the battle seemed to be out of our guns' reach.

'When are the English going to come to our defence?' the men asked angrily. The Royal Air Force certainly did their best to help, sending Hurricanes and Kittyhawks which shot down a total of twenty-two German planes. They bombed Rommel's forces on the ground too, but the Germans just seemed to wait until they'd gone before starting up again.

The general, however, sent an appreciative telegram: '*Merci, la RAF.*'

A delighted RAF responded: '*Merci à vous pour le sport.*' Thereafter the pilots took special care to protect and defend Bir Hakeim.

On one particularly bad day, I seemed to be the Germans' prime target. One shell fell behind my dugout, then one in front of it and another on each side. The whole earth seemed to be groaning all around me. Watching and waiting, unable to make a run for it and feeling like a sitting duck, I was certain that the next one would be a direct hit.

'I'm not a wretched military target!' I yelled aloud in indignation as the shells continued to fall. Fortunately, the guns moved away at last. I was spared once more.

The British were delighted with General Koenig and his men. On 4 June they sent him a telegram which read: '*Excellent work. Hold fast. All the best. All will be well.*'

The general responded that if Rommel wanted to bring the French to their knees, 'he would have to wait a long time'.

The world's press trumpeted the French success. Headlines such as 'Heroic defence by the French' and 'Magnificent feat of arms' were on the front pages of newspapers in London, Washington, Cairo and Sydney. General de Gaulle sent a special telegram to us from his headquarters in London: '*General Koenig, know and tell your troops that the whole of France is looking at you and you are her pride.*' It was the first time in this campaign that the French had fought on their own, apart from the Allies, and we were putting on a brave show of defiance in the face of sledgehammer blows. We had restored the nation's honour.

Attack after attack continued while the general's men carried out an effective harassment campaign against the enemy, with raiding parties seizing fuel, water, supplies, prisoners of war and vehicles. One group even returned with large bars of chocolate and bottles of eau de Cologne. But it was dangerous work. Even Amilakvari was trapped the wrong side of the minefield one evening and had to be rescued by Pierre Messmer and his men. Amilakvari was so angry at being caught that he went out again the next night and destroyed five German tanks. He was a man who took the business of war personally.

Once more Rommel sent surrender terms, this time via three German officers who came in an armoured vehicle at 4 a.m. only to be turned away at the gate.

'We wouldn't dream of waking our general at such an early hour,' our guards told the officers.

As they departed, their vehicle hit a landmine, wrecking the car but not injuring them. Mortified, the officers had no choice but to walk back to their lines, under a barrage of taunts from German-speaking legionnaires.

The fresh onslaught which followed raged for eight days, a non-stop bombardment by ground and air forces as the enemy grip tightened still further. The RAF did marvellous work, sending in a wave of twenty fighters to attack enemy positions at a vertical angle despite the dense curtain of enemy fire. In retaliation, Rommel sent in his best tank corps, the 90th Light Division. Shells, mortars, heavy-calibre machine-gun fire, tanks and automatic weapons were all used against us and our little patch of desert called Bir Hakeim.

Fighting stopped only when the cutting, sand-filled winds whipped up from the Sahara, or at night when each side collected its dead and wounded and licked its wounds. Then the silence of the grave prevailed, and became almost as unnerving as the noise of the day. It was hard to imagine that thousands of men were all sleeping, sometimes little more than a few feet apart, before trying to kill each other again the next day. When battle resumed, at six o'clock sharp each morning, it was relentless. Hour upon hour, attack and counter-attack followed each other in intense heat. The sky was never clear – a great cloud of sand thrown up by the shells hung suspended in the air, making it even harder to breathe.

French gunners fired more than 40,000 shells during the siege. More than a hundred Stuka dive-bombers and forty Junkers heavy bombers flew 1,400 missions and pounded the French position with 1,500 tons of 500 lb high-explosive bombs. The RAF lost seventy planes.

I hated the Stukas most of all, their incessant screaming and the awful silence which followed as I sat alone on the floor in the middle of my dugout, with only my tin helmet to protect me. Each morning brought coffee and Stukas for breakfast. Every day brought fresh artillery shells whining across the no-man's-land of coiled barbed wire and anti-tank minefields. Machine-gun bullets rained on us almost constantly and the scorching desert sun sat unchallenged in the sky for fourteen hours a day, baking us dry.

The eighth of June was one of the worst days. It started with a fog, which meant that the Stukas and Junkers could only guess where to drop their bombs. Sadly, they were just as effective. As the morning mists cleared, artillery fire opened up and Bir Hakeim was subjected to a ferocious enemy barrage. The German guns drenched it in a wave of high explosives. Then the Stukas and bombers came back, this time severing all our communication links with the front lines. No sooner had the aircraft finished than the German infantry launched another full-blown assault. Finally there came the fire-spitting tanks, Rommel's 15th Division, brought in to finish us off. Dozens of Free French soldiers, mainly legionnaires, were killed or taken prisoner. The ground was peppered with craters and piled with smouldering debris. Several French vehicles were destroyed by the shelling and some went on burning into the night.

That evening, the Germans could be heard mine clearing just a few hundred yards away. Rommel was said to be in situ on one of the *mamelles*, his cannon all lined up ready to fire again in the morning. Later, air raids were carried out for the first time after dark against our little fort, the Stukas dropping baskets of grenades which exploded on impact. By keeping us awake with a non-stop bombardment, Rommel hoped to crack our men and break camp morale. And the Luftwaffe's intention was clear: to blast Bir Hakeim off the face of the desert.

The following day, it soon became apparent that our situation was completely without hope, especially when the Stukas deliberately targeted the hospital and surgical theatre vehicle a few hundred yards from my dugout, even though they were clearly standing alone and marked with huge red crosses. The shells blew to pieces most of the twenty-four wounded men inside and some of the medical orderlies. As the reserves of medicine were also destroyed, there was little anyone could do. The RAF had dropped urgently needed supplies of plasma earlier, but when they landed the bottles were all shattered and useless.

The lack of water compounded our misery, as supplies fell from two litres each a day to a quarter litre, less than a cupful per man. And it tasted horrible, thick and murky like tea. Every drop had been carefully recycled for weeks, with shaving and washing water poured into car radiators or filtered through gas masks to use time and again. Shirts and shorts were washed in shallow bowls of petrol and laid out to dry. Dishes and mugs were scrubbed clean with petrol and sand. Not a drop was wasted.

Now, with supplies so short, men sat together, slumped and dejected, fantasizing about ice-cold beers and pitchers of lemonade and cool water from mountain streams. Thin of face, stubbly of skin, exhausted from sleeplessness and strain, they steeled themselves for the inevitable.

On 9 June a hundred Stukas bombarded the north of Bir Hakeim, where Pierre Messmer and his company were dug in. Artillery attacks followed, and the German infantry tried to enter the camp and were driven back. Six hours later, the Stukas returned and the bombardment continued.

In desperation, the general radioed Allied headquarters that afternoon: *'Water and ammunition virtually exhausted. Cannot hold out much longer'*. By the end of the day, surrounded as we were by enemy divisions, there were no shells left for our best defender, the 75 mm cannon, and few mortars or cartridges for anything else.

We had hardly a drop of water left, apart from some filthy green muck sloshing around in the bottom of some old petrol tins which had to be poured away lest the men drank it, and a few fastidiously guarded private supplies which had all but been shared out. Some ice had

207

been dropped by the RAF for the wounded to suck on but this had long since melted.

As the sun set low on the horizon, all we could see were the menacing silhouettes of the German and Italian tanks, pressed in so close around us that they could no longer open fire for fear of hitting each other. I feared that none of us would survive another day. It was not without reason that Rommel radioed his headquarters that night: '*I shall be in Bir Hakeim in the morning.*'

The general too sent a telegram that night. Addressed to the Eighth Army, it read: '*We are surrounded. Our thoughts are always near you. We have confidence. Long Live Free France!*' It was clear that he anticipated the end and was prepared to sacrifice his life and those of his men if he had to. For me also, a hostage to fortune in my tiny dugout, death seemed very near.

At six o'clock that night, the general received fresh radio instructions from Allied Command and summoned his officers for urgent talks. We saw the exhausted men heading for the general's dugout and knew there was something going on. The smell of defeat was in the air and it made us deeply uneasy.

Amilakvari was the first to leave the meeting, his green cloak flying, his black kepi with its gold brocade perched jauntily on his head. I thought for a moment I detected a trace of his familiar smile. Dear Amilak, he refused to wear a tin helmet out of respect for the great First World War French general and 'Father of the Legion' Paul Rollet, who did likewise. 'Death knows when it is your turn, with or without your helmet,' Amilakvari had once told Pierre. The other officers followed him from the general's briefing just as briskly and made for their own command posts, each one resolute of expression and saying nothing.

I sat cross-legged on the floor of my dugout and waited for further news, as I had done throughout the siege. On this evening, I knew the reports could only be grim. The heat that day had been unbearable, the perspiration had

Rommel's ultimatum: 'To the troops of Bir Hakeim. Further resistance will only lead to pointless loss of life. You will suffer the same fate as the two brigades which were at Got el Ualab and which were exterminated the day before yesterday. We will cease fighting as soon as you show us the white flag and come towards us unarmed. Rommel, General Oberst.'

Advancing in a Bren carrier during a Jock Column reconnaissance.
© *SIRPA/ECPA France*

Facing Rommel's panzers, we fired back day after day with everything we had.
Imperial War Museum (E13306)

Patrolling on foot. Pipes and cigarettes were among our prized possessions.
Imperial War Museum (E13310)

On the wire at the periphery of Bir Hakeim.
© SIRPA/ECPA France

Our troops endure yet another bombardment.
The men at the rear were lucky enough to be
able to use palm fronds as camouflage; for
those ahead there was just the desert sand.

© SIRPA/ECPA France

A rough wooden cross marks dear Amilakvari's grave. El Himeimat, Libya.
Imperial War Museum (K3964)

General Koenig (*left*) with Lieutenant General Willoughby Norrie.
Imperial War Museum (E13290)

Generals de Gaulle (*left*) and Koenig (*right*) accompany Field Marshal Montgomery and M. Diethelm, French Minister of War, across the courtyard at Les Invalides in May 1945.

Imperial War Museum (BU6766)

In the same courtyard over a decade later my general pins the Military Medal to my coat. It was the last time I was to see him.

Dressed in a white Legion uniform which I had had
specially made, and carrying a bouquet of red and green
tropical flowers (the colours of the Legion), I married
Nicholas Schlegelmilch. Indochina, April 1947.

Happy days. Nicholas and I on the verandah with baby
François and Rebecca, my dog.

poured off me and soaked my already sweat-stained clothes. I'd not been able to wash for several days, my hair was lank and greasy and my face and hands were streaked with dust. Sand mingled with the sweat to form a filthy sludge that collected in every crevice of my skin – in my armpits, in my groin, around my neck. It scratched and grated, a constant source of irritation to flesh already sensitive from the heat.

I rested my head on my hands and tried to forget the discomfort and the fear and the dirt. I allowed my mind to float away, far above the doom-laden desert skies. Pressing my eyes shut, I conjured up the smartest of French restaurants, a chic Parisian brasserie lined with huge gilt mirrors to reflect the glowing candlelight and staffed by a small army of waiters all dressed in crisp white jackets and black bow ties. The tables were set with hand-embroidered damask and rows of silver knives, forks and spoons, cut-crystal glasses for wine and water and adorned with porcelain vases of the freshest flowers. As I picked my way carefully towards my table, I could almost hear the sound of cutlery clinking on bone china, and the murmur of polite dinner talk. I could feel the satin of my lilac dress swishing against my legs, and the slight sensation of silk underwear against scrubbed alabaster skin. The general was waiting for me, dashing in his uniform, rising to his feet with a broad smile as I approached and accepted his hand. I took my place and inhaled delicious scents of herbs and wine, garlic and roasting meats wafting towards us from the kitchen.

I'd dined in such restaurants in some of the most fashionable capitals of Europe, and in my dream's eye I had spent enjoyable evenings there with my general since. If ever I got out of Bir Hakeim and made it to somewhere civilized, I promised I would take myself off to such a place once again and buy an extravagant dinner. I knew exactly what I should eat. A huge platter of oak-smoked salmon, followed by a dish of delicious duck with orange sauce and all the trimmings, finished off with a really rich vanilla ice cream with tiny almond biscuits. All washed down with a very good chilled white Burgundy.

Thinking about wine made me thirsty and I opened my eyes and checked my few provisions in the stinking dugout. Brushing the cockroaches and rat droppings from my provisions box I opened it and looked inside. My supplies were low – a few inches of gritty water sloshed around in the bottom of my canteen, and four indigestible tack biscuits were infested with weevils. Spurning them, I tried to decide whether to drink or wash with the water I had left. I knew the general had more water in his personal stores, and would give me some if I asked. The cupful I used to wash my face every other day didn't seem too extravagant to me, even though I knew that the men had stopped shaving to conserve their supplies. Deciding to neither wash nor drink for the moment, I slumped back onto the sandy floor and closed my eyes once more.

When would we know what the general had decided, I wondered. If we surrendered, I would become a prisoner of war, the only woman in the hands of hostile captors. I very much hoped that I might be able to pass myself off as a man again. Maybe I would ask the orderly to cut my hair even shorter, or try to conceal my face with my gas mask. I wondered where I might be able to hide my pistol, in case I needed to use it to defend myself. If only the general would tell me what was going on, I might feel slightly better prepared. But he'd never confided in me before, so why on earth should I think that he might do so now?

He had once told me that it was a deliberate policy of his never to share any information with me. 'If you're ever unfortunate enough to be captured,' he'd said, 'and they discover that you are my driver, you can tell your interrogators, quite honestly, that you know nothing.' Holding my face in his hands to emphasize the importance of his words, he'd added: 'If you tell the truth, they will believe you.' He'd then pulled me to him suddenly, wrapping his arms around me as if he was truly afraid that someone might one day try to hurt me. For the first time

210

since I'd met him, I understood the loneliness of command.

Just as I was about to succumb to the deep sleep of the exhausted, I heard the sound of boots on gravel and realized that someone was approaching my dugout. Sitting up and peeling back my canvas roof, I looked out. In the darkness I recognized the unmistakable outline of the general. This was only the third time in three months that he had deliberately sought me out. I jumped to my feet and brushed down my shabby uniform as best I could.

His features were creased with dust and I could see the tiredness in his sunken eyes. Poor Pierre, he was bearing such a heavy burden. He had been responsible for one of the toughest battles fought in Africa, returning honour to the Free French for the first time since the debacle of Dakar. Yet his next step was equally crucial, for the lives of nearly three thousand people depended on him. Gone were all traces of the laughing man whose life I'd shared during those carefree days at Aley.

Smiling, I tried to offer him some crumb of comfort, but his eyes were distant and cold. He was miles away, and well beyond my reach.

'Get everything ready,' he said, under his breath. 'We're going to break out through the enemy lines tomorrow night. Don't say a word to anyone. It's an absolute secret.'

'Where are we going?' I asked. Sweat trickled into my eyes.

He paused. 'To a rendezvous,' he replied at last, his jaw set.

Fear pinched my heart. I knew that one of his favourite poems was 'Rendezvous' by the Legion poet, the American Alan Seeger, written during the First World War. Pierre had found it in a book he'd borrowed from the library in Beirut, a well-thumbed volume that he took out repeatedly and carried with him everywhere. On a day not long after he'd told me that we'd have to leave our idyllic cottage in Aley and move back towards the theatre of war, he'd opened the book at a familiar page and asked me to sit down.

'I want you to read this, La Miss,' he said, as I arranged some roses in a crystal bowl. 'It's a poem I'd like to share with you. A young American soldier wrote it in 1916, a month before he was killed fighting for France. His words mean a great deal to every man in the Legion.'

Kneeling on a cushion at his feet, watching him as he leaned back on the soft chintz sofa we'd chosen together, I took the book from his hand, opened it at the page he'd marked, and read the poem quietly to myself. Stopping after the first few lines, I looked up at him again.

'Read it aloud for me, *chérie*,' he murmured. 'I like to hear your voice.' Taking a deep breath, I sank further into the cushion and leaned against his legs as I began to recite the poem he loved.

> *'I have a rendezvous with Death,*
> *At some disputed barricade,*
> *When Spring comes back with rustling shade,*
> *And apple-blossoms fill the air*
>
> *'I have a rendezvous with Death*
> *When Spring brings back blue days and fair.*
> *It may be that he shall take my hand*
> *And lead me into his dark land*
> *And close my eyes and quench my breath –*
> *It may be that I shall pass him still*
>
> *'I have a rendezvous with Death*
> *On some scarred slope of battered hill,*
> *When Spring comes round again this year*
> *And the first meadow-flowers appear*
>
> *'God knows 'twere better to be deep*
> *Pillowed in silk and scented down*
> *Where love throbs out in blissful sleep*
> *Pulse nigh to pulse, and breath to breath,*
> *Where hushed awakenings are dear . . .*

> 'But I've a rendezvous with Death
> At midnight in some flaming town
> When Spring trips north again this year ...'

I never forgot that night or the poignancy of those immortal lines. Taking in the words now, a year later and in this godforsaken spot, I thought that perhaps even then Pierre was trying to prepare me for death.

My heart pounding, I racked my brain to remember the final stanza of the poem so that I could say it to him once more. But before I could even open my mouth to speak, he had turned on his heel and gone. There were no kind words, no thin smile of encouragement, no wishes of good luck. Just orders, from a general to an *adjudant*. Every man – and the lone Englishwoman amongst them – must do their duty, unflinchingly.

As I watched him go, the words suddenly came to me. I recited them softly to myself.

> 'And I to my pledged word am true.
> I shall not fail that rendezvous.'

12

THE BREAKOUT

'They gave their bodies for the commonwealth and received
Each for his own memory, praise that will never die,
And with it the grandest of all sepulchres,
Not that in which their mortal bones are laid,
But a home in the minds of men where their glory
remains fresh.'

PERICLES (495–429 BC)

I had twenty-eight hours to get ready, twenty-eight long hours in which to pack my belongings, which could have been done in less than five minutes, and prepare myself for what seemed like nothing less than a suicide mission. Trying not to think too closely about the massive German firepower we would almost certainly encounter as we forced a passage through enemy lines, I carefully went over all that I was responsible for: the car, fuel, water, tyres and oil. I lined the inside of the car with sandbags to protect us against mines and bullets, and placed the general's papers and Tommy guns in the back. The larger of my belongings, my bed and bath, were stored in the general's caravan. With everything packed and loaded, checked and double-checked, I still had hours to kill. It seemed like a lifetime.

Looking around at our sorry encampment, our home for the past four months, I could see hardly any flat piece of earth between the multiple craters where shells had landed. Small fires burned everywhere, as equipment and secret papers were destroyed so the enemy couldn't get its hands on them. The fires served a double purpose in keeping the men warm that chilly night. Someone was piling up bodies in a corner of the compound while the chaplain, Père Mallec, stood over them, his bible open, reading a few lines. When word got out that we were leaving, the burial of the dead became a priority. As the digging parties set about their task, marking the graves with simple wooden crosses on the general's orders, a sweet, familiar stench pervaded the air.

I found Arad, eating greedily from a tin of bully beef that had been given to him by someone in the Chad battalion. Claude le Roux, one of the officers, told me that in the last fifteen days Arad had become their lucky mascot – a white dog for a battalion of black soldiers. Apparently he'd overcome his fear of air raids and shelling and had taken to barking at the Stukas. He even chased a shell across the desert, and the men were proud of his courage.

'We'll look after him for you, La Miss, and we'll take him out of Bir Hakeim with us,' the officer added, his eyes bright.

Patting Arad on the head and stroking his silky ears fondly, I nodded my assent and wished him and Claude courage.

Wandering back to my car, I saw one of the secretaries emerge from the general's caravan with the last few jerrycans of water. I helped him strap them to the back of the vehicle.

'There's been an order to smash all the windscreens,' he told me quietly. 'If a bullet hits the glass, it will shatter and you won't be able to see out.'

I looked askance at him and only just prevented myself from pointing out that if a bullet hit the screen, I would almost certainly be dead. Irked by the thought, I stalked off to fetch another can. When I returned, I found the windscreen smashed with a hammer and the glass neatly swept away. The secretary then told me that all the officers were shaving with their final supplies of water, a last act of defiance in the face of the enemy. Equally defiant, I went to my dugout and poured the last dregs from my canteen into my mug so that I could wash.

The general's plan was simple. After the British had finally agreed that his position was no longer tenable and given the order for us all to withdraw, he'd rejected the most obvious options of surrendering or tiptoeing out with only his able-bodied men, leaving the wounded, heavy arms and vehicles behind. 'For a legionnaire,' he had told his officers, 'there is no such option.' Instead, he decided on a mass breakout through the south-west gate, straight into the minefields and the enemy lines, thus taking the German and Italian forces by surprise.

'I know your men haven't eaten or slept for two days, but this is the last thing I will demand of them at Bir Hakeim,' the general told his officers. 'At H hour, we shall give General Rommel a slap in the face and end this great battle in glory.'

His plan was that the sappers would create a new fifty-yard-wide path through the minefields by defusing their own mines. Special lamps, whose soft beams of light pointed down only, would be used to light their way. Three battalions of troops, led by the legionnaires, would push forward silently on foot, their remaining Bren guns ready to draw any enemy fire if the alarm was raised. One battalion would go right, the next left and the third straight ahead, crushing any resistance and creating as wide a corridor as possible for the rest of us to escape through. Gabriel de Sairigné and his men were to organize the vehicles to convey the wounded and the heavier equipment to safety.

The general and I, with Amilakvari and his men following on, would lead the hastily assembled convoy out through the sleeping enemy. An assortment of vehicles and trucks carrying two hundred of the most seriously

216

wounded would follow after we'd ploughed our way through the minefield. A final contingent of legionnaires would bring up the rear on foot, firing until the last, hoping to make the enemy think that Bir Hakeim was still occupied. Using a familiar Jock Column route, we would all then make our own way to the agreed rallying point, known as B837, a British-held position twenty kilometres south and marked with only three red lights. Simple, if a little hastily thought out.

As H hour – midnight on 10 June – drew closer, everyone made ready. What couldn't be carried had to be destroyed. The orders were not to leave a single useful item behind. If necessary, we were to set fire to our own vehicles rather than let them be captured. The mood was very tense as rumour after rumour flew around the camp. The wounded feared they'd be left behind, some of the legionnaires doubted they'd have enough time to escape and the drivers worried that they'd be the easiest targets of all. Amilakvari, de Sairigné, Messmer and Simon did their best to quell our jittery nerves, moving through the camp issuing strict orders.

'You must keep in an absolutely straight line,' they told us. 'Silence is vital. Don't stop and don't make a noise.'

Trying to ignore the butterflies in my stomach, I started the car carefully, edged it out of its dugout, threw in my few belongings and made my way to the assembly point. I sat in the driver's seat, watching the rev counter fearfully. The car had been subjected to extreme temperatures and sandstorms in the past few months and hadn't been driven for nearly three weeks. It had played up badly on the last two Jock Columns we had been on, stalling suddenly and not starting again easily. A shell splinter had punctured the radiator during one of the Stuka raids, and I had had to enlist the large Indo Chinese corporal who drove the general's *camionnette* to help me empty it, unhitch it and carry the heavy thing across to the field workshop for welding. When I begged the mechanics to mend it, they had been most reluctant as we were still in the middle of an air raid.

I'd checked the car over every day since and asked the mechanics to look at it several times, but I still feared it might break down. Leaning my head on the steering wheel, I listened to the steady ticking of the engine and whispered a quiet prayer.

'Please don't let me down tonight,' I said to the dash-board. 'Please, whatever you do, don't stall on me.'

Exactly on cue, the general emerged, freshly shaved and washed, his uniform remarkably crisp. He looked around in the darkness at the hundreds of anxious eyes blinking back at him. The vehicles had been lined up since nightfall, our car at the front of the HQ convoy, and the men were in position, waiting silently. The news of the breakout had fired them with enthusiasm. No-one wanted to surrender after all we'd been through, and despite a few last-minute nerves the audacity of their commanding officer's escape plan only renewed their ardour.

It was a moonless night, bitterly cold, and we were as ready as we would ever be. Stepping into the car beside me and staring straight ahead, the general said quietly, 'You're to do exactly as I tell you, when I tell you, for both our sakes. I will stand behind you on the back seat and look through the hatch in the roof. We will follow Route F, which we have used countless times on the Jock Columns.

'If I tap your right shoulder with my foot, you're to slow down. If I tap your left shoulder, you must stop. If I press hard on either shoulder, you must go faster.' Turning to me for the first time, sensing the anticipation in my eyes, he said very deliberately, 'Do you understand what I'm saying?'

Unable to answer for the lump in my throat, I nodded violently, nearly dislodging my beret, whereupon he feigned anger.

'And for goodness' sake, put your helmet on,' he added.

Trying to return his smile, I picked up the tin helmet from my lap, whipped off my beret and rammed the helmet as forcefully as I could onto my head.

218

Yanking the Ford into first gear, I allowed it to creep steadily forward as the Bren carriers rolled slowly towards the minefield in the darkness ahead of me. The tension was palpable, the silence broken only by the low rumbling of our engines as we crept from our besieged position in the dead of night. The 2nd Battalion were the first to descend the steep slope into the minefield and take their place at the head of the narrow corridor that was being cut through ahead of them. The column stopped while we waited for the path to be cleared. The general ordered everyone out of their cars for their own safety and he and his most senior staff sat some way away. I squatted down beside one of the wheels of my car, foolishly thinking that it would protect me if we were attacked.

Silence was the key. The general and his officers had sent out word that if we all remained silent and kept calm, we might have a good chance of escaping while the Italians and Germans slept in preparation for their big push tomorrow. I felt increasingly nervous in the silence as my eyes grew accustomed to the dark. I was afraid that I would do something silly, that I might panic. In such a state, I might be unable to restart the car if it stalled.

I was very grateful for the sudden appearance at my side of Captain Simon, with his trademark black eye patch, who crouched down beside me and found a seat on the running-board of the car. I'd been right about him in Syria. He did look very dashing.

'Hello. What are you doing here?' he whispered, as if we were idling time away in the middle of a minefield through choice.

'Feeling rather silly,' I whispered back, the fear evident in my voice.

We chatted quite amiably for several minutes, talking about what we both planned to do once we got out. Before too long, he'd almost managed to make me forget where we were.

It was the general who reminded me. 'Shut up over

219

there!' he said sharply. Duly chastised, we sat silently side by side, waiting for the order to move on.

The order came half an hour later. Back in our cars, knowing that the escape route was ready, we started our engines again and waited. The Bren carriers were the first down the slope and into the minefield. We followed on as stealthily as we could, in single file because of the narrowness of the path, with the others in a long-drawn-out line behind us.

Maybe it was because of the eerie silence that had prevailed in the previous few hours that the sudden shattering of it seemed so shocking. In any event, I jumped so violently at the sound of the first explosion that my head hit the roof of the car. A few yards ahead of us, the first of the Bren carriers had inadvertently strayed from the designated path in the darkness and rolled over a landmine. The blast illuminated the minefield and alerted us to the fact that we, too, had mistakenly followed the Brens and were several feet away from the safe route marked out by the sappers. The conflagration had, not surprisingly, awoken the sleeping enemy on the first heavily defended line we had to cross and they immediately jumped to their positions and opened fire. Frozen to the spot as I watched the mayhem unfolding right in front of my eyes, I fully believed this to be the end.

Suspecting that someone from Bir Hakeim was trying to make a run for it, the Germans sent up dozens of green and red flares and we found ourselves trapped under heavy fire in the well-lit corridor. Tracer bullets now lit the night sky too, criss-crossing in a great arc in front of us. Before anyone could prevent it, the second Bren gun exploded in a shower of sparks and flame and then the third, as they tried to manoeuvre a way back to the safe path. Legionnaires at the front of the line threw themselves at the heavy guns a few hundred yards away, sacrificing their lives for us, their comrades, as we tried to find a way back. But several of the trucks reversing past the crippled Brens were hit before making it across. They burned in the middle of the corridor, making it impassable and rendering us even easier targets as silhouettes. Some drivers, in their panic, leaped from their burning vehicles only to be blown up by anti-personnel mines.

Shells were falling around us like rain and sudden, violent explosions tore the night, showering our car with burning metal. The German cannon were upon us, and all the vehicles stopped, unsure of where to go or what to do next. The wounded who could walk were ordered to get out and continue on foot, to lessen the weight of the vehicles picking their way through the mines. From starting off as a reasonably well-planned evacuation, it had become a shambolic flight.

The general was beside himself with anger and distress. His face lit by the phosphorous flares, he scowled down at me through the hatch in the roof. 'Why aren't we moving? Turn the wheel right and go round that car!' he yelled, ordering me this way or that, tapping my shoulders with his feet, barking instructions at his men to continue their running fire-fights, and attempting to retain control of a chaotic situation that was fast slipping from his grasp.

Trying to see if I really could negotiate a safe way round, with the general still shouting and using his feet to bruising effect, I was staring into the gloom ahead when there was an almighty bang and, for a moment, I thought we'd hit a mine. But I was wrong. It was the car directly in front of us, carrying Amilakvari.

We both watched aghast as it was thrown up into the air like a toy. Stopping myself from screaming Amilakvari's name, I stared through my glassless windscreen as the smoke cleared and a slightly blackened Amilakvari trotted towards us in his ubiquitous cloak, a gun in one hand, a grenade in the other, outlined against his now blazing vehicle. He seemed completely unaffected by the blast and carried on shouting out orders to his men. His chauffeur, a man called Van der Wachler, also emerged uninjured.

Inspired by Amilakvari's fearlessness and keen to knock out the guns that were aiming directly at us, one of his

221

captains immediately ordered the infantrymen who were on foot to turn left through the minefield and towards the German gunners to engage them in hand-to-hand fighting. To his fury, the men didn't immediately do as they were told, as some of them were still clinging to the sides of the lorries for protection from the constant gunfire. They were completely terrified.

As the bullets continued to rain down, the captain ran to Amilakvari to ask for his help. Without a thought for his own safety, the White Russian prince deftly avoided a bright blue trail of tracer fire, ran to where the troops were and told the men to fix bayonets. Giving the order for them to move forward, he cried, '*Baïonnettes aux canons. A moi la Légion! On avance!*' His arm held aloft, he looked hugely impressive with his cloak flying. There was little hesitation after that. The men would have followed Amilakvari to hell and back. Fired up with *esprit de corps*, determined to restore the glory of Free France, they regrouped as best they could, assembled in serried ranks and charged headlong into the curtain of fire.

Seeing what he had done, the general yelled Amilakvari's name over the noise of battle and waved him back towards us. Still standing on the rear seat, among the sandbags, the general ordered Amilakvari into the front seat next to me. We were now, once more, the leading car and I was responsible for both their lives. Gulping, I tried not to think of my responsibilities.

'Drive straight ahead, as fast as you can,' the general yelled, his foot pressing on my left shoulder. '*Vite! Vite!*'

I turned to my left for a moment to stare at Amilakvari, not sure whether I should pinch myself. He'd survived the mine explosion completely unscathed. A huge grin broke across his face and he patted the Thompson submachine-gun on his lap.

'Drive!' he repeated, whereupon I decided that, whatever happened, I was going to get these two lunatics out of this bedlam.

The general kicked my left shoulder and shouted again.

'There's nothing for it. If we go, the rest will follow.' As Amilakvari crouched down in his seat, waiting for me to move off, I put the car into first gear again, skirted his burning car as best I could in the darkness, and tried not to think how vulnerable my feet were. I'd seen what a landmine could do to feet, I'd bandaged Dr Lotte's bloodied stumps myself and that thought frightened me more than anything else.

Somehow I managed to find my way round the long line of halted traffic without getting blown up or running over any of the soldiers rushing backwards and forwards across my path. At the head of the stalled convoy some medical vehicles had found a way through the mines but then stopped. Avoiding a car burning fiercely in front of me, I roared on across the minefield, heading straight for the tracer fire, not having time to think or even be afraid. In fact, by this time I was exhilarated. It was an amazing feeling, going as fast as I could in the dark towards what looked like a mass display of beautifully coloured fireworks dancing towards me, bringing what seemed like almost certain death. This was what I had come for – to feel what it was like to be a man, in the very heat of battle.

The reality of the matter was that I was probably more likely to be killed by my own poor driving than by a bullet. Unable to assess the rocky terrain into which I was heading, I seemed to drive into every hole there was in the desert floor. The ground was uneven at the best of times and had not been improved by all the recent shelling. It was pitted like Swiss cheese and the general shouted constantly at me, telling me to avoid the craters.

'Be careful, you're going to break the car to pieces! Turn left! Right!' he instructed, but with my headlights switched off and unable to see a thing in the pitch blackness, I could only plough straight on regardless. I just kept going, I couldn't stop. My main concern remained that the engine would stall, the general and Amilakvari would be taken prisoner and that it would all be my fault.

Behind us there was carnage. Explosions lit the night

sky as vehicles were thrown up into the air and the firestorm raged on. Wave after wave of tracer fire zigzagged across the desert towards us, and the parachute flares falling from the sky bathed the battlefield in a preternatural light. The running firefights continued all around us as the men on foot ducked and dived under the coloured lights and did their best to knock out the enemy guns, using grenades. The stalled convoy, seeing us get through, followed my lead, jerking their engines into life again. I drove at the tracer fire ahead of us as if the car were the bow of a great ship, parting a sea of bullets.

But it was not a smooth crossing. We slithered from one hole to the next, our wheels skidding as I reached speeds of forty miles per hour. 'Keep out of the shell holes!' the general kept yelling, as if I had a choice in the matter. A lot depended on him, and on me, so I resisted the temptation to respond. He stood or sat in the back, a gun in his hand, shouting instructions and trying to see if the others were getting through as well.

The din inside the car was awful. The engine was revving, the rocks beneath us were banging the underside of the car, the two men were shouting and the sound of explosions and shooting reverberated around us.

'Slow down!' Amilakvari shouted. 'You'll break up the car and lose us all.'

I slowed a little but not much, too afraid of what might be behind us. From the back, the general told me not to go too far left in case I hit a mine, and then he told me to go right for fear of overturning on a huge boulder. I just did as I was told.

At one point the general leaned forward to Amilakvari and yelled above the din, 'Stop firing your gun. I can't hear myself think and they'll be able to locate us.'

Amilakvari, who by then was crouching on his seat, popped his head up, his gun in his hand. 'I'm not shooting,' he said. 'That's the sound of bullets hitting our car.'

The general flopped down into his seat and I pressed the

accelerator pedal to the floor again, withdrawing my helmeted head even further into my shoulders.

It was sheer luck that we managed to cross the minefield and break through the first enemy cordon, with several vehicles safely behind us. But our troubles were only just beginning: there were three concentric rings of enemy lines, eight hundred metres apart, each one slightly less heavily defended than the last. We had two more yet to cross. Needless to say, having been alerted to the commotion further forward, the enemy started to shoot at us all over again.

Once more, confusion reigned. Fresh tracer bullets fell on us. Sparks flew from the car as it was peppered with machine-gun rounds. Both men were shouting at me now: 'Left! Look out! Turn right! Go faster!' Their conflicting instructions were more of a hindrance than a help and I just kept driving as fast as I could.

Amilakvari, a little pocket compass in his hand, was shouting fresh directions to me. 'Left here, left, left!' he yelled as I yanked hard on the steering wheel, my chin tucked so far into my chest that I could barely see over the dashboard.

Behind me, the general was standing up again, looking through the hatch, trying to see where we were going and whether he could spot enemy vehicles. He banged on the roof with his hands, or kicked me with his foot whenever he spied another crater looming. Behind us, vehicles and men were burning, gunfire echoed across the great plain and none of us seemed to have any idea which way we were going.

We drove on and on through the barren landscape. It took hours to get through all three lines of enemy armour, our route twisting this way and that to avoid the heaviest fire. We had set off shortly after midnight and four hours later we were still in the danger zone. Thankfully, a thick early morning mist descended, which shielded us. Unfortunately, it also blocked our view of what lay ahead. At one point, there was a tremendous bang on the side of

225

the vehicle and I thought we must have been hit or driven over a mine. I spun round in my seat to check the damage, but Amilakvari, who'd seen what had happened, reassured me.

'Don't worry,' he said, 'it was just Masson's car. His driver ran it into the back of you. It's wrecked and Masson's been thrown out of the roof, but he's OK. Carry on.'

I thought of the gleaming new staff car I'd driven so carefully back from Tobruk and cursed inwardly.

After driving for so long, we felt that we must surely be the other side of the enemy lines but we couldn't be sure. None of us could. We were slightly better off than the rest because we had a compass and Amilakvari was an excellent navigator. Behind us we knew that solitary soldiers and groups without compasses who had become separated from their units would be wandering around aimlessly. Some would be picked up by English patrols, some by German. We all worried that those who were lost in the desert might never be seen again.

The general ordered me to stop the car in the middle of a plateau so that Amilakvari could take a proper bearing on the compass, which wouldn't work well inside the metal car. I did as I was told, releasing my grip on the steering wheel for the first time in four hours and stretching out my cramped and bloodless fingers. Every muscle in my neck and shoulders ached, every bone cried out for rest, but I knew there would be none for some time yet and I rode the pain. I refused to switch off the engine, for fear the car wouldn't start again. My head resting on the steering wheel, fighting to calm my thumping heart, I waited for my next set of instructions.

It was Amilakvari who took the initiative. He opened his door and stood on the running-board to listen and try to get a reading. He could hear nothing, no vehicles following us, no men on foot, not even the sound of distant gunfire.

The general stuck his head out of the roof and started to

speak. 'We're going to have to get a move on now—' he began.

Amilakvari suddenly reached across and clamped his hand over the general's mouth. He'd heard what we could all hear now, German voices, speaking very close to us in the fog.

'*Halt! Wer ist da?*' a German soldier barked. '*Stehen bleiben!*'

I was tempted to respond in the German I had learned in Vienna all those years ago. I wondered for a moment what they would think if they heard a woman's voice speaking in aristocratic tones in the middle of nowhere.

'Drive! *Vite!*' Amilakvari shouted, jumping back into the vehicle at the same time as the general kicked my left shoulder ferociously. I floored the accelerator once more, bumping off into the white shroud. Gunfire rang out again, and the vehicle juddered as the bullets found their mark. Looming either side of us in the mist, we could just make out the sinister shapes of German tanks. We had inadvertently driven straight into a magnificent laager of panzers, no doubt resting up at the back of the lines before their planned attack on Bir Hakeim in the morning. My heart was in my mouth as I flew past the menacing silhouettes and on into the darkness, speeding as fast as I could across the desert floor. Behind us, in close pursuit, were several enemy armoured cars, headlamps full on, their beams cutting through the mist like searchlights. Somehow I managed to pull ahead some five hundred metres and take a curve down into some dead ground, up a crumbling slope the other side and behind a small cliff, finally losing our pursuers.

Once we were back out in the open, Amilakvari asked me to steer straight ahead, following the path of a single bright star we could just make out above the mist. So, with one eye on the star and the other trying to see in front of us, I bumped along. We didn't know where we were or in which direction we were heading, but we didn't dare stop.

I continued driving at speed until we were several miles out in the middle of the desert.

Finally, as rosy streaks of light on the horizon heralded the dawn and the fog began to lift, we found ourselves quite alone. There was not another soul to be seen for miles and the silence of the desert was deafening. It was hard to comprehend, but by some miracle the three of us were all still alive.

The car was still going as well as it had when we started and I thanked my lucky stars for that. Now all we had to do was find B837 and see how the others had fared. We estimated that we had gone too far west and needed to head south-east again to reach the rendezvous point. Under instructions from Amilakvari with his compass, I carried on driving for another two hours, until the general ordered me to stop so that we could drink some water. He had also decided to take over the driving.

'At least now we might have a smoother ride,' he added grumpily, swigging from his *bidon* as he walked round to the driver's door. When we went to fill our flagons, we found that German bullets had punctured almost every jerrycan. The general was, I thought, extremely disagreeable, especially considering I hadn't done so badly. Exhausted from wrestling with the unwieldy car, I allowed him to take the wheel and slid into the back among the sandbags and the weapons. I was pleased to note, when we started up again, that his driving was even worse than mine and the car continued to crash upon almost every hidden rock.

I lay down on the back seat for a rest, while the General and Amilakvari sat in the front discussing where to head for next. According to Amilakvari, we'd driven in a wide circle round Bir Hakeim, were several miles from the rallying point, and might still be in danger. It occurred to me, as I lay on the back seat trying unsuccessfully to sleep, that no-one had bothered to tell me where the rallying point was, so that if anything had happened to my two companions I should not have had the faintest clue where I was meant to be heading.

But the destination was not now their greatest concern. Believing that we must have been the only escapees from Bir Hakeim, the general was beside himself.

'I'm a general in charge of nobody,' he said. 'All my men are dead. It's been a complete disaster. I should never have attempted the breakout.'

Listening to the two men talking so earnestly, I was distressed at the anguish in their voices. The general sounded like a broken man, bitterly disappointed at the failure of his mission.

As the dawn turned to morning and we drove wearily on, his sense of dishonour seemed to become too much for him. 'There's only one thing for it,' he announced suddenly. 'I'm going to give myself up to the next enemy vehicles we come across. At least then I can lead my men in captivity.'

Amilakvari was as shocked as I was. 'Think what you're saying, *mon général*,' he urged. 'You'd be a gift to German propaganda. Can you imagine what mileage they'd make of your capture? Besides, for nothing in the world would I, Prince Dimitri Amilakvari, become a voluntary prisoner of war. I beg you, please, to wait until we have more information.'

I listened to all of this in astonishment. I couldn't believe that, after all we'd gone through together, the general was prepared to give himself up so easily. Displaying what the general used to call my '*flegme britannique*', I sat up and told him to stop feeling sorry for himself.

'I've gone to a great deal of trouble to get you out, and now I think that the least you can do is to try and stay out of German hands,' I told him crossly. 'I've stuck with you for this long and I'm not prepared to be separated from you now.' Like Amilakvari, I was also quite adamant that the last thing I wanted to become was a willing German captive.

I took the wheel again and we continued across the

desert for several more hours without seeing another living thing – just a convoy of abandoned British cars in the morning fog, their seats empty, their fuel and water almost certainly stripped. We didn't dare touch the cars in case they'd been booby-trapped, as they so often were. The only signs of life were the hundreds of tracks criss-crossing the desert, evidence that the might of the Panzerarmee had passed through on its way to Bir Hakeim.

My eyeballs burning with tiredness, I stopped the car at a little New Zealand cemetery entirely on its own in the desert. Lost in the silence and the sun, it appeared like a mirage on the horizon. Stepping from the car, a soft breeze buffeting us, the three of us walked up to it in reverential stupor, marvelling at how beautifully maintained it was, here in the middle of nowhere. I almost had to pinch myself to believe it was real. Saluting our dead comrades, we moved on.

We were alone in the desert for much of that day. We didn't know it then, but the British were listing us as missing, presumed dead, along with so many others. The general and Amilakvari grew more and more depressed, and Pierre became increasingly determined to give himself up. When we eventually found the rallying point, at the 837 drum pile, the British 17th Motorized Brigade were very surprised to see us, but the men with me had only one question on their lips.

'What news from Bir Hakeim?' the general asked.

'Nothing,' came the ominous reply.

We were directed to a French position further back at Gasr el Abid where we found the 1st Battalion, who'd been waiting to enter Bir Hakeim and join us for nearly two weeks. The general and Amilakvari went into immediate conference with Colonel Garbay, Captain Thoreau and the other officers, who did their best to assure them that all might not be lost.

But nothing could lift the general's spirits, and it was with a heavy heart that he sent a radio message to General Willoughby Norrie expressing his view that the breakout had been a complete disaster.

'As a result of our crushing defeat, the First Free French Division should almost certainly be considered as incapable of continuing in battle,' he concluded, before returning to his fellow soldiers in deep despair.

Tired of all their talking, I went to the kitchens to get a cup of tea and found that my hand was shaking too much to hold it. Abandoning it, I took a mouthful of water from my canteen instead, sloshing the foul-tasting liquid around my mouth and spitting it into the sand. I tried to eat some lunch but found the food sticking in my throat, so I abandoned my plate three-quarters full.

Leaving the general and Amilakvari deep in discussion, I took the car to the workshop to get it checked over. As the mechanics counted eleven clear bullet holes in the bonnet, several in the radiator and multiple other direct hits which had sheared off part of the bodywork as well as damaging water and brake pipes, I started to shake. The shock absorbers had gone completely with all the bumpy driving, the radiator was splintered and the rest of the car was peppered with shot.

'I can't believe this vehicle's still running,' the astonished chief mechanic told me. 'One round passed through the seat directly between you and your passengers.'

My knees wobbling, I felt suddenly exhausted and lay down in the shade of the car to get some sleep. I wondered why I had such a thumping headache and then realized I'd forgotten to take my tin helmet off. It had been wedged on since the previous night. Lying on my back in the dirt, my head half under the car to keep cool, my hands crossed on my stomach, I fell into a deep and troubled sleep, in which bullets whizzed past me like insects and tracer fire peppered the inside of my eyelids as the general barked his commands in my ear and stamped on my shoulder.

I awoke an hour or so later, at around four o'clock in the afternoon, still with a splitting headache. Sitting up blearily, my eyes thick with sleep, I thought I was hallucinating. What I saw was a thin line of men and vehicles on the unbroken desert horizon. Blinking hard to clear my vision, I assumed I must be witnessing one of the many mirages that tricked the unsuspecting almost every noontime in the desert. But the mirage kept moving towards us. Jumping up, I cupped my hands over my eyes and strained to see what was in front of me. To my astonishment and delight, I suddenly recognized the raggle-taggle group winding towards us as the remaining survivors of Bir Hakeim.

I opened my mouth to yell, to call the general and Amilakvari from their nearby tent and let them know the wonderful news, but nothing but a hoarse, rasping noise came out. Running for the tent instead, my eyes filling with tears of joy, I managed to find my voice just as I reached the door.

'General! General!' I shouted. '*Venez!* Come quickly. Look!' Pointing to the horizon, I ran back outside, my heart pounding in my chest, almost afraid that the mirage would have melted away into the hot afternoon sun. But it hadn't, it was still there, and close enough now for me to identify the various ambulances and vehicles that, in what seemed like another lifetime, had been lined up behind us at midnight in Bir Hakeim.

The general stood beside me, clasping his chest and trying to catch his breath. Amilakvari paused only for a moment and then ran headlong through the sand towards the convoy, his kepi falling to the ground in his haste. We followed on, rushing to meet our friends and colleagues, each of us overcome with emotion, having thought that we'd never see the others again. Amilakvari was hugging everyone, kissing the men he'd fought and nearly died with on both cheeks, his own face wet with tears. The general was embracing them all, shaking their hands vigorously and patting their backs.

The men were in equally high spirits, the officers overcome – de Sairigné, Simon, Messmer, Père Mallec, Captain Arnault and all the others I knew. Everyone was laughing and crying and shouting all at once. Finding Gabriel de Sairigné, that warm and friendly soul who'd first called me pig-headed on the ship from West Africa and whose path seemed somehow inextricably linked to mine, I cried: 'I never thought I'd see you again!' and fell into his open arms.

He hugged me to him and wept openly. 'No such luck,' he said. 'You don't get rid of me that easily. I can't tell you how good it is to see you, too, La Miss.'

Each had a terrible story to tell of confusion, disaster and – ultimately – freedom. Simon told how he had driven his car, one-eyed, into a huge trench full of Germans, crushing several of them. He and his sergeant had to fight their way out with guns and grenades. Then they fled on foot, although not before they'd gone back for an injured comrade, shot in the knee. Those driving the ambulances spoke of the terrible agony of the wounded as the vehicles bumped and bounced their way to safety. They said they would always be haunted by their cries of pain.

Messmer, who'd proved himself time and again at Bir Hakcim, had been instructed to stay to the last with a company of men to give the impression that the French were remaining in their positions. Fortunately, the future prime minister had finally made it through the enemy cordon with another officer, Lalande, only to find themselves in the middle of a German company of a hundred men, armed with only one working pistol and no knowledge of German between them.

Just as they were about to accept their fate, a cluster of French armoured track vehicles, also lost, came lumbering into view, scattering the Germans before them. The two men ran after the French vehicles and managed to cadge a lift. Further on, they lurched into a German command post, its astonished officers so amazed to see them that they didn't even open fire. The legionnaires shot them dead and moved on.

Pierre Ichie, an officer in charge of several ambulances, managed to get his group beyond the enemy lines and, in the pitch black, formed a square in the middle of the desert, determined to fight it out to the last. When dawn

233

broke and holes began to appear in the mist, his men spotted a camp with trucks lined up some distance away. Unsure if they were English or German, he peered at them through his binoculars. Suddenly he laughed out loud.

'They're playing football!' he cried with delight. 'They must be English!'

Somehow he and his men had found their way to within a few hundred yards of the rallying point.

It had been a difficult journey for all of our company and the men were delighted to see us – even more so when the British came rushing over and handed out free beer and cigarettes. The general was completely overwhelmed.

'It was a miracle,' he said later. 'The impossible had happened and in spite of the pain caused by the loss of several friends, an immense joy entered my heart.'

Even My Fen and the corporal driving the general's caravan had made it, along with Arad, who'd run through the enemy lines with the Chadians. So too had the 75 mm guns, the lorries and the anti-aircraft guns, some of which were carried out by hand.

On learning of the great success of the operation, and hearing that so many had escaped only because they'd followed our car, Pierre softened considerably towards me, patting me warmly on the back in a rare show of public affection.

'Well done, La Miss,' he said, his eyes filling with tears, the first time I had ever seen him cry. 'Between us, we did it. We got them out.' Taking my hand in his, he squeezed it and my own eyes filled.

Despite our months of separation in Bir Hakeim and our many difficulties during the breakout, the events of the previous night had sealed our relationship and made us closer than ever. In Aley and Damascus, I'd been apart from Pierre's military life; a diversionary love interest to while away the long months between campaigns. After Bir Hakeim, having endured its rigours and been with him at both his worst moment of despair and his time of greatest triumph, I had become more important to him than any woman before. I was a comrade in arms. Amilakvari was included in our special bond, a staunch ally with whom we had shared something precious on that perilous road to freedom, something those who hadn't been there would never understand. I had never felt more proud.

Of the 3,700 men who had been with us at Bir Hakeim, 2,400 had managed to cross enemy lines in the dead of night. More than half the vehicles and almost all the soldiers wounded during the siege had made it, following our lead. Stragglers were still coming in on foot, and it was hoped that more would yet be found.

There were, of course, many dead. Amilakvari was especially distressed at the death of one of his dearest friends, a company commander called de la Haze, and scores of Free French, including much of the African battalion who had been the rearguard and who were nearly all killed or taken prisoner. I was deeply saddened to hear that Lofty, the workshop corporal who had always been so courteous to me, had also been killed.

In all, 763 men were missing, presumed dead or captured, 72 confirmed dead and 21 wounded. The two battalions of the 13DBLE had suffered the most and were left with only 650 of their thousand men. They'd also lost most of their equipment. But they were the heroes of the hour, having stayed until the end to protect the other escapees. Instead of being a rendezvous with death, as I had feared, the breakout had been a *rendez-vous d'honneur*.

It was a moment of great glory for the Free French and for my general in particular, who had bought time for the Eighth Army and who received the DSO from General Alexander. The British media compared the battle to that of Verdun in the First World War, one of the longest and fiercest battles on the Western Front, in which 350,000 French and 300,000 Germans had lost their lives under a torn and shredded tricolour.

Rommel had no idea how many men had slipped

through his fingers. His tank division had advanced on Bir Hakeim at 8 a.m. on the morning of 11 June with 'irresistible force', and had 'taken Bir Hakeim by storm', according to Axis Radio. After firing on the outpost for several hours in a last show of strength, the Germans and Italians were astounded to find it empty, but for a few dead and wounded. The two hundred men left behind had fought the Germans to their very last breaths.

Rommel, who admitted that he'd underestimated the Free French, was amazed to discover no fewer than 1,200 separate dugouts for men, guns and vehicles burrowed into the rock and sand. Despite the fact that his side had triumphed, it was a hollow victory. 'Seldom in Africa was I given such a hard-fought struggle,' he conceded later.

In a momentary fit of pique, the German High Command threatened the lives of the captured men. Berlin Radio issued a communiqué declaring that those taken prisoner 'do not belong to a regular army . . . and will be executed'. General de Gaulle issued an immediate response, threatening to execute all the German troops captured by his men. By the end of the day, Berlin Radio had capitulated and announced that 'General de Gaulle's soldiers will be treated as soldiers.'

The plaudits for General Koenig and his men came thick and fast. General Auchinleck was fulsome in his praise. 'The United Nations owe it to themselves to be full of admiration and gratitude towards these French troops and their valiant general,' he declared.

De Gaulle came to Cairo to thank those at Bir Hakeim personally. The success of the Free French at Bir Hakeim had done more than any other event of the war so far to make him a serious political figure. Awarding Pierre and Amilakvari the Cross of Liberation, he told our men, 'Under the command of the intrepid General Koenig, you have for fifteen days and fifteen nights taken the force of the enemy's increasingly fierce attack . . . Neither the sea of tanks nor the thunder of the Stukas have dulled your courage and you have not abandoned your defence until ordered to by the Command.'

Pierre then stated, 'Bir Hakeim was a French victory. I salute our dead, our brothers in arms fallen in battle, whose blessed memory will sustain us in battles to come.'

On his and Amilakvari's recommendation, I was later awarded the Croix de Guerre and the Ordre de Corpes d'Armee for my role. General Catroux presented them to me on a blistering day at our camp just outside Cairo a few weeks later. The brigade bugle band played, as well as the Marseillaise and the *Marche Lorraine*, the regimental song, '*Sous le soleil brûlant d'Afrique*', which had never seemed more appropriate. My general was there, along with a smiling Amilakvari and the whole brigade. Standing to attention in front of them, receiving my accolade along with the rest, I was filled with pride.

My citation read:

> *Having proved her courage and composure in the course of two previous campaigns, notably in Eritrea, and having further confirmed these qualities during the Libyan campaign, Susan Travers, on the night of June 10, on a sortie from the main force at Bir Hakeim, drove the general's car when it came under enemy assault while negotiating a minefield. Miss Travers' bravery in the face of several barrages of intense artillery fire, numerous bullet strikes to her vehicle and pitch blackness, resulted in the safe delivery of General Koenig and Colonel Amilakvari to safety.*

The soldiers who had seen me that night said I'd simply put my head down and pressed hard on the accelerator, seemingly oblivious to the war raging all about me in my determination to save the life of my noble general and Amilakvari. The love and respect I engendered amongst the Legion for that one day and night of madness was to support and bolster me throughout the rest of the war and beyond.

13

THE BLOOD OF OUR HEARTS

'The victory was not without price
Paid with the blood of our hearts
We are leaving thousands prostrate
In graves in the dust of El Alamein.'

MALCOLM MACLEOD, WHO SERVED IN NORTH AFRICA,
FROM *THE VOICE OF WAR*

The war went on. Our actions had done little to halt its relentless flow, and as soon as we had rested we were expected back in the fray. On the night of 11 June we slept where we fell. I felt almost too exhausted to sleep and the day dawned all too soon. The following morning, the entire brigade was sent north-east towards Alexandria, to regroup and recover from our losses.

Ours was to be the lead vehicle in the Free French convoy. The general climbed into the car and I started it up as the brigade moved out.

'I want you to drive slowly past the men so that I can salute them as we pass,' he instructed me. His eyes bright with the glory of the last few days, he stood up through the observation hatch, waving triumphantly and saluting them in grand style. I drove very carefully so as to avoid any bumps that might cause him to lose his footing. The road began to slope downhill and I pressed the brake pedal to keep us at a steady pace. To my horror, nothing happened and we started gathering speed.

'You're going too fast!' the general yelled through the roof. Clinging to the edge of the hatch, still trying to salute the men who were saluting him, he kicked me hard with his right boot. 'I said, slow down!'

I couldn't answer. I gripped the steering wheel, staring straight ahead at the slow-moving convoy of vehicles in front of us.

Unable to maintain an upright position, he crashed back onto his seat. 'Didn't you hear me? You're going too fast!' he shouted again.

'I don't have much choice, *mon général*,' I called back, not daring to take my eyes off the road. 'The brakes have failed.'

He watched me helplessly pumping the brake pedal as the speedometer reached fifty kilometres an hour. Studying the solid line of vehicles snaking away ahead, he too must have wondered what was to become of us.

Directly in front and looming up fast was a great army truck, piled high with provisions.

'Brace yourself!' I yelled, my arms rigid in front of me as I put my head down and waited for the impact. We both held our breath as our car crashed violently into the back of the truck, sending up a shower of sparks and bits of metal. Locked together in an unhappy coupling of number plate and tailgate, we bumped along as I hooted my horn repeatedly to try to grab the attention of the driver. Eventually he spotted me in his wing mirror and, realizing what had happened, put on his brakes. Using my gears I managed to bring us to an undignified halt, our nose deep in the back of the truck.

After several seconds' silence, the general spoke. 'Once again, you've saved my life,' he said, his hand squeezing my shoulder. 'What would I do without you?'

I turned to him and smiled, the perspiration running into my eyes. We climbed out to examine the damage and thank the truck driver, who'd emerged from his cab scratching his head in confusion. Steam hissed from the engine of the poor old Utility and its front was badly crumpled, but it was otherwise intact. The general was most impressed, until he suddenly noticed that approaching us at a march was the column of men we'd just overtaken. Unable to do anything but wait until they'd gone, he clicked his heels together, stood rigidly to attention and stayed in a fixed salute for a full ten minutes as they passed. I buried my head under the bonnet so as to hide my smile.

Taking the car to the mobile workshop, I discovered that an enemy bullet from Bir Hakeim, previously unnoticed, had passed clean through the engine housing a few inches from my feet, rupturing the brake pipe. Brake fluid had been leaking for two days before eventually running out. Another lucky escape. Having no brake fluid available, the mechanics filled it up with ordinary oil when I wasn't looking, a mistake the general blamed me for later as the car soon failed and everything had to be purged. That night we slept in a clearing at the side of the road, me in the car, the general in his caravan, barely speaking to each other.

The next morning, I drove him to the Spears hospital to visit the wounded. The place was crowded with shot and shattered men; it was an awful sight to see. Once-proud soldiers and legionnaires lay broken in their beds, blinded, limbs missing, heads bandaged and bloodied. The nurses did a wonderful job tending to them all, and to the German and Italian wounded who lay alongside their former enemies. War was a great leveller. I watched the general move from bed to bed, shaking hands, dishing out cigarettes and charm and I fell in love with him all over again. He really was a great leader of men; you could see the love and respect in the eyes of those he spoke to. After Bir Hakeim, he'd become a living legend and I couldn't help but adore him too.

To my delight, I found that Kelsey was in charge. I hadn't seen her in many weeks. When she saw me she came straight towards me. I thought she was going to give

240

me a hug and congratulate me on getting out. But she was furious.

'Travers! How dare you go back to Bir Hakeim when you were specifically barred from the place!' she fumed. 'Our name will be mud with the English when it gets out that you disobeyed orders. What were you thinking of?'

My eyes suddenly smarting, I fought my inclination to burst into tears. Softening, she squeezed my hand and led me to one side. 'Was it very bad?' she asked.

I nodded, unable to speak. Looking around me at the maimed and dying, I realized for the first time how terrible it had been.

The journey to Alexandria was unexpectedly hard. Everyone was dog-tired and all we wanted to do was sleep. Climbing back over Halfaya Pass, one of our trucks slid off the road and into a deep ravine, killing an NCO and a legionnaire and gravely injuring several others. It seemed so senseless after all the men had just gone through. For some of the soldiers watching, the sight of the accident was too much and they were overcome. At the chaplain's suggestion, a short service was held the following day in memory of all those who'd died.

The main coast road was unrecognizable. Just a few months before there had been nothing, just desert, a few fig plantations and some well-worn ruts in the sand. Now, after months of activity, it bristled with the flotsam and jetsam of war – petrol stores, piles of spare parts, oil drums, even hastily erected food stalls. The bumpy road, always appalling but worsened by overuse, was teeming with traffic; the efficient British military police kept everyone on the move. As we headed east, we passed great numbers of Australian troops in their wide-brimmed hats, heading back to the front. They were all singing and as happy as could be, going off to fight in the desert and keep the Germans at bay.

After a brief regrouping at the battered coastal resort and fortress town of Sidi Barrani (which had the first metalled road we'd travelled on in months), we arrived in Alexandria where the French population gave us a tumultuous welcome. Even the British soldiers treated us with respect. Only the Vichy sailors on board the neutralized French warships in the harbour were hostile.

For one whole week we were allowed to rest, repair our equipment, treat our wounded and reflect on our losses. We swam in the sea, ate proper food, slept, drank and wept. I was with the men when they listened to the famous rallying broadcast by de Gaulle from London on the second anniversary of his call to arms. 'When a ray of reborn glory touched the bloodstained brows of her soldiers at Bir Hakeim, the world recognized France,' he said. The broadcast was followed by 'Lily Marlene', which reduced many to tears. I could hardly believe it was only two years before, huddled around a wireless in Finland with my fellow nurses, that I had first heard of General de Gaulle. It seemed like a lifetime ago.

At a series of celebration dinners afterwards, including a sumptuous feast at the home of Madame Zarb at Meadi, outside Cairo, the men presented the general with gifts as tokens of their esteem. One, from the officers, was a toy rabbit, in recognition of his *'vieux lapin'* nickname. The other was a toy lion, because the general had also become known as 'the lion of Bir Hakeim'. Handing them to me for safekeeping, the general promised that he would treasure them both always. Secretly, I knew, he much preferred the lion.

The general was then dispatched to see de Gaulle, who wanted to thank him personally and discuss his glorious future. His absence gave me a few days off in Cairo, my first leave in four months, and I decided to fulfil the promise I'd made to myself during the worst of the shelling. Putting on my smartest uniform and beret, I marched into the best restaurant in town, Le Petit Coin de France, and ordered the meal I dreamed of during so many lonely hours in the desert. The restaurant was full of officers and I was the only woman present. I was probably also the only NCO. Everyone was staring at me.

Sadly, as with most fantasies, the reality did not quite match the dream. As a woman dining alone and an NCO to boot, I was given the worst table in the room, near the kitchen. I ordered from the à la carte but they had run out of smoked salmon, so I had to have a herb omelette to start instead. When my main course arrived – the *canard à l'orange* – it was tepid and I had to send it back to be reheated. So disillusioned was I with my first decent meal in months that I didn't even bother to stay for the vanilla ice cream. Finishing my half bottle of good wine, I walked out of the restaurant without leaving a tip, the greatest possible snub to the imperious Egyptian waiters.

The Legion was enjoying itself in Cairo too – wining and dining as if there were no tomorrow. 'We have fifteen days' drinking to catch up on,' Amilakvari told me. 'We plan to drink every nightclub in Cairo dry.' Gathered together in a smoky bar one night, they watched aghast as an Egyptian comic took the stage and began to mock Rommel, imitating him and strutting the goose-step. The bar fell silent, but the comic carried on. Unable to take any more, Commandant Bablon rose to his full six feet six inches and marched up onto the stage. Pushing the comic to one side, he berated him for targeting the great German general.

'When you mock Rommel, you mock us,' he told the hushed crowd. 'Rommel and the Afrika Korps deserve our greatest respect. They are tremendous soldiers. We fought against them and we should know.' He received tumultuous applause.

There were moments of levity too. The general returned to Alexandria and was asked by the English to help arrange a boxing match between some mighty Cairo boxers and his finest legionnaires. Large amounts of money were riding on the outcome. Only too happy to oblige, the general agreed, and the match went ahead with a young legionnaire called Adjudant-Chef Dormoy in the ring. For the first three rounds it looked as if Dormoy would not survive. He barely fought his monster of an opponent and took a severe beating. The English, who'd placed their money on the Egyptian, were delighted. But then, completely out of the blue, the young Dormoy landed a mighty blow to the chin of his opponent, felling him. It was a knockout. The referee lifted Dormoy's arm and named him the winner. Collecting their winnings, the general and his men left the building rather hurriedly with their young pugilist, failing to tell the English that his real name was Francis Jacques and he was a European boxing champion.

But there was no more time for play. The general had returned from his debriefing with orders that the brigade was to be mustered to resume battle. Despite the success of Bir Hakeim in keeping the enemy busy, a 'box' fort fifteen kilometres further up the Gazala Line and manned by the British 150th Infantry Brigade had been smashed with great loss of life. I thought of the Yorkshireman who'd told me of Bir Hakeim's 'hell on earth' nickname, and wondered who'd had the worst hell.

In Rommel's great sweep onwards, some 250 of the 300 British tanks had been lost. He had broken through the Gazala Line, and was hammering the British defences mercilessly in what became known as the Battle of the Cauldron. Tobruk had been overrun, and now Rommel was threatening Cairo itself. There was mass panic in the city. Civilians mobbed railway stations, so many official documents were burned in one day that it became known as 'ash Wednesday', and the Egyptian people prepared to welcome their Nazi 'liberators' by tearing down the Union flag and icing cakes with German lettering.

Desperate to stop Rommel's inexorable advance, Winston Churchill sacked General Claude Auchinleck and appointed a new commander, a relatively unknown general named Bernard Montgomery, giving him control of the Eighth Army.

Montgomery was a feisty man, diminutive and terrier-like – a professional soldier who exuded confidence, inspiring fear and admiration in equal measure amongst his men, most of whom liked his direct approach and his insistence that there would be no further withdrawal. He told his men that if Rommel attacked, they would stand and fight 'alive or dead'. He drew a curved line on the map, forty miles long, south of a little-known railway station called El Alamein and on the edge of the unstable and shifting valley of sand known as the Qattara Depression.

Keen on peak physical fitness, high moral fibre and focused minds, Montgomery wanted nothing to distract his men from the task ahead. As the general and I led the Free French convoy to the Alamein Line, stopping only to eat and sleep, word came back that all female staff were being turned away by the military police at British check-points ahead. The order had come from the highest quarter: 'Monty' was insistent that no women should be at the front line.

I hadn't survived Bir Hakeim and the minefields only to be turned back now by an imperious British general. My female nursing colleagues did as they were told, but I carried on. Still in my androgynous uniform, with my chiselled features and cropped hair, I was confident that neither the general nor the men would give me away.

When we reached the Alamein Box, formidably edged in coiled barbed wire, we had to pass through various military checkpoints with their barriers and armed guards. One by one the military police peered in through the general's window, asked for his documents and spoke only to him. Just once did an MP stare at me suspiciously and ask the general for my papers. Concentrating on the desert road straight ahead, I tried not to panic.

To my great relief, I heard the general's roar. 'I am a French general, on urgent war business for General Montgomery,' he told the young soldier. 'I will not be delayed.' Terrified, the MP waved us on. With the general's support, and my new family following on behind, I made it through every checkpoint.

On Montgomery's orders, two battalions of the Free
French were instructed to mount an attack on a strongly
fortified flat-topped mountain called Qaret El Himeimat
in the Qattara Depression south-west of the main battle
area. El Himeimat had a sheer cliff face on one side and a
gentle slope on the other. It was occupied by German tanks
and Italian paratroopers, whose heavily defended
machine-guns were dug in at every rocky outcrop. All
around were minefields, booby-trapped and doubly served
by thick, shifting sand.

The French were not told that their attack was to be a
diversionary one, only designed to keep enemy forces
occupied while the British, New Zealand and South
African troops prepared for a much bigger attack further
to the north-east. Such was the secrecy of the main attack
that the generals themselves only knew about it five days
in advance, the captains one day and the soldiers one hour.
Montgomery toured all the divisions, giving pep talks to
the officers right down to the rank of captain, warning
them of the dire conditions they faced but urging them to
keep going and to help make Alamein a great victory. 'We
shall beat Rommel,' he told them and they believed him.

When Amilakvari first heard of the French attack on the
sheer cliff face, however, he described it as complete madness. The general agreed wholeheartedly and tried to have
the order changed or modified, going to see General
Alexander personally. But when he returned, he told his
officers that the attack would go ahead. 'Alexander says
that if we're not up to it, he'll bring in someone else who
is,' he reported, still looking shocked. I saw both the
general and Amilakvari later that day and I don't think I'd
ever seen them more concerned.

The French mission, which began at 7.30 p.m. on 23
October, was a shambles from the start. The men and
vehicles had to cross sixty kilometres of the most inhospitable terrain. No heavy vehicles could get through,
only jeeps, and they quickly became bogged down in the

sand. Many had to be abandoned in the tremendous heat, despite the fact that the men had taken everything out of them (even the radios) to try to lighten the load.

When they arrived at the unmapped minefields on the plateau of Naqbrala, they were the worst they'd ever come across. The sappers, lying on their stomachs, tried desperately to find a way through, but the German and Italian troops had moved our warning signs into the middle of the minefields, so that no-one would know of their exact location until it was too late.

To complicate matters still further, the Axis forces had added hundreds more of their own, more sophisticated mines, many of them booby-trapped, deliberately placing them along the narrow roads through the minefields which had been made by the English. They would then roll a tyre from one end to the other, so that we would think that a vehicle had passed through safely. The result was catastrophic, with many men lost in the first few hours.

As the men approached the 1,300-foot-high mountain, the alarm was raised and the enemy opened fire with 105 mm guns, making it even more difficult to cross the last part of the minefield. The cliff was much better defended than anyone had imagined and when the soldiers reached it, it loomed up at them in the moonlight, an enormous unassailable façade. All their radios stopped working the minute they arrived in its shadow, making communication with each other, and with their commanding officers, impossible. Trapped and, for a few moments, surrounded by total silence, they wondered what they'd been let in for.

The silence was shattered by the opening barrage of the main Alamein offensive, which began at 9.40 p.m. with Montgomery's thousand guns pounding the enemy positions relentlessly. The carefully synchronized flashes from the guns taking part in Operation Lightfoot turned night to day. The desert sky blazed with light from tracers and fires. After an opening barrage of fifteen minutes' duration, the guns fell silent for five minutes, the air still

247

thick with their smell. Then at 10 p.m. they began again, with an even more deafening crescendo. It was a vast orchestrated war requiem.

The distant fighting sparked the El Himeimat defenders into action and they opened fire on the Free French. English aeroplanes flew overhead and put down a curtain of smoke across the battlefield to make the enemy think that armoured vehicles were approaching. Unimpressed, the 11th Panzer and Italian Ariete Divisions, supported by two more Italian units, kept firing relentlessly on the trapped men and vehicles below. Seventeen of the twenty-four anti-tank vehicles under the command of Jean Simon were hit and burst into flames. The guns were unhitched and, wherever possible, pulled along by hand.

Commandant de Bollardière, the white-gloved, impeccably dressed French gentleman I'd first met on the *Neuralia*, was ordered to attempt an assault on the enemy positions. With three companies and a Bren gun he made a valiant effort, but it soon became a massacre and he withdrew to a crater, still trapped. When he went on a further recce in a jeep, he hit a mine, seriously injuring his right arm. His driver lost a leg. They could do nothing but lie where they were and wait for help.

The night was freezing and the men, dressed only in their summer fatigues, had little protection from the cold. At 4.30 a.m., Amilakvari told Commandant Bablon that it was his turn to attack. 'For the honour of the Legion, you must achieve some success,' he told Bablon, patting him on the back encouragingly. The huge *commandant* and his two companies of men pushed forward, running at the cliff face in one movement, elbow to elbow, their white kepis all that could be seen in the dawn light. Pierre Messmer was among them. Somehow they managed to pull themselves up the escarpment and overwhelm the Italian defences, destroying some heavy artillery and taking control of a gun emplacement and observation point. But with no-one following them and no heavy arms to support them, they were soon outnumbered by

248

advancing German forces, described later by the men as a 'black mass of advancing tanks'. With Pierre Messmer and another captain wounded, the men had no choice but to retreat.

Under a constant barrage of fire, our troops tried to find shelter. But raked by machine-guns, trapped at the foot of the cliffs and unable to escape, they had little chance. It was a terrible day for the Free French. Communications had broken down completely, but a messenger arrived from Montgomery to tell them to try harder, 'even if it meant serious loss of life'. Further efforts were made but eventually, utterly exhausted and with huge numbers of dead and wounded, General Koenig ordered his men to retreat across an open plain swept by continuous fire.

Watching and waiting for news on the rear edge of the front line, I found that time dragged by interminably. Sitting in my car, my ears straining for every sound, imagining all too clearly the chaos of the battlefield, I heard the opening barrage. All the next day we could hear the shelling in the distance and at night, as we slept in our vehicles, we saw tank fires burning. The other drivers chain-smoked as we talked endlessly of what was happening, speculated on the outcome of the morning's battles and passed on what little information we were able to glean. Having survived the rigours of Bir Hakeim, it felt wrong not to be with the men now. I feared for Pierre and for all my friends. I pictured Amilakvari, bravest of them all and certainly the most handsome in his green cloak; Messmer, already legendary for his valour and destined for still greater glory; Simon, courageous and dashing in his eye patch; de Sairigné, funny and kind and able to rally his men to the most difficult of tasks. Even Arad was out there somewhere with the Chad forces, braving such a vicious and continual attack.

And so I waited with the other drivers. Because our vehicles were too heavy and bulky to manoeuvre in the fine Libyan sand, American jeeps had been brought up from the rear to ferry the commanders about. Temporarily redundant, we lined up in a row at the front of our tented encampment, about ten of us looking out across the moonlit stage, listening to the forces programmes, the BBC, Radio Mondiale and Tunis Radio, and waiting for our respective commanders to return.

The first major round of fighting stopped almost as suddenly as it had begun, leaving in its wake a silence more disturbing than the thunderous noise that had preceded it. It was a few minutes before dawn on 25 October 1942 when slowly, sombrely, a line of vehicles and men appeared on the far horizon making their way towards us. As they came into view, we could see that at the head of the convoy was an ambulance, a large American Dodge of the type we'd seen more and more of since the United States had joined the war. It trundled past us as fast as it could go in the sand, on its way to the hospital tent. There was nothing unusual in this: there were bound to be wounded on board. But something about the expressions on the faces of the drivers and the fact that the ambulance was flanked by two command jeeps bothered me.

I didn't dare move. Instead, I stood squinting into the rising sun trying to see who it was that was being carefully lifted out of the ambulance on a stretcher and rushed inside.

'Please don't let it be Pierre,' I whispered under my breath. 'Not Pierre, God, please.' I closed my eyes and thought back to the last time I'd prayed for his safety, on Christmas Day in an incense-filled church in Cairo almost a year before. Our blissful days in Aley scrolled up before my eyes and I ached with the memory.

Van der Wachler, Amilakvari's chauffeur, could stand it no longer. Dropping his half-lit cigarette and grinding the butt into the sand, he walked across to the hospital tent.

He emerged a few minutes later, and I could tell that the news was bad. His shoulders were stooped, and as he neared our line of cars I saw that his cheeks were wet. Yet again I couldn't move. I felt breathless, flushed with heat and anticipation. I remember thinking that I might faint.

'It's Lieutenant-Colonel Amilakvari,' Van der Wachler said in his thick Flemish accent. 'He's dead.'

We struggled to take this in. Amilakvari? Dead? Our prince among men. The valiant officer most beloved of the legionnaires, adored by all the women he had ever whispered to in his sensual, Georgian accent. The man with the black kepi perched jauntily at an angle, who, in defiance of death, had always refused to wear his officer's tin helmet. It seemed impossible that he could be killed. He had always seemed immortal.

'How?' I heard a strange voice ask. It was several seconds before I realized that the voice was mine.

Van der Wachler crumbled completely. Holding his head in his hands, he sobbed openly. 'That's just it,' he wailed, his mouth forming peculiar shapes. 'It was a fragment of shrapnel from a shell. It hit him in the head and passed clean through and out the other side of his kepi. If he'd been wearing his helmet—'

'It would have saved his life.' I turned and walked away from him, the other drivers and the cars, treading softly across the sand, heading towards the horizon, my heart pounding. I stopped only when the sinister hump of El Himeimat was all that I could see ahead of me, silhouetted dark against the dawn.

I knew that Amilakvari had died the way he'd lived, with great courage. Having sent so many of his men to their deaths that fateful night, he had insisted on supervising the retreat, standing in the middle of the battlefield in his green cloak from Narvik, the folds of its hood already peppered with shot. Shouting orders and words of encouragement to his men, he was waving them back and was determined not to leave until the last man was out. He had just spurned the offer of a lift in an armoured car sent by General Koenig. 'My place is with my men,' he told the driver.

Minutes after the armoured car had left, everyone heard a shell whistling in from above, and dived for cover. The shell landed a few feet from Amilakvari, who'd turned to face it. A two-inch-long piece of jagged metal flew from the burning heart of the explosion and went straight into his eye, passing through his head and out the other side. As his men watched aghast, dear Amilakvari clutched his eye and slumped to his knees, making a most dreadful death rattle in his throat. One of his officers, Bernard Saint-Hillier, told us how he'd run forward and dragged him to one side, behind a rock, screaming to his comrades for help. They pulled the prince to shelter, eventually lifting his body onto a tank as the Italian battery began to fire all over again.

Amilakvari was pronounced dead at the advanced dressing station later that afternoon as his shattered men sat waiting for news. The general decided to have his body laid out on a table in the control tent that night, so that the men could file past and pay their last respects. There was no shortage of volunteers to carry him; exhausted men scrambled to their feet as a troop of legionnaires emerged from the medical tent, carrying Amilakvari's body high on their shoulders as the sun was turning red. Ahead of and behind them, pacing slowly, were other legionnaires, holding up burning torches to light the way. The poignant sight was too much for some of the men, after such a terrible day. That torchlit procession across the Libyan dust at sunset was an image that was to remain with us all for the rest of our lives.

I found myself unable to cry either over Amilakvari's death or at his deeply moving funeral service, held a few days later at the highest point of Quor El Laban, facing El Himeimat in the middle of the desert. The men erected a simple wooden cross and pinned a photograph of Amilakvari to it. The general was inconsolable at the loss of his best friend and could barely lead the prayers. He stood by the rocky mount strewn with desert orchids and vowed revenge, urging his demoralized men, weeping openly, to do likewise.

Watching the display of grief around me, I tried to convince myself that Amilak wouldn't have minded dying a hero. He had died as he had lived – afraid of nothing. After all, General de Gaulle had conferred on him the Croix de Guerre with enamel palm for being 'always to the fore in most dangerous situations and a symbol to all by his calmness and his disregard of death'.

Turning away from the rock-piled burial mound for the last time as the strains of the Last Post sounded mournfully on a bugle, I bumped into Claude, the Chadian officer I'd last seen on the final day of Bir Hakeim.

His eyes too were full of tears. 'It's your dog,' he told me sadly. 'I'm afraid he's disappeared. He ran off into the desert the morning Amilakvari died and no-one has seen him since. We think he must have been killed, probably by a mine.'

I closed my eyes against the flood I felt sure would come, but when I opened them again my eyes were dry. In my imagination, I pictured Arad, our carefree white dog with whom I had shared my happiest days at Aley, disappearing over the horizon of sand dunes and rocks into the sunrise, his soft ears flapping. His death seemed fitting on such a dreadful day.

There was more bad news to come. That evening Bernard Saint-Hillier came to my tent. 'There's been a radio broadcast,' he said, standing in the canvas doorway, half-afraid to enter. 'It's only nonsensical Italian propaganda, no doubt started in Cairo, but I think it might affect you.'

'Go on,' I said, my heart in my mouth.

'It was very derisive,' he said apologetically, trying to prepare me for the worst. 'It said that General Koenig, hero of Bir Hakeim, had taken his mistress to battle.'

I sat on my little camp bed listening to him as waves of shock and humiliation swept over me. Mortified at being called the general's mistress, feeling so much more than that, and furious that our love for each other had become public knowledge in such a tawdry way, I rocked myself in pain.

'It said you had been a great personal comfort to him throughout the North African campaign,' Saint-Hillier added softly.

Seeing that I was completely unable to respond, he apologized for being the bearer of bad news and left. It was several seconds after he'd gone before I was able to exhale. I was devastated, both for myself and for the general. These propaganda broadcasts – usually a tissue of lies – were monitored scrupulously and if General Catroux or the puritanical General Montgomery got hold of this information, it could be the end for us both. Cairo was a hotbed of spies and word must have got out that I'd been with the general during the breakout, when women were meant to have been banned from the front.

For the remainder of that night, I lay on my canvas bed unable to sleep. When I did drift off, my sleep was fitful and filled with dreams of Pierre, Amilakvari and Arad. I'd lost two of them and now, it seemed, I was about to lose the most precious one of all.

I was right. General Montgomery was upset with General Koenig, but chiefly for what he deemed his military failure to take El Himeimat. He believed that sixty-nine wounded, eleven dead and ten missing was not a heavy enough toll to justify his retreat. The French hadn't been the only ones to fail in their initial task; the South Africans and the New Zealanders (later to be hailed as the heroes of El Alamein) had also failed to get through similarly impenetrable minefields. But, unlike the French, they had gone on with the British and Commonwealth troops to engage in what became a mighty victory. Striking while General Rommel was resting in a German sana-torium, exhausted by war, Montgomery had capitalized on the mental and physical depletion of the Axis forces without a leader, and he'd won.

El Alamein was hailed as the great turning point of the North African campaign, even though some 13,500 British and Commonwealth troops had been killed. 'Before Alamein, we never had a victory, after Alamein,

254

we never had a defeat,' Churchill famously declared.

Still the momentum had to be maintained, and four days after the conclusion of Alamein, the biggest invasion fleet the world had ever known landed assault troops at various points along the French North African coast between Casablanca and Algiers, commanded by the American General Dwight D. Eisenhower. The routing of the German army had begun. The heroes of the hour were sent after the retreating Germans, while we were withdrawn from the front lines and dispatched ignominiously to the Mediterranean shore.

Many of the French felt very bitter about their treatment at the hands of the British. Hadn't they achieved their objective, to keep the forces at El Himeimat busy? And hadn't they sacrificed enough in the process, with many dead – Amilakvari among them. What more did Montgomery want? After our great success of Bir Hakeim, our perceived failure was a bitter pill to swallow, especially as Montgomery refused to call our troops back to the front until the final stages of the Tunisian campaign many months later – a decision which affected the already battered French morale greatly and marked a period of regimental history still referred to as '*le temps d'oubli*', the time to forget.

French troops were sent to Gambut in Tripolitania with few supplies and little idea of when they would be engaged in battle once more. There was even talk of the 13DBLE being disbanded, or of being merged into one giant unit. 'As you are an Englishwoman, La Miss, perhaps you could tell us what kind of sauce the British will serve us with when they finally eat us up? Or will they just roast us alive on a spit?' one officer asked me drily. I didn't know what to say.

My own troubles were far from over. The general and I were based near Alexandria when I heard that Madame Catroux, the much-feared wife of our commander-in-chief, had written to the general's wife and informed her of the Italian broadcast. I don't think that Madame Catroux, now referred to as 'Queen Margot', had ever liked me very much. Not one to shy away from supporting her husband's career, Madame Koenig let it be known that she would shortly be making an unprecedented trip, travelling from the safety of her home in Morocco, via Portugal, to visit her husband at the Free French camp.

I was depressed and hurt by the thought of what her visit might mean. I remembered Pierre's first comments to me about her – 'wealthy, well connected, an aristocrat, overprotective and overambitious for me'. The thought of her made me shudder. Worried as he was for his own future, the general refused to discuss her arrival with me. He had clammed up and we barely spoke. When he eventually did, it was to send me on my first formal period of leave in over two years, to Port Said on the Suez Canal for 'a rest'.

Nothing about the characterful old tourist port could raise my flagging spirits. When I returned to Alexandria ten days later, I discovered that Madame Koenig was not only still in situ but appeared to have little intention of leaving her husband's side. They had toured the circuit of officers' clubs, dined out at the famous Cecil Hotel and the Colossi Cossus restaurant and appeared to be a devoted couple.

The general did his best to keep us apart, sending me on leave and on errands – anything but have me driving them around. After three days back in the desert, I still hadn't met her. Finally I asked one of the general's aides what she was like.

'A gendarme,' came the frosty reply, and I almost laughed.

When I eventually set eyes on her, I was completely taken aback. Pierre's wife may have been older than he, heavily made up and with dyed blond hair, but she was unexpectedly charming and had clearly once been beautiful. A chic Parisian, she wore skirts to the knee and rich furs. A determined woman, more than ten years my senior, she looked me straight in the eye, extended a bony hand and smiled politely.

'How nice to meet you, Adjudant Travers. I've heard *so* much about you.' Her expression was fixed and stony. 'And I understand I have you to thank for saving my husband's life. Well done.'

For once, I found myself lost for words.

Keeping eye contact with me, she spoke to the general standing uneasily at her side. 'Come on, Pierre. It's time we were leaving.'

In the great tradition of deceived French wives, she obviously didn't want a confrontation. She had let it be known that she was there simply to redress the balance. In my presence, she instructed her husband to take her to Cairo and book her into Shepheard's, the very hotel where he and I had spent some of our happiest nights.

As I watched her step neatly into the car, I reflected on what my feelings were about this woman I'd so feared. Smiling slightly to myself, I decided that, in spite of everything, I admired her. She wasn't like a gendarme at all. On the contrary, she was a very attractive and determined woman. Married once before, she'd eloped with the general when he was a mere captain, giving up a great deal for love. Now she lived in Marrakesh – a long way from her friends in Paris – with her children from her former marriage. She didn't seem to me to be a woman who was about to give her husband up.

Madame Koenig and I understood each other completely, I reflected later. We were, after all, in love with the same man. Only she had the quiet confidence of someone who knew that she had won. I realized to my shame that I didn't even know her Christian name.

The next few weeks were tense and miserable for the general and all the Free French. Confined to Cairo and Alexandria on Montgomery's insistence while the English chased the Germans west, trapped by the arrival of his wife, Pierre and I could meet privately only when she was out or sleeping. When we did, he was nervous and jumpy.

'You see the impossible position I've been placed in,

don't you?' he pleaded. 'My hands are completely tied while she's here. I owe it to her to be at her side.'

'And what about me?' I'd complain, cross with myself for my petulance. 'What about what you owe me?'

His face would darken and I'd fear I'd overstepped the line. We were both in this together after all, grown-ups who'd always known how things might end. But I was filled with such longing and such a torrent of confused emotions that I didn't know if I was coming or going. Holding me, stroking my hair with his long, bony fingers, he'd kiss my forehead tenderly and whisper for me to hush.

But Madame Koenig's arrival had changed everything and the longer she stayed the more bereft I felt. I missed him dreadfully and wondered what he was doing when he was with her. The thought of them together physically clawed at my heart. I tried to busy myself with books and newspapers, and with swimming daily in the sea, but my mind was always elsewhere and I could never finish an article or even a page.

The only thing that kept me going was the fact that, despite all the gossip, I'd somehow managed to hang on to my job. When Montgomery issued new orders that the French be moved to another forsaken outpost in the desert, and Madame Koenig decided to stay in Cairo, I dared to hope for some time alone with the general at last.

I should have seen it coming, but I didn't, not then. The general told me we were going to visit the field hospital an hour's drive away and that he would drive. I didn't mind. I knew he liked to drive, and I walked round happily to take my place by his side.

'No! Sit in the back,' he said brusquely. 'Captain Thoreau's coming with us.' Momentarily taken aback by his manner, I looked askance at him, but he turned away hurriedly and started up the engine.

Sitting in the back, studying the familiar outline of his broad neck and shoulders, the way his cropped blond hair bristled with silver at the nape, I remembered his first visits to me in hospital in Damascus. How charming he'd been, how attentive and kind, sitting in the sunlight by the window, a box of chocolates on his lap. I think I'd known, even then, that I loved him.

Captain Thoreau, the officer in charge of our transport arrangements, got in and we set off on the bumpy desert track to the north. The two men talked politely and intermittently about the situation west of our position and how the enemy was being beaten back to Tunisia by the British. Both men expressed their eagerness to see some action and were bitter at their treatment by Montgomery. A companionable silence descended after a while, and I sat quietly in the back waiting for the field hospital to materialize on the horizon. It seemed to take ages.

Suddenly the general broke the silence. 'Adjudant Travers,' he began rather formally. 'There's something I have to tell you. I'm being sent to Tunisia to join General de Gaulle in a liaison capacity.'

I sat up, interested suddenly, and leaned forward to hear him above the engine noise. I wondered when we would be leaving.

'My orders are that you won't be coming with me,' he said, as casually as he could. 'The British have said that, in the circumstances, I can't have a woman driver any more.'

I caught the general's eye in the rear-view mirror and frowned. We had been inseparable since June 1941 – it seemed much longer – and now he was abandoning me. He reached up, adjusting the mirror so that he could no longer see my pained expression, as Thoreau shifted uncomfortably in his seat. It was clear to me now why our fellow passenger had been invited along – so that I wouldn't make a scene.

I slumped back into my seat. I couldn't speak. I couldn't breathe, I couldn't even think. I felt more bereft than I had ever felt in my life.

Finally catching my breath, I asked bitterly, 'Where are you sending me then? Cairo? To Madame Catroux?' I couldn't imagine anything worse than being under her beady eye.

'No,' the general replied. 'You're to be attached to the field hospital and offer your services as a driver there.'

The silence between us became almost unbearable as I blinked back the tears and sat rigidly in my seat. Thoreau didn't dare look at me, and the general's hands gripped the steering wheel so hard that his knuckles showed white. Not another word was spoken for the next twenty minutes. I wanted to scream, to shout at Pierre that he was being unfair, to ask him how he could do this to me after all we'd been through. But I couldn't. I'd never stood up to him in all the time we'd been together and I was certainly not in a position to do so now. He knew that and was using it against me. For the first time since I'd seen him emerging dustily from under a truck during that air raid near Damascus, I felt real anger towards him. He had ill-used me, and I deserved better, especially after Bir Hakeim.

When the interminable car journey finally came to an end, I leaped out as quickly as I could. Keeping my head down as Thoreau beat a hasty retreat, I tried to gather together my things.

Pierre watched me fumbling with my few belongings – my bed, bath and suitcase. 'Here,' he said, handing me the car keys. 'You can fetch them later. I'm staying at the hospital overnight.'

As I let the keys drop into my hand and closed the boot lid, he spoke once more. 'Please try and understand. The orders came from the very top,' he said, the sadness evident in his voice. 'I know it seems hard, after . . . after everything. But you must understand, I really have no choice . . . La Miss?' Grabbing my wrist as I turned to walk away, he held it so firmly it hurt, forcing me to look into his eyes. 'Please don't leave like this.'

Releasing his grip with my other hand, I turned away from him silently and headed towards the field hospital as steadily as I could, not allowing him to see the tears spilling down my cheeks.

I can't remember where I went or what I did for the rest of that day. I must have reported for duty and possibly even done some nursing, but none of it registered on my numbed mind.

It was several hours later, and in the mess, when a stranger approached me at the table where I was sitting alone, staring into a cup of coffee.

Clearing his throat to attract my attention, he introduced himself. 'My name is Brandt and I am General Koenig's new driver,' he said.

I looked up distractedly, my eyes wild, and wondered at what he'd just said. 'I beg your pardon?'

Holding out his hand, he shifted uncomfortably from foot to foot. 'I'm the general's new driver. I've been looking everywhere for you. I'm afraid I need the car keys. I've been instructed to take the general to Cairo first thing tomorrow morning.'

Standing up, I drained my cold cup of coffee and, turning my back on him, gathered my things together.

Confused, he placed a hand on my shoulder. 'Adjudant Travers? Did you hear what I said? I need the keys to the car.'

I spun round. My expression must have surprised him for he dropped his hand and took two full paces back. 'I heard you!' I spat. 'Now leave me alone!'

Marching out of the mess, I barked at a hapless orderly to tell me where I could find Captain Thoreau, and headed for his tent. He was sitting behind a desk, a pile of papers in front of him, an even larger pile at his side.

Banging my fist down on the table, sending several papers flying, I lost my temper. 'What the hell is going on?' I demanded. 'Some other driver's asking for my car keys.'

Up until that moment, I think I'd been in limbo, hoping and praying that the general would be able to get round the new orders so that we could be together, as he always had done before. Relinquishing my keys to another driver meant it was final.

'Tell me this isn't happening,' I cried. 'Tell me the

general didn't really mean it when he said I'd have to go.'

Captain Thoreau listened to my outburst in silence. '*Sic transit gloria mundi*,' he said quietly. His eyes were fixed on mine.

I ran a hand through my hair and shook my head in confusion. 'What on earth does that mean?'

Thoreau allowed a smile to tug at the corner of his mouth. ' "So pass the glories of this world",' he replied.

I knew then that I'd lost my general for ever.

It seemed to me then, quite literally, that my life was over. Amilakvari was gone, Arad too, and now Pierre. The times we'd shared, the cottage in Aley, the vast distances we'd travelled together – they were all in the past. The war which showed no sign of ending and the cruelties which continued unabated were only bearable because I had had Pierre by my side. Now there was nothing ahead of me but a void.

Some time later, I found myself sitting alone in the front seat of the general's Ford Utility – the car in which my destiny had been shaped, our chariot to safety at Bir Hakeim. I stroked the tattered seats on which we had driven thousands of miles side by side, the huge steering wheel and the unwieldy gear stick. I turned to look in the back, where I had passed so many nights, wrapped up in my sheepskin coat, and where the general and I had once slept huddled together with a soldier during that dreadful sandstorm. Snatches of conversation and disjointed fragments of memory haunted me.

It seemed to me then that this car had been my whole life: my home, my work, my vehicle to freedom and to love. It had saved my life and kept me safe from heat, cold, sun, sand and storms. I had tended to its every need, fed and watered it, and sheltered it from harm. In return, it had been shot at and shelled, shunted and crashed, patched and repaired. It was unbearable now to be asked to give it up to a complete stranger. To have another driver sitting where I should be sitting, someone who didn't understand its strange ways. To have someone else driving the general, my beloved Pierre.

Throwing my head back to blink away my tears, I caught sight of a bullet hole in the roof above my head, a near miss I hadn't noticed before. I had come so close to losing my life in this car, its four walls now seemed to be my only sanctuary. 'How can you do this to me, Pierre?' I cried aloud. 'How can you make me leave you?'

Gripping the steering wheel, my head leaning against it, I allowed my tears to splash onto my lap. Then, wiping my nose with the back of my hand, I tried to regain some sort of mental control. 'You have to pull yourself together, Susan,' I told myself. 'Just take what you came for, hand in the keys and get on with your life.'

Inhaling deeply, I reached across to the glove compartment and opened it to see what mementoes of our travels were inside, what fragments of our time together I could take with me. As the little door fell open, I started. Nestling between the faded linen maps that we had used to criss-cross our way through North Africa was my Beretta pistol.

In less than a heartbeat, everything seemed clear. Here was a way out of my dilemma, a chance to escape the pain, the humiliation and the empty future.

Leaning forward, I stretched my fingers towards the gun I'd swapped two years before with an aviator in the Congo, the weapon with which I'd planned to protect myself when the enemy arrived at the end of the siege of Bir Hakeim. It glinted invitingly in the moonlight.

Picking it up and laying it in the palm of my hand, I felt its weight and the coldness of its metal against my skin. It was simple. I could place it against my temple and apply a small amount of pressure to the trigger. It would be a private conclusion to a very private war.

'There is no future,' I whispered to myself, the warmth of my breath sending a fine cloud of mist into the cold air all around me. I watched the mist evaporate and imagined doing the same, disappearing into thin air.

My hand was steady as I lifted the weapon. Nobody would hear the shot. The car was parked at the very edge of the encampment and everyone was dining in the mess tents. I would be found the next morning, preferably by the new chauffeur, a man for whom I'd already developed an unreasonable dislike. As the barrel reached my temple I pressed it deep into the soft flesh, relishing its coolness. The chauffeur would cry out and run for help, knowing all the while that I was beyond any assistance. The doctor would be called – Dr Godou perhaps. One look would tell him all he needed to know.

The general would be found. One of his aides would take him quietly to one side. Thoreau perhaps. *Sic transit gloria mundi*. I imagined Pierre's face as he was given the news and wondered how he would feel. Would he cry as he had done at Amilakvari's grave, his tears brushed away hastily to spare his embarrassment? Probably not. He would attend my funeral, say a few kind words, and then go on his way. In this car. The car in which his lover had taken her life.

I allowed my forefinger to curl itself around the trigger. With just the tiniest bit of pressure, I could feel the torque. 'A hot pain and then oblivion,' I muttered, closing my eyes in readiness, pressing the barrel still further, until the metal almost cut into my skin. My finger twitched.

The silence overwhelmed me. No sound. Not even my breathing. My heart seemed to have stopped beating.

Concentrating, afraid of losing courage, I prodded my temple still harder, willing myself on. The general. Me. This car. It was a perfect ending.

Yet something was holding me back. Perhaps it was the Travers spirit – 'Neither Afraid nor Timid' – clawing its way back into my brain. I wasn't a quitter and never had been.

Lowering the pistol slowly, I opened my eyes and looked around me. With vivid clarity I saw how futile my death would be. What end would it serve and who would I be punishing? The general couldn't help it: duty always came first with him, and he was simply obeying orders. The new driver? A man I barely knew and who surely deserved a better start to his promotion. I realized guiltily what a terrible mess my suicide would make in my treasured car. The general would be furious – so angry, in fact, that he would probably not even attend my funeral. He'd have to borrow a new car to take him to Cairo and de Gaulle in the morning while this one was cleaned up. He would have lost me, and maybe even his 'lucky' vehicle – the one that had got him through hell and back at Bir Hakeim. He would be livid. Apoplectic!

I found myself almost smiling at the thought. Shaking my head at my foolishness, I plunged the Beretta into my pocket, slammed the glove compartment shut, and fled. Taking a very long walk in the dark, plodding over loose, cool sand, I distanced myself as far as possible from the car.

As the moon rose and flooded the sea of sand before me with silver light, I managed to compose myself. I was never to contemplate suicide again.

Knowing that work was the only salve, over the next few months I threw myself into my new job, ferrying doctors and nurses to and from the front, volunteering for extra duties and unpopular tasks. My only companion day and night was my new dog, an Alsatian puppy called Josephine, a much-loved replacement for Arad whom I'd bought from a legionnaire.

There were other women drivers, Spearettes, six of them, who drove medical staff and the wounded in the rear echelon but I was the only one on the front lines. To begin with I drove an elderly French doctor around, but then, for a few happy days, I was reunited with the lovely Commandant Lotte, back in the war after an extended convalescence and now walking with a stick. I was very pleased to see him.

'Susan, my dear,' he called, welcoming me warmly. 'How marvellous to see you again.'

I ran over to where he stood leaning on his stick, and gave him a hug. He looked a little older and fatter, but otherwise unchanged. Looking around for Assab, I asked him where his trusty 'boy' was.

'He disappeared after my accident,' Lotte said sadly. 'He must have thought I wouldn't be back and went off with someone else. You haven't seen him, have you?'

I thought of the tall native covered in pots and pans and shook my head. 'I think I would have remembered if I had,' I said.

Dr Lotte was moved on and I had to drive Dr Godou again. Swallowing my resentment, I retreated further and further into myself. 'At least you're still alive,' I kept telling myself, thinking of Amilakvari and all the rest. But the truth was that I felt half-dead most of the time, thin as a rake and tired to death.

Asking for time off that winter, I went to stay with Eka, Amilakvari's sister-in-law in Cairo, who was very kind to me and gave me plenty of fresh fruit and milk.

'I think you're more than just exhausted,' she told me after a few days in her lovely home. 'I think you're sick inside.' She clasped her hand to her heart to indicate what she meant. I told her nothing. I felt too raw to talk about Pierre, and she respected my silence.

When she felt I was up to it, she asked me about Amilakvari's death. Unable to get over his loss, she was determined to remain close to the Legion for the duration of the war. 'Just by talking to those who knew him, being with them, I feel in some small way that he is still alive,' she said.

In Eka's tender care, I recovered my strength and my sanity and decided that the best thing to do would be to get on with my life and try to forget the general.

But the general clearly couldn't forget me. Whether Eka contacted him or not I don't know but, hearing that I was unwell, he came to see me. In his hand was a bunch of white roses.

'I'm taking a trip back to Bir Hakeim,' he said, his eyes shining as he took my hand in his. 'I feel there is an invisible thread pulling me back and I'd very much like you to accompany me, La Miss.'

I thought of the desolation of the place and of the many ghosts it would hold. 'I-I don't know . . .' I stammered. The last thing I wanted right now were reminders of my time with him. I wished he hadn't come.

But Pierre was most insistent. His visit was, he said, partly a homage to those who had died and partly a personal test of all that had gone before. 'I need to go and see the place again,' he urged. 'Please come with me.'

Against my better judgement and partly to see how being in his company made me feel, I decided to accept his invitation, only to find that we wouldn't be travelling alone but with Dr Godou and the redoubtable chaplain, Père Mallec, both of whom had invited themselves along.

The general drove the Ford Utility himself, Dr Godou at his side. I sat in the back with the chaplain, unable to take my eyes off Pierre in the rear-view mirror. To my great shame and anger, my overwhelming emotion was of joy just to be with him.

When we arrived at the barren outpost we'd lived in for so many weeks almost a year before, we hardly recognized it. The new Free French brigade in charge had done a wonderful job, filling in the shell craters and tidying the place up. They were halfway through the construction of a cemetery which was to feature a large stone monument bearing the Cross of Lorraine. Within its low walls were the dozens of new mounds, each one marked with a cross. The sight of them all together like that reminded me once more how many had lost their lives. My breath caught in my throat.

Dr Godou got out to stretch his legs and talk to the men, but the general wanted to retrace our exact path on the night of the breakout, so he asked a young Free French lieutenant to jump in and show him the way.

'Can you take me to Route F?' he asked. 'I'm not sure now which way it is.' Confused by the changes since we'd last been there, the general drove forward without waiting for directions and we bumped and bounced our way across a particularly uneven piece of ground.

The colour drained from the young lieutenant's face as he realized where we were. 'Excuse me, sir, but I think you've just driven into the minefield,' he blurted.

For the first time we saw that there were sappers all around us, with their metal detectors, earphones round their necks and long poles. The white tape which was supposed to mark out the minefield had become tattered and torn in a recent sandstorm and was fluttering on the ground. We were in the very middle of the same minefield in which we'd nearly lost our lives a year earlier.

'Oh dear, have I?' the general muttered, as if it was no more than a minor matter.

Slamming the car into reverse, he tried to back out the way he'd come. Before he'd moved more than a few feet, there was an almighty bang and the most colossal jolt as the whole car lifted up and crashed down, sending up a huge cloud of dust. Flying up into the air and landing again, I felt a searing pain in my left buttock, as if it had been hit as hard as it could be with a cricket bat. After all his orders for people like me to be careful not to drive over landmines, the general had done exactly that, nearly killing us all.

I was the only person injured, with a suspected broken hip. I was also extremely shaken. In the flash of the explosion and the few seconds of pain and shock that had followed, I'd thought that my time had come. Looking across at Pierre, mouthing a scream, I'd been momentarily grateful that I was with him at the end. But by the time the car and I had come back to earth, I realized I was hurting far too much to be dead.

The rear wheel had been blown clean off, directly under me. Carried from the car by the lieutenant and Pierre and laid on the ground, groaning, I caught sight of Pierre's anxious face.

'I'm not dead yet,' I told him, as help was summoned.

My plight was made worse by the fact that I had to be

stretchered back to the field hospital, bounced across the bumpiest of roads under the care of Dr Godou. He examined me – hastily, I thought – and, with a quick and painful poke in the hip, announced: 'You're perfectly all right. Nothing broken – just some bruising. Go and have some lunch.'

But I was in so much pain I couldn't walk, let alone eat.

The general came to see me in the hospital. 'You look like a piece of cheese,' he said, looking at my pale face. 'You'd better stay lying down.' He smiled fleetingly to let me know he was pleased that I was all right, but I knew he could show no further emotion in such a public place.

In truth, he was so angry with himself that he forbade anyone to mention his embarrassing mistake. Word soon got out when I was seen hobbling around with a bad limp a few days later, my leg, hip and buttocks black and blue. The legionnaires ribbed me mercilessly about the episode, pointing, laughing and rubbing their backsides in mock pain. All I wanted was to get better and to see the general again.

After I'd been run ragged for months by Dr Godou and the hospital staff, the Legion took pity on me and offered me a job as an ambulance driver. It was April 1943 and the brigade had finally been ordered to Enfidaville in Tunisia. I accepted gratefully and drove two thousand kilometres in eleven days across the most inhospitable terrain in a heavy, hard-to-manoeuvre ambulance, via Tobruk, Derna, Benghazi and Tripoli and into Tunisia. The terrain in the high mountains was precipitous, with roads pocked with shell-holes and dizzying hairpin bends, made even more challenging by the slippery mud and cold grey drizzle.

I was on hand throughout the final fighting with the 43rd Battalion of the Afrika Korps on what became known as Ridge 245 at Jebel Garci, where the 13DBLE suffered many casualties. They were the last French soldiers in action on African soil in the Second World War.

Overhead, British planes dropped propaganda leaflets in German, inviting the remaining enemy forces to surrender.

Later I took part in the victory of my division at Cape Bon and saw the great tide of demoralized and defeated German prisoners of war trudging wearily to the Allied lines. A month afterwards, at eight minutes to eight o'clock on 12 May 1943, with the enemy all but defeated, it was announced that all German resistance had ended in Africa.

The Legion and I had been together from the very beginning, when I sailed with them on the ship to Dakar in 1940, to the bitter end of the North African campaign, when 125,000 Germans and 100,000 Italians finally surrendered. I even took part in the Allied victory parade in Tunis that May, driving one of the senior medical officers, celebrating the fact that not a single enemy remained on North African soil. The last remaining Vichy French now formed an uneasy alliance with their former enemies, the Free French, as part of the 1st Brigade as they prepared to carry on fighting the Germans in Europe.

In preparation for that important next stage of the war, we were moved on to the Tunisian town of Zuara, where the desert meets the sea, and set about preparing our camp. Rows of white tents were erected on a slope down to the beach, and I looked forward to a chance to rest and swim and catch my breath after the exertions of the previous few months. It was not long after we'd arrived that I saw something which stopped me in my tracks. The old Ford Utility and the general's *camionnette* were parked on the front, overlooking the ocean.

'How long has General Koenig been here?' I asked an orderly hurrying past me with some boxes of provisions. I'd believed him to be still abroad with de Gaulle.

He shrugged his shoulders. 'A couple of days, I think.'

I had my tent erected not far from the front, facing the sea, so that I could sit inside and watch the comings and goings a few hundred yards below. I didn't expect to be given a chance to see the general privately, but I did hope

270

for a glimpse of the man who had come to mean so much to me. Within a few hours, sitting with my arms around my dog Josephine's great shaggy neck, I had my first sight of him in months, and was angry with myself for the way it still made me feel. Seeing him come and go in the Ford Utility, his new chauffeur at the wheel, nearly reduced me to tears.

For two days I watched out of the opening in my tent. At night I lay on my camp bed restlessly aware that the man I'd loved more than any other was only a five-minute stroll away. I longed to lie in his arms once more, to inhale his special scent and listen to his slow breathing as he drifted off to sleep. I felt the loss of his physical presence in my bed more keenly than ever before. I ached for him and wished that there was something I could do which would allow me to be with him once again.

On the third morning, just as I was drinking my coffee and preparing to report to the hospital tent for duty, I heard someone make a little coughing noise at the entrance to my tent.

Lifting the flap, I looked out to see My Fen, the general's diminutive orderly, shifting from foot to foot awkwardly in the dust. Seeing me emerge, he looked relieved. 'I've something for you,' he said, holding out his hand coyly. In it was a copy of the *Illustration*, the newspaper for the men at the front, which the general and I had read avidly at Aley.

Looking up, I studied My Fen's expression carefully. It was clear that he realized he was being asked to deliver some sort of message to me, although he didn't understand what it was.

'Is it from the general?' I asked, my hands trembling slightly as I took it.

'Yes,' My Fen replied timidly. 'He thought you might like to read it.' He looked impatient, eager to get away.

I recognized the general's handwriting instantly. There was only one word: 'Koenig.' Lowering my head so that My Fen wouldn't see me smile, I composed myself hastily.

271

'Thank you,' I told the orderly, my features rearranged into a serious expression. 'And thank the general.'

He scurried off, his tiny figure heading down the incline to the general's camp. Peering after him, squinting into the bright Mediterranean light, I thought I saw a net curtain flicker slightly in the window of the caravan.

The rest of that day seemed endless, waiting for the night to come. I took Josephine for a walk, collected some medical supplies from Bizerte and found a private place to have a bath. My cleanest uniform on, my hair freshly washed, I slipped out of my tent at ten o'clock and padded softly past the other tents and down to the sea in the darkness. The oil lamp was burning in the general's caravan when I approached, its light glowing through the closed curtains. Breathing deeply, I reached the door and tapped on it lightly before entering.

Pierre was sitting at a low table at one end of the small vehicle, papers and maps strewn before him, a glass of red wine in his hand. 'Come in, La Miss,' he said, smiling. 'I've been expecting you.'

Locking the door behind me, I sat down next to him and watched in silence as he poured me a glass of wine.

'*Santé*,' he said, raising his glass and leaning closer. I sipped the wine, my eyes locked with his. Before my glass was lowered, I was in his arms once again, our mouths tasting the wine on each other's lips.

For a few blissful weeks, I was reunited with Pierre on a nightly basis. Meeting him secretly in his caravan, which was parked overlooking the ocean, I became his lover once more. I knew what a risk he was taking – the British knew, the Italians knew, the whole world seemed to know of our affair. Pierre's career, his reputation and his marriage were on the line, but he seemed to believe me a risk worth taking. As always, it was hard to know what he was feeling, but I didn't care. All I knew was that he wanted to be with me again and, for a brief moment, I felt almost as happy as I'd been in Aley.

But my happiness was to be short-lived. Our clandestine and rather haphazard method of communication – with My Fen bringing me the *Illustration* on the evenings the general expected me – broke down. One night My Fen forgot to deliver the paper. I waited, watching, but when My Fen didn't come, I assumed that the general was busy or in a meeting, and didn't go to the caravan.

Annoyed and upset, his pride wounded as he waited in the lamplight a few hundred yards away, the general believed that I was ending our relationship.

He came up to my tent first thing the next morning. 'I suppose you did that on purpose?' he began, fire in his eyes. 'You made me wait there all night like an idiot, watching and hoping, knowing all the while that you weren't coming.'

'No, Pierre,' I protested. 'My Fen didn't come. I sat here wondering if you'd changed your mind.'

Despite all my protestations, however, I don't think the general ever quite believed me. We had one last bittersweet night together in his caravan, the moonlight glistening on the white tents behind me as I stole silently down to the sea for our final rendezvous two days later, but he was never to send for me again.

Within a few days, news sped round the camp that he had been promoted to General of the Division and had been summoned to join de Gaulle's administrative staff in Algiers, to help set up the historic Comité Française de la Libération Nationale, the provincial government of the French Republic. I didn't even have a chance to say goodbye. As I watched his car disappear into the distance, I berated myself for such an ignominious end to what had been the pivotal relationship of my life.

Picking up my Beretta once more, this time to fire it in anger at a wild dog in the desert who was bothering Jooophine, I pulled the trigger. But the gun failed to go off. It was broken, and had been for years, apparently. There was a bitter irony in the knowledge that, even if I had wanted to, I could never have killed myself with that gun.

14

THE SMELL OF VICTORY

'Until at length with bridled hopes we came upon
this little land
So like the sea-girt shores of home it seemed
That head and heart and eyes had spanned
The continents between . . .'

GWENYTH HAYES, FIRST NEW ZEALAND VADS,
FROM *THE VOICE OF WAR*

By the summer of 1943, the Free French were posted to a little fishing village called Hammamet, drinking arak and eating *mezze*. There were a handful of white villas and some wonderful beaches, where I swam every day with Josephine. It was a restful time and a chance to recover my senses. My heart had been broken more than once in the course of my turbulent love life, but nothing compared with the pain I now felt at the loss of Pierre. I doubted if I could ever allow myself to love again.

In the outside world, events became increasingly momentous. With the Americans fully involved in the war, Tunisia had fallen, Sicily had been taken and the big push was on. Unhappy with each other, the French and British agreed that it would be better for everyone if the Free French were seconded to the US Fifth Army, under the overall command of General Alexander and under the direct control of US Lieutenant-General Mark Clark and the French General Alphonse Juin, whose orders were to help clear Italy of German opposition. Having been a strange sort of legionnaire, I supposed I was now to become an unusual GI.

On learning that I was to leave North Africa for good, I shed no tears. Proud to be serving alongside my colleagues in the great sweep up through Italy after the retreating Germans, I braced myself for the next phase in my private war. The saddest part was that I couldn't take Josephine with me on the ship to Italy. I cried as I left her with friends in Tunisia, hugging her huge shaggy neck and promising that one day we'd see each other again. '*Au revoir, ma chère amie*,' I whispered in her ear. '*A bientôt*.'

The news from Italy was good. Naples had been taken and, travelling on a British cargo ship due to leave from the recently recaptured north Tunisian naval base of Bizerte, we were told that we could disembark there. Word came that women weren't going to be allowed on the ship or to land in Italy and that the American military police waiting for us in Naples were more scrupulous than their British counterparts. In the previous three years, however, I'd become a sort of honorary male, and I thought nothing of the American orders.

In April 1944, donning the smart US Army uniform I'd been issued with amongst the avalanche of new equipment, I tucked my hair up into my helmet and climbed the gangplank at Bizerte along with the rest of the Free French. There were two banks of armed British sentries waiting and, head down, my heart in my mouth, I managed to get past them both. It was only when I was on board that Commandant Arnault pointed out the mistake I'd made.

'Your gaiters are back to front,' he whispered.

Looking down, I realized with horror that the unfamiliar ankle coverings I had to wear were on the wrong way round, with the myriad hooks, eyes and buckles showing on the outside. Swapping them over quickly while Commandant Arnault and his men huddled round to cover me, I thanked my stars that no-one had noticed.

The multinational officers on board the boat were charming and looked after me kindly. Some of them – Arnault and de Sairigné, Simon, Bablon and Saint-Hillier – were familiar to me but many others weren't. One, a young *aspirant* or officer cadet called Hugo Geoffrey, was very sweet and seemed to regard me as something of a legend. (He later became a highly respected Legion general.)

'What was it like breaking out of Bir Hakeim?' he'd ask time and again, his eyes eager and his face fresh. He never seemed to tire of war stories.

'Oh, average, I suppose,' I'd reply and he'd wander off, disappointed.

The officers arranged for me to have my own cabin and to dine with them each evening. They were warm and friendly without being predatory and that is how my relationship with them was to remain.

Naples was full of Americans, all smart and as yet un-affected by long-term warfare. They smoked Lucky Strike cigarettes and seemed permanently tuned in to Glenn Miller and jazz. Their uniforms, equipment and vehicles were so new and clean, they put our battered old kit of Bir Hakeim to shame. But they were very efficient and well organized and the long-awaited Italian landings that April ran like clockwork.

Once on Italian soil we were told to prepare for battle. I was to be a general ambulance driver again, this time behind the wheel of an old American Dodge. With Moroccans, Chadians and Legionnaires in our number, we were now renamed the French Expeditionary Corps. We formed the western prong of a great sweep up Italy, part of the unbroken line of Allied forces from coast to coast scooping up those Germans who chose to stand and fight, and pushing back those retreating.

Monte Cassino stood in the middle of the Allied path, a heavily defended monastery astride a mountain top and a place which was to acquire its own legendary signifi-cance, with Polish, English and Indian forces tested to the very limits. We were to the south-west, taking part in the push to the Garigliano river, up through the Aurunci mountains and on to Rome – a city the British, French and Americans were all desperate to reach first.

H hour was fixed for 11 May 1944 at 11 p.m. The offensive began with a violent artillery barrage similar to that of El Alamein. It was mountainous terrain, partly volcanic, and the twisting narrow roads were heavily mined. The American tanks were unable to get through and in many key areas of battle, only men and mules could pass. The Germans used fixed flame-throwers hidden in shelters, which inflicted terrible burns on those unfortunate enough to cross their path. There were some serious losses, and the German snipers picked off those they couldn't kill en masse. Morale sank to an all-time low. This was not what the men had been trained for, and they were losing comrades every step of the way. The redoubtable Bablon, *commandant* of the DBLE, he who had defended Rommel's reputation in an Egyptian night-club, was injured by a splinter of shrapnel from a hand grenade.

My task was to keep to the roads as much as possible, driving French and American wounded and various medical staff to and from the field hospitals. Bablon was one of my first passengers, nursing his head wound. 'You were lucky,' I told him, handing him my *bidon* filled with cognac and examining the shard of metal which had caused the damage. 'It was a piece not much bigger than that which killed Amilakvari.'

For a large part of my first few months in Italy, I also had to act as personal chauffeur to a doctor and his mistress, taking them to their clandestine rendezvous. It was a sad reminder of my affair with Pierre, and I was privately aggrieved by my subordinate role. So, too, were the Legion, and when they discovered the indignities of my position, they applied to have me rejoin them as a front-line ambulance driver. I was flattered and full of gratitude, happy to be back with my *famille*.

My transfer back to the Legion, however, marked the end of 'easy street' for me. Daily I braved heavily mined roads, air raids and spartan living conditions to fetch the wounded from the front and bring them back to the repairing stations – or the more seriously injured to the base hospitals. I became little more than an automaton, closing in on myself emotionally, feeding on the memories of my happiest times with Pierre and praying that, one day, I might see him again.

The work was both physically gruelling and emotionally draining. There was one severely injured man I remember clearly, an American who'd lost both legs to a landmine. Summoned to his side, I watched as the American doctor who'd done what he could to stem the bleeding from his bloodied stumps stepped away, shaking his head. Leaning over the freckle-faced young man, I squeezed his hand, lit a cigarette for him and placed it in his mouth.

'Here you are, Joe,' I said, using the universal name the Americans seemed to adopt. The cigarette stuck to his dry bottom lip and he inhaled deeply, closing his eyes as the smoke curled upwards. Coughing violently as the smoke filled his lungs he spluttered and choked in pain.

Lifting his head and taking the cigarette, I reached into my pocket and pulled out my *bidon*. 'Here,' I told him, 'try this.'

Swallowing a slug of cognac as best he could, the amber liquid still trickling down his stubbly chin, the man who was little more than a boy looked up at me and smiled.

'Thank you, ma'am,' he muttered, his green eyes fixed on mine. 'Cigarette?'

I placed it back between his lips.

Moments later he was dead. Looking down, I saw something clutched in his right hand. Opening his fingers, I retrieved a creased black and white photograph of two people who must have been his parents. Taking his half-finished cigarette from his mouth and grinding it into the dirt, I closed his eyes.

*   *   *

278

Italy marked a time of great darkness for me, a period when the momentous events of the previous years began to take their toll. I felt isolated and lonely, and missed Pierre dreadfully.

As fighting raged on all around us, with comrades fresh from the Anzio beachhead now engaged in fierce battles at Monte Cassino, the Free French pushed up the centre line, forming part of a single Allied front stretching right across Italy. At the wheel of my American Dodge ambulance, I drove through countryside rendered virtually impassable by the heavy rains. Mines were everywhere, anti-vehicle and anti-personnel mines, lining the roads, hidden in derelict buildings and placed beneath dead bodies, waiting for some hapless hospital orderly. Having been blown up once myself and seen, at first hand, the devastation a mine can cause to vulnerable limbs, I was especially careful where I drove or stepped. It became a constant anxiety, niggling away in the back of my mind.

Curled up in the back of my ambulance at night under a starry sky, I would lie awake, overwhelmed by sadness. Sometimes misery threatened to engulf me. But each cold dawn, exhausted and alone, I would arise again, put on my uniform and go out to face another arduous day, always quick to unload my cargo of wounded so that I could fetch the next. My duties kept me going although I sometimes wondered if I would ever again enjoy the normality of a comfortable bed, running water and the certainty of living through another day.

Stripped of all luxuries and often my dignity, I rarely longed for anything from my former life, although I still occasionally fantasized about the smallest fragments of luxury and convenience, and oh, how I longed for the smell of fresh flowers. In Syria and Eritrea my chief quest had been for a regular bath, in Bir Hakeim it had been a dream about a lavish meal in an opulent restaurant. By the time I reached Italy, where I was able to get an occasional fresh egg for the first time in years, I began to long for a far more basic requirement – an eggcup.

Ridiculous as it now sounds, finding as insignificant an object as an eggcup from which to eat my egg became a near obsession for me, and, accompanied by a young armed legionnaire called Philippe who refused to let me go into dangerous areas alone, I scoured the shattered ruins of every devastated Italian hill town I came to.

The once magnificent countryside was in ruins. Bridge after bridge had been destroyed, rebuilt and destroyed again. Ancient medieval towns, once crammed with art treasures and exquisite pre-Roman architecture, had become a wasteland of derelict and hollowed-out buildings, ringed by hidden mines. Fierce fighting, often house-to-house across the ancient stone streets, had laid waste to whole communities. In Pico, manned until recently by the 26th Panzer Division and taken in a bloody battle by French and Italian joint forces, and Pontecorvo, the fronts of houses in the main piazzas had crumbled, exposing the rooms like opened dolls' houses.

As I rummaged through the rubble of each town we came to, trying to find what had been a kitchen or a food store, oblivious to the constant danger of mines and falling masonry, my quest became a passion.

'Be careful, La Miss,' Philippe would call, his eyes wide with fear as I climbed into yet another abandoned building. 'It may be booby-trapped.'

Ignoring him, I'd plough on. But instead of finding what I sought, I'd stumble across the broken detritus of the simple life before the war: the pots and pans, the pasta boards and colanders of family kitchens, once warm and filled with the scents of cooking. Standing in the brick dust by a broken sink, looking out onto what had once been a peaceful olive grove but in which now lay the rotting corpses of German soldiers, I would close my eyes and conjure up an amply proportioned Italian matriarch peeling onions, her eyes moist as she chattered about her day.

Occasionally, I would happen upon some unexpected delight – a whole salami, some Parmesan cheese or a case of the very light white wine of the region. There was so much wine around that the men actually washed in it. I preferred to wash in water and to drink the wine. It was refreshing, and made a pleasant change from the bitter American coffee that we were now provided with night and day.

Every now and again, I would come face to face with local peasants, ravaged by hunger and poverty, trying to salvage what they could from the wreckage of their homes. Retreating ashamed and mumbling: '*Mi dispiace*,' I would offer them anything I'd found and leave them to their work. Numbed by war, shattered by the political turmoil their country had endured for the last few years, these people had lost the light in their eyes. Their *bambini* would stare blankly at me, their dirt-stained mouths a testament to their foraging. Even the few scrawny dogs I came across seemed to have lost the ability to wag their tails.

By early June 1944 we had reached the outskirts of Rome, where we camped. The Italian capital had been taken on 4 June, to the satisfaction of the legionnaires especially, who – despite the Italians' change of heart and their move to our side – couldn't forget their actions of the previous four years. While the demi-brigade went on to capture the town of Tivoli, I managed to make my way to Rome with some of the Free French officers to savour the moment of glory.

General Clark, sitting astride his jeep, had led the rush to be the first in the Eternal City, knowing its capture – the first of the Axis capitals to fall – to be of great psychological value, if of little strategic use. US tanks rolled along the Appian Way and there were only minor skirmishes. American bombers patrolled the skies overhead as we went in, swooping down on any German resistance and crushing it. The city had remained remarkably intact, thanks to the Nazi officers who had disobeyed their Führer's orders to destroy it.

The people of Rome couldn't have provided more of a

contrast with the Italians we'd met before. They were overjoyed to see us, lining the streets, thronging around the vehicles, throwing kisses, flowers and gifts. The crowd saw us as their liberators. '*Viva la Francia!*' they shouted as soon as they saw the tricolours fluttering on our cars. It was a relief for everyone after months of hard and bloody conflict against crack German troops.

Returning to the Tivoli region, I continued to sleep in the ambulance. I ate my meals with a Free French doctor and a charming dentist, a man called Celerier, who was very good company and always found something to smile about (his teeth being an excellent advertisement for his own work). The French Expeditionary Force was sent on, north through Montefiascone, Bolsena, Acquapendente and Trevignano to the fortified town of Radicofani set atop a grand massif. Radicofani was finally taken in mid-June after two days of bloody fighting, thereby opening up Tuscany to the Allies. The Legion was later awarded the Croix de Guerre with palm for its valiant efforts.

By now the Germans were on the run. Low on supplies and ammunition, they had taken to requisitioning horse-drawn carts and wagons to get their men and equipment away. Victory was within sight and we pushed on, our spirits lifted by the long summer nights.

But no sooner had we begun our march north than our orders changed and, at the end of June, we were instructed to make our way back to the Albanova camp near Naples. Not for us the push up through Italy in pursuit of the Nazis. Other plans, it appeared, were being made on our behalf.

The news of the Normandy landings three weeks earlier, on 6 June, had been received with considerable bitterness amongst the Free French. The Legion, especially, felt it had earned the right to be among the first to land on French soil. But instead it was American, English and Allied forces, minus the French, who took part in the biggest combined land, sea and air operation of all time under General Eisenhower. Great inroads were now being made

282

in France and it was de Gaulle's most fervent wish that his various forces, scattered to the four winds, should be reunited in France once more – the first time any of us would have been back since 1940 – to take part in the final push for Paris. Our new destination was to be the south of France and German-held Toulon.

Turning and heading wearily back towards Naples, we were leaving behind us 106 legionnaires and officers dead and 360 wounded – nearly a quarter of our strength. We travelled back through the heart of the country, still wary of undiscovered mines or lingering snipers. The land seemed even more desolate since our last passing.

Naples was heaving with Americans; the bay was awash with vast ships, the skies full of planes. There was hardly a room free or a restaurant table unbooked. General de Gaulle, fresh from a visit to Rome, flew in to bestow medals on those who had served France so well at Radicofani and elsewhere.

Naples was a pleasant interlude after the rigours of the Italian campaign and the Legion were in high spirits at the thought of their return to France. In their company, I, too, allowed myself to smile again. One night I even pretended to be a man to get into the popular men-only French Club with its legendary 'hostesses'. The men were delighted at my success and toasted me copiously.

'You truly are a sheep in wolf's clothing, La Miss,' de Sairigné had told me, and I knew I was supposed to be flattered.

We were camped in a shady field near a small ravine. It was blisteringly hot that Italian summer and the sea breeze was most welcome. I had the luxury of a tent to myself, although it was so small that it was difficult to dress and wash myself in privacy.

As preparations got under way to leave, I was told that the ambulance I'd driven through Italy for the 13DBLE was not being taken on to France with the Legion – all such vehicles and their drivers were to follow on separately. This news threw me into a deep despair, as I knew only too well that when one was separated from one's unit, one rarely caught up with them again.

Asking around, determined to find some way of staying with my family, I came across Lieutenant Blanc, a kind Frenchman who was *commandant d'armes* of the Legion 1st Brigade.

'Please, sir, do you have any work for me so that I can travel to France with the Legion?' I asked plaintively.

The lieutenant took my arm. 'Of course, Adjudant Travers,' he said. 'We can always use an extra man.'

He agreed to take me on as a truck driver so that I wouldn't be left behind. I was very grateful until he showed me my new vehicle, an enormous American GMC lorry. Fortunately, it went marvellously well, and the other truck drivers were very nice to me.

We were told to carry our own packs and make our way by landing craft to one of the 'Liberty Ships' taking us back to France. A friendly Polish corporal showed me how to fill my rucksack correctly, although when we'd finished it still weighed a ton. After years of warfare, I was too thin and weak to carry very much. Weighed down, I had great difficulty even standing up. The American MPs began to get impatient with me. Waiting in line, I overheard one of them addressing a legionnaire whose pet dog could be seen poking out from his jacket. 'Sorry, buddy, no dogs,' the MP said and pushed him away.

Pretending I'd forgotten something, I dropped my pack, much to their exasperation, and hurried back along the line to tip off the legionnaires, many of whom kept small mongrel dogs with them throughout the war. Some of these valiant animals had been with us since long before Bir Hakeim and were as familiar to me as the men who cared for them. As if by magic, all the little *chiens* disappeared from view, only to reappear miraculously on the ship later.

Once on board, we found that the ship had a British crew and was captained by a former member of the old

Royal Naval Reserve, who clearly hated the French. There were two American officers who despised us even more, and a number of black Americans whose task it was to load and unload. Not since South Africa had I seen such segregation.

There was little room for niceties on the week-long voyage, and because the French were so despised we were put in a kind of hold halfway down the ship. Couchettes were rigged up around the walls and I found I was expected to sleep with the men. Hoping for some privacy, I draped my couchette with a ground sheet as a blanket.

The lavatories were all lined up in a row on the deck with no partitions between them. I didn't fancy sharing a seat with someone so I asked the chief engineer if he would mind me using his. Eventually, the kind chief steward, sensing my embarrassment, allowed me to sleep in a cabin the stewards used to eat in.

'Thank you so much,' I told him. 'It's a blessing you're on board.'

The poor man laughed. 'You wouldn't say that if you knew how unlucky I've been. I've been sunk three times already in this war. The bloody Germans seem out to get me. I've lost twenty of my unit to fires and torpedoes. Next time I might not get away with it.'

Listening to his ghastly stories, I realized what a frightful time the navy had endured.

We weren't allowed to eat in the officers' mess to begin with – the Americans refused, then reluctantly agreed to let us eat there only after they'd finished. We disliked them heartily. Other than this, however, the voyage was peaceful enough and after ten days we arrived at Cavalaire-sur-Mer near St Tropez on the French Riviera on the evening of 16 August 1944. It was my first return in many years to the region of my childhood. All was quiet when we sailed into port and, to our great delight, a barrel of rum was produced. (This was an idea left over from the First World War, when a tot of rum was given to each man before they went 'over the top'.)

285

It was frightful stuff and very strong. Even the most hardened legionnaires couldn't drink it, but ships were dry during the war and the man ladling out the stuff gave generous glasses to the crew and sent some to the captain. The blacks who were unloading loved to drink although they weren't allowed to, and had been issued with handy little rifles even though they never went ashore. So we did a brisk trade in exchanging their rifles for our rations of rum.

'Please, can't you tell the men not to give the blacks any more to drink?' one of the American lieutenants complained, but I told him it was too late. Everyone was drunk except us, and we had lovely new rifles.

The captain, who'd been sent several flasks, was completely incapable. He couldn't even find our correct mooring position. Then a small plane flew overhead and the anti-aircraft crew were so drunk they opened fire on it, lying on their backs and firing into the night. It felt like some sort of mad regatta.

The Americans decided to get off while they still could. They had two amphibious cars, known as 'Ducks', which they loaded up with all their packs. But when the first amphibious vehicle was lowered into the water, it sank like a stone, much to our amusement.

When everyone had sobered up, our lorries were loaded onto barges and we were told to climb down the netting fixed to the sides of the ship. A kind sergeant carried my heavy pack down for me. If I'd had it on my back, I too would have disappeared under the waves. Fortunately the Germans had been pushed back, so there was no resistance and the barges reached the beach without incident. Standing on French soil again, I looked around me as dozens of legionnaires dropped to their knees and kissed the sand. Reaching down and picking up a handful of it, I allowed it to trickle from my fingers and blow away in the night breeze. 'Welcome home,' I heard a voice behind me say.

That night we slept on the beach, waiting until morning for the sappers to clear the minefields that surrounded us.

We moved on to Hyères, just outside Toulon, the first French town we'd seen since 1940, where we were received with sympathy and understanding by the local populace, who offered us bread and wine and wished us well. Still attached to General Clark's Fifth Army, we were to take part in what the Americans called Operation Anvil. It was the first time the Free French had been allowed to participate in the invasion of France. Like my fellow legionnaires, I felt very proud to be back and about to contribute to my adopted country's liberation from the Mediterranean to the Vosges. As in Italy, I followed in the footsteps of the French Expeditionary Corps during the battles for Mont des Oiseaux, Toulon, Avignon and Lyons, driving a huge lorry as, ahead of me, German resistance was systematically snuffed out.

At Lyons, Captain Miville, a very amusing Swiss who had trained horses in Ireland before the war, saw me struggling with the GMC truck and took me to one side.

'You can't go on like this,' he said, seeing the weariness etched in my face. 'I'll take you on if you like.'

He took me into his company to drive a much smaller truck which towed an anti-tank gun. The vehicle was much easier to handle, but its cargo meant it was far more dangerous to drive. It was my job to manoeuvre it into position, unhook it, turn round and go back for the next. There was a fair amount of shelling whenever I appeared because the Germans were very keen to knock me out before I got the gun into position.

Working with the anti-tank company, I was briefly reunited with Lieutenant Germain, the man who had given Arad to the general in Beirut. We reminisced fondly of the lovely white dog he had known as Georges.

'Do you remember how soft his ears were?' I asked him.

'Yes,' he said. 'I always said they'd make lovely gloves for de Bollardiere!' His talk made me mourn Arad's loss, and even more heartsick for Pierre and Aley. It also made me miss Josephine all the more. Whatever happened, after the war she and I would be reunited, of that I was determined.

After the battle for the medieval town of Autun, near Dijon, the 13DBLE recaptured a large English ambulance and I was asked to drive it. I also had a Citroën car in which I occasionally ferried the company commander around. The ambulance was a heavy vehicle to drive and I often had to change the tyres by myself, which wasn't at all easy. I went back to being on my own, lost in my own thoughts. Some days I barely spoke to a soul, and at night – once again – I was alone in the back of the ambulance, with nothing but memories for company.

By September, we were in the Vosges mountains. For the next two months, as the weather grew colder and the leaves turned, we fought our way towards the German border. By November, when we reached the towns of Belfort and Mulhouse, the going was especially hard. Belfort had been the venue for invasion after invasion for centuries, and a giant lion carved into the sandstone cliffs on the way to the red fortress bore testament to a celebrated former siege.

In the course of the fight for the Vosges, the 13DBLE lost 145 men, with 643 injured and more than two hundred cases of frostbite. In the mud, rain and snow for two long months, our supplies low and constantly short of fuel, we attacked without rest despite very heavy losses. The only thing that kept us going was the knowledge that Paris had been recaptured by the Allies, who had been led into the city by the French 2nd Armoured Division under General Leclerc. The swastika was wrenched from the Eiffel Tower and Parisians took to the streets in droves to celebrate their city's release from occupation.

General de Gaulle cried, '*Vive Paris!*' and the next morning he proclaimed the Fourth Republic.

For those of us still in the middle of a war, however, there was little cheer. The retreating Germans fought for every inch of land, destroying whole towns as they retreated and laying a series of mines and booby traps for those in pursuit. I divided my time between driving an ambulance or manoeuvring artillery as a member of the

101st Compagnie du Train and occasionally using my nursing skills to help treat the wounded.

In October 1944, I was promoted to the rank of *adjudant-chef* (warrant officer first class) for my role within the Legion. My uniform now bore the gold stripe with a fine red line across it. I also learned from one of the men that the Americans had taken to calling me 'that woman legionnaire' as they watched me drive back and forth past them all day. The latter title, more than the former, made me feel enormously proud. As for my promotion, I was just glad of the extra pay. Not that I had anywhere to spend it. I dreamed of treating myself to a hot bath, a sumptuous meal and a bone china eggcup when the madness ended.

Later that month, we heard some news that saddened us all. Field Marshal Erwin Rommel, the legendary commander and our erstwhile foe at Bir Hakeim, was dead. We learned much later how he'd met his end. He'd known of a plot to kill Hitler and the Führer had given him a stark choice. If he committed suicide, he'd be given a hero's funeral and his beloved wife Lucy and his son would be spared any dishonour. If he refused, he faced a trial and execution. Having said goodbye to his family, the legendary Desert Fox took poison. The German High Command claimed that he died from injuries received when his car was attacked by RAF planes, but no-one believed them. We received the news with solemn hearts. Unlike any other enemy commander, Rommel had inspired almost as much respect in us as he had in his own men.

In January 1945, after a Christmas Day that meant nothing more to me than all the days which came before, we were moved to Alsace, heading for Strasbourg via Elsenheim and Grussenheim. The Germans resisted forcefully in the forests surrounding these two villages and many were killed on both sides. I was run ragged ferrying the wounded back along narrow twisting trails to the dressing stations, my flask ever useful.

'It's much better to arrive at the surgeon's table a little

on the drunk side,' I'd inform my injured charges, before giving them a swig of rum or cognac or whatever I could lay my hands on. Among the wounded I offered drink to was young Hugo Geoffrey, shot in the arm at Elsenheim. A priest called Père Hirlemann helped me lift him off the battlefield and into my ambulance. He maintains to this day that by the time he arrived at the dressing station, thanks to me, he was in 'an advanced state of gaiety'.

In late January and early February, we were involved in Operation Nordwind, fighting to liberate the pretty half-timbered town of Colmar on the Adolf Hitler Line. Halfway through the battle, because it was so cold I was allowed to spend a few nights in the living room of a little house in the nearby town of Illhaeusern instead of in the ambulance. I was alone on the first night, just me and my little oil lamp in a room all to myself. The rest of the house was occupied by the other members of the American battalion. On the second night I was forced to share my room. Just as I was about to put out my light and go off to sleep, someone outside slid open my little window.

'Hey!' I yelled, reaching for a weapon and my greatcoat as an icy blast blew in. 'Who's there?'

'It's only us,' came the reply, and the heads of two stretcher bearers I knew very well poked in through the window. 'Sorry, Adjudant-Chef Travers, but we have orders to use this room.'

'Use this room?' I said anxiously, pulling my greatcoat closer around me. 'Use it for what?'

The two heads disappeared momentarily and then returned, pushing the fully clothed corpse of a legionnaire in through the hole. Four more followed.

'As a makeshift morgue until we can bury this lot in the morning,' they replied, climbing in and neatly arranging the bodies on the floor next to my bed.

'But you can't do that!' I protested, aghast at the sight of five dead men lying at my feet, their lifeless eyes staring at the ceiling. 'I'm sleeping in here.'

Climbing back out the way they'd come, the stretcher bearers popped their heads back in and smiled.

'Don't worry, Adjudant,' they said. 'These men won't be bothering you tonight.'

With that, they slammed the window shut.

Those last months of the campaign were among the toughest, in temperatures of -20°C (-4°F), in snow and ice, among tanks, mines, artillery barrage and snipers, and in vehicles largely equipped for desert warfare. The cold was paralysing, and yet throughout it the men were engaged in some of the most brutal battles of the war in Europe. Many suffered frostbite in the icy conditions and several died of it. None of life's cruelty was spared us.

The Free French losses had become so severe that two senior officers slipped away to Paris to see de Gaulle at the war ministry to complain that the Vichy generals were trying to destroy the 13DBLE. They were sending us on perpetual engagements, withholding recruits and supplies, and using us as a *'troupe de sacrifice'*, the officers claimed.

Oblivious to all the politics and the posturing, I closed in on myself once more, taking each day as it came and focusing on the need to stay alive, keep warm and get enough to eat. My hands numb and clumsy with cold, I'd pull my beret down over my ears and drive ambulances or huge gun carriers bearing howitzers through snowdrifts and along frozen roads twenty miles to the battle lines, as American troops saluted me. Never forgetting the comforts of life, I managed to arrange the rounding up and milking of the hundreds of scrawny cows abandoned on the higher pastures by fleeing farmers. In this way the troops could at least enjoy some warm milk. (I was hopeless at milking, so I enlisted the help of the stretcher bearers, who were far more adept.)

En route, I was awarded the Ordre de l'Armée, although I'm not sure what for. The citation read:

NCO of the highest order showing extraordinary selflessness and dedication. Having rallied to the cause of the Free French in 1940, she took part from that date in all the campaigns. Ever ready for the most risky missions, without any thought of danger to herself and with a coolness under fire which inspired the admiration of her fellow legionnaires. In all circumstances, she was an example of the finest qualities of the Legion. She was always the first to volunteer to bring the wounded back from the very front line, and was once again noted by all for the eight days of heavy fighting at Elsenheim from 22 to 30 January 1945, at her task night and day in the snow and the mud under artillery fire, mortars and deadly infantry attack.

The last few months of the war saw us struggling on as spring broke in the mountains and the news from the other fronts improved almost daily. The Allies thrust deep into the industrial heart of Germany, the Ruhr valley, and were closing in on Berlin. Roosevelt, Churchill and Stalin had met to work out the future of a free world. Then, on 28 April, Mussolini was shot and killed by Italian partisans. Two days later, Hitler was found dead in his Berlin bunker. Both men died alongside their long-term mistresses, Clara Petacci and Eva Braun.

By that time, our sojourn in the frozen mountains was over and we'd gradually been moved south to the much warmer climes of the Côte d'Azur, in an attempt to sweep up the last few pockets of German resistance. Our target was the massif of Authion thirty kilometres north of Nice, where men were still engaged in bitter fighting with a few recalcitrant Germans.

Waiting at the foot of the mountain on the evening of 7 May 1945, hoping that the casualties would be slight, I saw a corporal on the medical staff heading down from the village where the fighting was coming to an end.

'It's over! It's over!' he cried, driving his jeep full tilt towards us. We stood around staring at him and at one another, trying to take the information in.

'What's over?' I asked.

'The bloody war!' he shouted, jumping from his vehicle and running towards us. 'It's just been announced. An armistice has been signed.'

A young legionnaire lying in the back of my ambulance, his knee shattered by a sniper's bullet, burst into tears.

My initial reaction was of shock. I felt so winded by the news that I had to sit down. If what he·was saying really was true, then all that we'd been fighting for – the protection of France and of Europe from the Nazis – had finally been achieved. It had taken six years. And countless lives. But we had done it. We'd won.

Later that night, having dropped off my few charges, I gathered up some of my fellow officers, jumped in my ambulance and headed for Nice. I was taking them to a place I used to know quite well, a long time ago – the nightclub, Maxime's. Pouring from the ambulance in our droves, dirty and sweaty from the business of war, we quickly overran the club, which was filled with smart Niçois, ladies and gentlemen, waiters and bar staff, mostly people who had had a comfortable war.

'We demand free wine on the house for our valiant efforts on behalf of the citizens of France,' one of the officers announced, as the maître d' looked on impassively.

Sniffing at us as if we stank (which we probably did), he replied, 'I shall not be authorizing drinks on the house for anyone. Now kindly leave.'

Angrily, we left en masse, muttering under our breath about people like him having made money out of everyone during the occupation.

Further along the Promenade des Anglais, other bar owners were more sympathetic to us, toasting our success and allowing us to drink as much champagne as we could pour down our thirsty throats. Few would have recognized me – a scrawny woman in her American khaki – as a former customer. Dark round the eyes, gaunt, dirty and in army fatigues, I bore little resemblance to the Susan Travers of my youth, the gay young woman in sequinned dresses and cloche hats, drinking Manhattans and smoking cigarettes through an ivory holder, draped on the arm of her latest suitor.

It was hard to believe that after so many years the war was truly at an end. There was great happiness and pride. Over the next few days we celebrated madly, hugging each other and dancing and shouting our thanks that we'd made it through. There were parades and marches, barbecues and ceremonies galore. But inevitably there was great sadness too, chiefly for all those we'd lost along the way: for Amilakvari, and all the brave men of Eritrea, Syria, Bir Hakeim and El Alamein as well as those we'd lost more recently in Italy and France.

Although I was extremely glad that I was still alive, I couldn't help but fear that the armistice also meant an end to my great adventure. It was hard to make sense of it all after so many years travelling and fighting and being part of something so vast and consequential. I'd changed irrevocably. I was a different woman now to the shallow creature who'd listened, sipping a cocktail, to the declaration of war in a chateau near Poitiers. I'd become the person I'd always wanted to be from those earliest days of my childhood, the one I thought my father might be proud of.

If the end of the war meant an end to all that, then in some strange way I didn't want it to be over. Just as I had felt on that train journey from Rome all those years before, I knew I couldn't go back to the life I had previously led. I was thirty-five years old, single and altered beyond all recognition. In many ways I wanted to start again, with a new name and a new identity, and pretend that the old Susan Travers had died with the end of the war.

To help make up my mind, I took a few days off and drove myself to Cannes to have a look at Casa Longa, the house where I'd lived with my parents. I found it straight away but was surprised how much smaller it looked; more

294

faded, and of a different time. Some other family was living in it now, no doubt trying to pick up the threads of their life after German occupation. Children played in the garden where I had played with Chipmunk and Münch; a woman was brushing her hair in the upstairs window of the room that had been my mother's. I wondered if a man, smoking a pipe, was sitting in the drawing room reading the newspaper as my father so often had. I could hear a maid singing somewhere out the back, perhaps hanging out the washing or lifting home-made croissants out of the oven. Catching the eye of the woman in the window, I felt suddenly embarrassed and wandered shyly away.

I drove round to the humble single-storey home of Jeanne Martin, our former housekeeper, the woman who had helped me pack my bags for Florence and England, and was delighted to find her still there.

'Hello, Jeanne,' I said, holding out my hand.

Perplexed, she hesitated and stepped back from me slightly, wary of the stranger at her door.

'It's me, Susan,' I told her, smiling. Still her face remained blank. 'Susan Travers?' I tried to remind her.

Her eyes suddenly lit up and her face cracked into a huge grin. 'Susan! Susan!' she cried, holding my face in her hands. Tears spilling down her cheeks, she pulled me towards her and held me as if she never wanted to let me go. Her own face told how much she had suffered during the war. Her eyes were heavily lined and her skin ashen. Her hair, which had once been dark, glossy and thick, was grey and thin. There had been little work for her during the war, and her only son, accused of being a partisan, had been taken away by the Germans. 'Do you know anything? Can you help?' she asked, her eyes filling with tears. I promised to find out what I could.

She was clearly shocked by my appearance and asked after my health. 'But you're so thin,' she cried, poking a finger in my ribs. 'Haven't you been well?'

'I'm fine, Jeanne,' I replied. 'Really. It's just been a long war for us all.'

I was surprised to find how emotional seeing her made me feel. My head crowded with ghosts, I stood up abruptly and took my leave. Getting back into the old ambulance, shivering slightly from my brush with the past, I came to a decision about what I was going to do. I would go to Paris and try to find Pierre. He had been my *raison d'être* for so much of the war, and I had to know if it was really over between us. If it was, then I had to try to find a way of pulling together the torn threads of my life and starting anew.

What I desperately wanted, more than anything, was to stay with the Legion, my adopted family, the people with whom I felt most at home.

In the general confusion which followed the end of the war, I was able to make my way to Paris, where I was invited by the Free French to take part in the latest victory parade in front of General de Gaulle in May 1945. I thanked them warmly but refused to share their honour.

'Only the brave should march,' I told them, 'and I don't think I've been terribly brave.'

It was just as well I refused because when de Gaulle saw the Spears nurses lining up to take their place in the parade, he sent them all back, telling them there was still work to be done. The Spearettes were deeply hurt by this and many never forgave him for his Paris slight.

The parade went on regardless, and was certainly an event to be etched in the memory. Thousands of Parisians lined the streets, waving little tricolours and cheering happily. I stood amongst them, an anonymous face in the deliriously enthusiastic crowd, watching my many friends and colleagues march proudly past. Quietly, I saluted them.

In the weeks that followed I found lodging in a commandeered house at Meaux, east of Paris – which was the only place with any room left – and, after making discreet enquiries, found Pierre. Having been appointed senior commander of the French forces in both Germany and Britain at the end of the war, he was now on de Gaulle's personal staff as commander of the FFI, the Forces Françaises de l'Intérieur. He had also recently been appointed the Military Governor or Maréchal of Paris.

Living in Paris with his wife – who'd taken to her sickbed after the strain of the war – he was, among many things, in charge of the billeting of soldiers. Paris was full. Virtually every room was already spoken for, but I wanted to escape from the environs of the military camp. With the excuse that I needed something for the ambulance I still had use of, I managed to get an appointment to see him. It was the first time we had been together since Tunisia.

'Good afternoon, *mon général*,' I said, standing briskly to attention, as I was ushered into his rather grand office at Les Invalides. 'Or should I say, *mon maréchal*?' I clasped my hands together to stop them shaking.

He looked up. Remaining seated behind a huge desk, he appeared pleased to see me. 'At ease, *adjudant-chef*,' he said, acknowledging my promotion, as I stood down. Extending a hand, he smiled. 'Please, La Miss, sit down.'

Sitting opposite him, nervously fingering the beret on my lap, I began to tell him about the ambulance I was driving, the part I needed for it, and all manner of inconsequential matters. A secretary wandered in and out of the room as I spoke, handing him sheaves of papers to sign and documents to read. He took them from her, but never once took his eyes off me.

'Have you found somewhere to stay yet?' he interrupted.

I told him I was in Meaux, sharing a small house, and he shook his head. 'That won't do at all.' Sifting through some papers on his desk, he found the one he wanted, signed it and handed it to me. 'Move your belongings to a room at this address. It is a small but comfortable hotel and I'll know where to find you.'

Taking the piece of paper, I was just about to thank him when his secretary appeared once more, tapping her watch to remind me that I'd overrun my allotted two minutes. Rising to my feet shakily, I saluted Pierre and stood for a few seconds just enjoying being in the same room as him. Pinched hard at the elbow by his secretary, I was led from the room.

Pierre had been more than kind. My 'room' was in fact a comfortable suite in the Hotel St Regis, not far from the Champs-Elysées. While my former comrades-in-arms were queuing up at the camp latrines and allowed only one shower a week, I had the luxury of my own bathroom, sitting room and a large double bed. For my first few days in Paris, I slept and ate, bathed and read, lived night and day in a soft towelling dressing gown, my sweat- and blood-spattered uniform dispatched to the laundry for a steam clean.

Paris after the liberation still resembled a town in the middle of a war. Shops were shut or their windows empty, there were regular power cuts and the telephones didn't work. A latticework of tape still protected the windows in case of bomb blasts, there were petrol coupons and food shortages and the black market ruled the economy. The once gay city now seemed very drab, a vast military garrison with army vehicles on every street and check-points in every arrondissement. Men and women in uniform jostled with the civilian population who had suffered great hardships during the occupation. When the gaunt-faced deportees and inmates of the prison camps returned, wide-eyed, to their former homes, with tales of mass extermination and torture, they found that few among those trying to put the war behind them were prepared to listen.

Pierre treated me very nicely in Paris and saw me at the hotel as often as he could. I think he was truly sorry for the way things had been before. But he was incredibly busy and constantly in demand, not least from his wife, who was supposedly quite ill and seemed to be perma-nently attended by doctors. Still, I saw him when I could, occasionally visiting him in his office or snatching a few moments with him on the move.

He had a new chauffeur, a discreet young Parisian from the diplomatic service, who drove a very smart black Citroën. Pierre would collect me from the hotel en route to a meeting, just to be able to have a few minutes alone with me, and then I would wait for the meeting to end so that we could go and have a drink or a meal together somewhere where no-one knew us. It was a very peculiar time for me. For the first time in six years, I found that I no longer had a specific role to play. Instead of being behind the wheel and in uniform, doing a job of work, having a legitimate purpose, I was confined to my hotel room or the back of Pierre's car, in civilian clothes, waiting impatiently and watching the driver in the rear-view mirror. I seemed to have returned to the unhappy days of my pre-war life. I felt restless and more than a little afraid that this was what the future held. Most of all, I felt cheap.

I agonized over the direction my life appeared to be taking. Ever since the war had ended, I'd felt cast adrift. Now that I was back in the company of the one man who could anchor me again, I wasn't sure if this was what I really wanted.

Pierre never told me what he was thinking or what his long-term plans were. I assumed he'd simply like things to stay the way they were. Then, one day, out of the blue, I learned otherwise. I was in the back of his car with him, returning to my hotel after we'd dined out particularly well somewhere, reminiscing about the war, when he turned to me suddenly with a solemn announcement.

'If my wife should die, La Miss, I'd like to marry you,' he said quietly, taking my hand in his, his expression thoughtful. 'We have been through a great deal together and I think we should make a good match.'

Turning to face him, to be sure that I had heard him correctly, I stared open-mouthed at the man who had already been more of a husband to me than any other man. I'd always hoped that he loved me in his own way. I knew that he'd admired my free spirit and was more than happy to have me around in places like Beirut, but in Paris it was quite a different matter. Here he was a highly respected general – a governor. It was one thing to have an affair with a foreign chauffeur, but to take that mistress for a wife would have been professional and social suicide.

Yet, when I turned to look into his eyes I could see that, for the moment, he was being honest. He meant what he said, even if we both knew that marriage was not a realistic option. I squeezed his hand and, unable to speak, turned my head away to stare out of the window and watch the grey boulevards of Paris flashing by. For the first time in all the years I had known him, I accepted that, deep down, he loved me almost as much as I loved him. He'd never really known how to show it.

As if she had suspected what her husband was up to, the indomitable Madame Koenig rallied greatly in the next few weeks and was soon back to full health. Thereafter, Pierre became busier and busier and I saw him less and less. It became clear to me that, under the wing of de Gaulle and with the encouragement of his ambitious wife, my general was on a meteoric career path that would take him even further out of my orbit. I knew then that I would never get him back.

Shaking myself out of my reverie, I realized that the time had come to make a decision about my life. My prospects looked bleak; there would be no opportunity for me to continue in the Legion any more. The 13DBLE – the only brigade allowed to keep its name after the war because of its glory at Bir Hakeim – was about to be posted to Tunisia. I suspected that Pierre would have liked me to remain in Paris, but I realized that, despite my deep feelings for him, I was no longer prepared simply to be at his beck and call. I felt instinctively that I had to get away.

The only work I could find in Paris was in the displaced persons bureaux, helping to deal with some of the 100,000 people from nearly fifty nationalities who had flooded into Paris. It was a clerical and administrative job that held little appeal. There was nothing for me in England either. My parents were very elderly and living in Kent, I'd lost contact with my brother, and my friends were scattered to the four winds by war. I had no idea if many of them were dead or alive. In any event, I doubted if we'd now have anything in common.

All I knew was that I no longer wished to remain in Paris. Ideally I wanted to find a way to stay with all my friends. Speaking to Gabriel de Sairigné over a glass of wine in the foyer bar or officer's club at the Legion camp, I asked what he thought I should do.

'It's a pity you're not a man,' he said, rubbing his chin. 'Then you could join the Foreign Legion officially.'

Looking across the table at him, studying his frowning expression, I was hit by a sudden wild idea. 'Why not?' I said, my face brightening at the thought.

'What? A woman in the Legion?' he asked incredulously. 'You don't mean that. It's just not possible.'

'Not just any woman,' I said, beaming at him, 'but Adjudant-Chef Travers, from Bir Hakeim.' Taking another sip of wine, I began to hatch my plan.

Deciding to seek the advice of my major in the Legion, the avuncular Commandant Arnault with whom I had travelled so far, I made an appointment to see him at the recruitment office in central Paris. It was a drab, grey building that gave no hint of the adventures associated with it. Sitting down opposite him in his gloomy office I told him there was something I wanted to do.

'What?' he enquired amiably. Arnault had always treated me as an equal, for which I was truly grateful.

'Stay with the Legion,' I said simply, knowing how ridiculous that must have sounded but hoping that an ancillary role could be found for me somewhere. No women had ever been accepted into the Legion, indeed, to my knowledge, none had ever applied. As a volunteer with the Free French for the duration of the war only, I was expected to leave the army and the Foreign Legion once that war was over. But I didn't want to. It was my life and I desperately wanted to stay.

'Then do so,' said the *commandant*, realizing that I was

301

deadly serious. He slid something across his desk towards me. To my astonishment, it was a formal application form to become a member of France's noblest fighting force, the Légion Etrangère. 'The Legion is desperate for new volunteers now that the war is over and so many people are leaving, disillusioned with all the infighting with the Vichyists,' he continued. 'The Commission in charge of applications is going to be processing something like thirty thousand new applications from ex-prisoners of war and displaced persons over the next few months. Do you think that they will study each form individually? And anyway, where on that form does it ask you which gender you are? They assume all applicants to be male, so you wouldn't even have to tell a lie. You could legitimately apply to join as an *adjudant-chef* in logistics.'

I stared back at him, open-mouthed. This wasn't what I'd meant at all. I'd hoped for a civilian role. But his suggestion sounded so simple, so cut and dried. It wasn't wicked exactly, just a little duplicitous. I liked it.

I was being given an opportunity in a million and, without a moment's hesitation, I grabbed it. With his help, I filled out the form carefully, in my best handwriting, giving my full service details: my time at Bir Hakeim, my military medals and my track record during the remainder of the war. I failed to fill in the section which asked me whose son I was, or the part headed *Actes Liant L'Homme Au Service* ('acts linking the man to the service'). Commandant Arnault acted as my referee, giving me a glowing report and quoting the citation for my Italian campaign medal.

I could have given a false name or changed my name if I had wanted to, but I signed the form 'Travers, Susan Mary Gillian, *nationalité anglaise*'. It wasn't my fault if they were processing hundreds of applications from foreign nationals with peculiar names, or that the name Susan (rather than Suzanne) meant little or nothing to the French. After all, the name Mary was similar to Marie, which was often used as a male prefix, as in Pierre's name.

There were no medical examinations for applicants at that time – if you'd survived the war, you were assumed to be healthy – so no doctor would have to look me over. Nothing more needed to be said.

Passing the form back to Commandant Arnault, I grinned at him broadly. I felt like hugging him there and then, but I held myself back. That would have been most *irrégulier*.

Now all I had to do was wait.

15

A PAGE TURNED

'Though now this grained face of mine be hid
In sap-consuming winter's drizzled snow,
And all the conduits of my blood froze up,
Yet hath my light of night some memory.'
WILLIAM SHAKESPEARE, *THE COMEDY OF ERRORS*

The impossible came to pass. For the first time in the history of the French Foreign Legion, a woman was admitted to its ranks as an *adjudant-chef* in the logistics division and allowed to have a special regimental roll number, 22166, as only legionnaires can. The official date on which I was accepted was 28 June 1945. I was a legionnaire heart and soul, as I had proved to all my comrades, and now I was one in body too. Yes, I'd bucked the system slightly, but I'd been accepted on my own merits as a soldier, having done my duty for the country I loved.

To this day I have no idea if I was accepted out of ignorance or because a special exception was made in my case. I know that if General de Gaulle had ever found out, he would almost certainly have forbidden it. I rather suspect that Pierre may have had a hand in it somewhere along the line, as he was on the board reviewing new applicants at the time. If it was him who'd secretly authorized the overturning of the 144-year-old rule forbidding women entry, then I believe it to have been his kindest farewell gift and, perhaps, his way of thanking me for saving his life.

Receiving orders that I was to leave for Tunisia in August 1945, I decided to go to England first and visit my parents. I hadn't seen them for nearly six years. Travelling to London and then down to Kent I was struck by the drabness everywhere. London had been badly damaged during the relentless bombing campaign and whole areas were now unrecognizable to me. But, in true British style, the trains still ran, the chimes of Big Ben still sounded on the quarter hour and people carried on working, living and coping, as they had always done.

My parents were pleased to see me, and seemed to have been buoyed by the war rather than diminished by it. Father still had his Home Guard uniform and Mother spoke cheerily of the household economies she'd made under strict rationing. Laurence, they said, was planning to return to the bar after his diplomatic service and Aunt Hilda was well and had steadfastly remained in London throughout the Blitz.

'How was your war, Susan?' Father asked me over a dinner of thin soup, boiled ham and cabbage.

'Oh, you know,' I replied, taking a mouthful of soup. 'Fairly quiet.'

My father nodded and carried on eating. 'And what are your plans now?' he asked, wiping his mouth.

I paused for a moment. 'I've joined the French Foreign Legion,' I said, pushing my soup plate away from me slightly.

My mother's silver spoon clattered onto her plate, making the kind of din I could only dream about when I was a child in Devon. I stifled a laugh.

Father stopped eating and studied my expression for a moment. Mother sat, her bottom lip trembling, waiting for him to say something, do something. Staring Father out with a new-found defiance – born of places like Eritrea, Syria, Bir Hakeim, and the killing fields of Italy and France – I didn't flinch from his steady gaze.

Realizing at last that I was more than capable of looking after myself, he half-smiled. 'Well, good for you,' he said, breaking off a piece of dark dry bread. 'Eh, Mother? I say, good for Susan.'

My mother sat stock still, staring at me as if she'd never seen me before in her life. I could almost see her wondering what on earth I was doing at her dinner table.

Back in Paris for August, I prepared to leave for Tunisia to start my post-war role as a legionnaire. Not keen to travel long distances across land again, I approached the wife of General Mast, the new Governor of Tunisia, and asked if she could advise me on the best way to get to the port of Sousse. Unlike any other junior legionnaire before, or probably since, thanks to the kindness of Madame Mast I arrived in Sousse in the general's private plane, along with the general himself and all his staff.

Throughout my time in Tunisia, no-one showed any astonishment at the idea of a woman in the Legion or asked why I was there. The men themselves were from many different nations and had joined the Legion for many different reasons, but they never asked each other why. It was an unwritten rule that you didn't. And so they didn't think to question me either. I was one of them, they accepted that fact and me with it. As an officer, I had my own room, excellent pay of £12 10s a week and ate three good meals a day, with coffee and wine.

There was no official Legion uniform for women and so, abandoning the male-issue trousers and shorts of the war, I adapted a khaki-coloured pencil skirt to make up the bottom part of my uniform. Placed in charge of the '*foyer des légionnaires*', a bar or canteen for the rank and file, I had to organize the staff, taste and buy the wine and keep the accounts. It was not particularly demanding work, nor did it allow me any military action or even to wear a kepi, but I felt I'd seen enough action for a lifetime. Most of all, I was with the Legion, back in North Africa, a place which held so many memories.

Sousse was a large and bustling port, with impressive fortifications flanked by beautiful sandy beaches and rolling verdant hills. The old port, below the modern city, had been heavily battered during the war and was only just beginning to emerge from the smoking rubble. Allied planes had attacked it relentlessly during the German occupation and left it in a state of blackened decay. Even the palm trees along the seafront were bent double with the weariness of war. As part of the considerable French force returned to help restore order and rebuild the once thriving port, we were welcomed back with open arms. Our encampment was on the outskirts and pleasant enough. I had good living conditions and plenty to do, and as the weeks passed I felt more and more able to lift my head and face the world again.

I took my job very seriously, sampling the red wine with the tastes of the fussy legionnaires in mind, and sacking my corporal when I first arrived after learning that he was illegally trading on the black market. I would taste the wine each morning after breakfast and then buy a barrel or two, asking an old legionnaire to load it onto a mule cart for me before we zigzagged home.

'Can't you make the mule go in a straight line?' I would have to ask the driver. More often than not, he had sampled a little too freely of the product himself and was letting slip the reins.

I was treated with the greatest deference by my colleagues, many of whom I knew from our years together in the war. I was loved and respected, but from afar. Given our shared history, my relationship with them was rather odd. I was an officer now and could no longer associate with many of those I'd been most friendly with. I was lonelier than I'd expected to be. Nobody approached me; nobody dared to. Many of them had heard whispers about my relationship with Conoral Kounig – by now a French legend – and, I think, feared me a little for it.

I was never more grateful for the companionship of a dog. I'd brought Rebecca with me. She was the daughter of my lovely Josephine, with whom I'd been reunited almost as soon as I returned to Tunisian soil. Rebecca was the spitting image of Josephine, who was happily settled with her adoptive family, 'married' to a handsome hound and far too accustomed to her way of life to want to move.

It was in Sousse that I first got to know a young NCO four years my junior. His name was Nicolas Schlegelmilch and he had the dark features and strong jaw of a central European. Born in Alsace, the Catholic son of a stone-mason, Nicolas had joined the Legion before the war and then fought with the 6th Regiment of the Legion (mainly against Australian forces) until the Vichy defeat in Syria, when he switched sides. He was confident and charming, and he clearly didn't hold with the view that I was someone to be admired only from afar. I'd met him several months earlier in the NCOs' mess at our camp just outside Paris when he had approached me, an inquisitive look in his eye, accompanied by a rather over-anxious young colleague.

'My name is Nicolas Schlegelmilch,' he said, extending a large, hairy hand. 'I understand you're the famous La Miss.'

I took his hand and shook it, slightly startled by his forward approach and his steely grey eyes deep set under dark eyebrows. I looked at the badges on his shoulder and noted that I was of a higher rank.

His colleague was beside himself with embarrassment and apologized to me. Taking Nicolas's arm, he began to lead him away. 'You shouldn't be talking to her like that. Only the officers are allowed to call her La Miss. She's way out of your league,' I heard him whisper.

Nicolas turned back to me and smiled. I noticed he had an attractive mouth and that his face was deeply creased around it, as if he laughed a lot. 'Good to meet you . . . La Miss,' he said, before walking away.

I was surprised to find myself returning his smile.

I'd forgotten all about him until he approached me again in Sousse, this time alone. It was his eyes I remembered first. They were almost black in the bright Mediterranean light.

'We meet again,' he said, extending his hand. 'Nicolas Schlegelmilch. You remember? Paris?'

'Yes, of course,' I said, shaking his hand. 'You were a little over-familiar, as I recall.'

He smiled again, the creases deepening on his face. 'That's me,' he admitted, unabashed. 'And as I'm already a condemned man, may I blacken my record still further by inviting the Legion's only female member for a drink?'

I was surprised by the attentions of this young man and more than a little flattered. It had been a long time since anyone had paid me a compliment. I accepted his invitation, and the next. He seemed gentle, intelligent and respectful. He never pried about my personal life, or my past, and I believed that he sensed my inner sadness.

Nicolas was nothing like Pierre in either appearance or manner; he was very physical and rather deep and thoughtful. Although I was correct in my suspicions about his mischievous side, he could also be quite sombre when he wanted to be. His sense of humour was certainly very different from mine, but he made me laugh again and I enjoyed his company.

Gradually, I found myself growing more and more fond of him. I looked forward to our dates and often thought of him when he wasn't with me. Before too long, and to my great surprise, I realized that I was allowing my heart to love him a little.

Pierre and all that he had meant to me was behind me now. I had to move forward and, with Nicolas's help, I was able to. After a long and enjoyable courtship that Tunisian winter, we became lovers. I had to admit that I relished being in the arms of a man again, especially one so passionate and intense.

In February 1946, the 13DBLE was sent on a two-year posting to Indo-China at the start of what was to become the terrible Vietnam War. The Japanese had occupied the

309

former French colony in 1940 and been defeated five years later. The rebel Viet Minh nationalists led by Ho Chi-Minh declared an independent republic and took to arms to prevent the restoration of French rule. The Legion were sent to try to restore order. It was to be a bitter and, ultimately, hopeless war, a fight without mercy.

Commandant Arnault came with us, along with Colonel Geoffrey (rising fast since our first meeting on the boat to Naples) and my old friends Gabriel de Sairigné and the future prime minister Pierre Messmer. My dog Rebecca came too. We were a battalion strong, four companies in all and the officers were allowed to take their wives. (In fact, very few of the legionnaires had wives. The men weren't allowed to marry; only the NCOs could take wives after a while. There were some who later lived with native girls and even married them in village ceremonies.) I knew some of the officers' wives, such as Mesdames Geoffrey and de Sairigné.

Arriving in bustling Saigon, the French colonial capital with its broad boulevards and Parisian-style pavement cafés, we found ourselves in a new, tropical environment, plagued by mosquitoes, heat and disease. Nicolas threw himself into life as a working soldier, fighting running battles with the local Viet Minh, while I ran the bar for the men at the rural base at Hoc-Mon and was in charge of supplies. I also spent much of my time visiting the sick and wounded in the hospital, because I spoke German and by then many of the legionnaires were German.

Occasionally, as with the Jock Columns, there were diversionary trips away from the humdrum life at the base. The men used to go out in armed groups to round up the Viet Minh from the bush to bring them in for questioning. After my experiences in Europe and North Africa, I was detached to follow on in an ambulance, in case it was needed. It often was. The danger with the Viet Minh was that if you had a gun and they wanted it, you were dead. It was unsafe for anyone to be alone in the bush, or out alone in the camp after dark. I'd gather up

310

many wounded and dead from both sides during those running battles and ferry them back to the hospitals. In some ways it was a return to the bad old days.

The climate was appalling. We felt permanently tired and looked awful. Everyone was yellow. It was very hot and sticky. You had to take something foul every day for malaria and you couldn't drink the water. We slept under mosquito nets every night and drank cold tea, made with boiled water. The soldiers ate and drank anything and, consequently, dysentery and malaria were rife. I tried to eat in the officers' mess as much as possible. Nicolas had to eat in the NCOs' mess and we'd meet up afterwards.

The only escape from the heat and the flies was a weekend trip to Da Lat, which was in the north, in the mountains above the rainforests and much cooler. Da Lat was similar to an Indian hill station, acting as a refuge for the wives and exhausted officers. But the road up to it was a perilous one, and convoys had to be accompanied by armed guards for fear of ambush. I loved to escape up there with Rebecca whenever I could, but some of the other women were too afraid to go.

Way out in the Far East, it was difficult to keep track of what had happened to Pierre, but I made discreet enquiries where I could. I discovered that, as I had suspected, he had done very well. Promoted to lieutenant-general and then to full general, he was appointed French commander-in-chief in Germany by de Gaulle, personally helping to negotiate the armistice with General Eisenhower and the Allies in Baden Baden. It was my general who'd arrested the former Vichy leader Marshal Philippe Pétain and who interned him in the fortress at Montrouge.

He'd been sent by de Gaulle to head the reception committee at the French border when Pétain was handed over by the Swiss. Famously, Pétain had tried three times to shake Koenig's hand and each time Koenig had stood rigidly to attention, his hands by his sides. For the sake of the Jews and resistance fighters and all those who'd been killed or handed over to the Germans by the Vichy government during the occupation, he refused to acknowledge him. Accompanying Pétain back to Paris for trial (where he was found guilty of treason and sentenced to death, a sentence commuted to life imprisonment), my Pierre had become a figure of national importance. Most importantly, he was still married and I knew that as long as that remained the case, he would never contact me.

My relationship with Nicolas was a great comfort. I grew to love him in my own way and, if I couldn't be with Pierre, I couldn't think of a better person to be with. I knew that, if he wanted it too, I was ready to spend the rest of my life with him. We were also very good friends. He was able to ease the pain in my heart and help me forget my former sadness.

He, too, had a troubled past. In Beirut, after a patrol, he'd accidentally shot and killed a comrade. He was given a choice between imprisonment or service on the front lines. He chose the front. But he'd never been able to forgive himself or forget what had happened. Nor was he able to talk about it. It was a tragic event which was to cloud the remainder of his life. He touched on it only once, at the beginning of our relationship, and never mentioned it again.

'I did something once,' he told me. 'Something I can never tell you about.' The anguish it caused him was still evident.

I felt that he was trying to tell me, in his own quiet way, that if I could find it in my heart to bury the ghosts of my past, then he would try to do the same. We came to an unspoken agreement and one which suited me very well. Nicolas was the kindest man I'd ever met – which was just as well because within a year, I needed his understanding more than ever before.

Walking in Saigon a few weeks later, I stopped and took his hand. 'I'm going to have your baby,' I said, blurting it out just as we were about to cross the busy street. 'I've just come from the doctor and he's confirmed it.'

312

Looking anxiously into Nicolas's face, I wondered what he would say and how he would react. I hoped that I wouldn't scare him off. Stopping mid-stride and studying my expression, he remained grim-faced and silent for several seconds. I felt vaguely sick and thought I might faint.

Then, without saying anything, he took my face in his hands and kissed me tenderly on both cheeks. 'Well then, my dear,' he said, 'we'd better get married, hadn't we?'

Unable to speak, I buried my face in his chest and held him very tight. Finally catching my breath, I looked up at him and smiled. 'All right then,' I said. 'We will.'

It was, I knew, a very gallant offer, and my first genuine marriage proposal in thirty-seven years.

It was an awful business getting permission to be married. French legionnaires weren't supposed to marry foreigners and we had a terrible time getting all the necessary papers signed and agreed. I needed something called a *casier judiciaire*, which is basically a police record. All the French have one, a clean sheet or a full one depending on their character. The British never issued such records but unless I could produce one I couldn't marry a French soldier: that was the law of the land. I had to go to the British consul and to the head of the Legion. Between them, they arranged for me to have a *casier judiciaire* drafted so that I could marry Nicolas.

We were wed in Hoc-Mon in April 1947 at a simple ceremony. Our 'bridesmaids' were Rebecca and Peggy, Rebecca's sister, who belonged to Commandant Arnault. We went to the mayor for the civil ceremony and then to the little Catholic church for a blessing, travelling in a flower-decked military jeep with the dogs sitting on the back seat, adorned with red, white and blue bows. Also present were Pierre Messmer, by then a principal private secretary in Indo-China, and his wife, Gabriel de Sairigné, now a colonel and in command of the Legion, and several other friends and colleagues from the Second World War.

Nicolas's many NCO friends came along too, and were a little uneasy in the company of so many high-ranking officials.

Dressed in a white version of my uniform, which I'd had specially made, and carrying a huge bouquet of red and green tropical flowers (the official colours of the Legion) and local grasses, I was given away by the kindly Commandant Arnault. Madame de Sairigné accompanied Nicolas, who was also dressed in white and looked extremely handsome. The *aumônier* or chaplain was Père Hirlemann, who'd served with us in Italy. Our fellow legionnaires gave us a guard of honour with fixed bayonets as we left the little church, watched curiously from the wings by the natives.

There was a big dinner afterwards, at which we were presented with a beautiful leather-bound book of traditional songs of the Legion, with the famous grenade emblem embossed on the cover. I was very touched and have kept it ever since. I can honestly say that on that day I felt truly happy. I had found a kind of peace at last as the wife of a legionnaire, settling for someone I knew would protect and care for me.

We began married life at Nicolas's little flat in Hoc-Mon, which was above an old theatre. There was no honeymoon as I was four months pregnant and it was too dangerous for me to travel anywhere in a war zone. After a night on our own in the flat, it was back to work as usual.

The next few months were spent preparing for the birth of our child. I took on a native *femme de chambre* and a female Chinese cook called Assam, who was nothing like the marvellous Selim of the past. Being an officer, I had an orderly, whom Nicolas shared. I was very well during my pregnancy, although because of the heat and general discomfort I had to be regularly checked for high blood pressure and other possible problems. To be expecting my first child in my late thirties was very unusual for the time.

When I went into labour, one of the drivers drove me to

the Clinic St Paul in Saigon, run by nuns. It was a long and difficult labour and the doctor had to use forceps to get the baby out. I was so tired by the end of it all that when this howling little bundle was finally laid in my arms on the afternoon of 4 September 1947, I was unable to feel anything very much.

Nicolas was over the moon. He came to the clinic as soon as he heard and rushed in to see me and the infant.

'Is it a boy?' he asked excitedly, and one of the nuns nodded. His face lit up like a firecracker, and he beamed at me with such love and happiness that I couldn't help but feel happy too. It was considered a great triumph for a legionnaire to have a son.

The next night, he threw a huge party for the other NCOs in Hoc-Mon and they all got so drunk they fired off the mortar guns, waking the *commandant*.

Contacting them by telephone, Commandant Arnault asked anxiously, 'Are you being attacked?'

'No,' said a drunken Nicolas. 'But I have a son.'

Baby François had everything done for him and wanted for nothing. He had a beautiful lace-covered crib and the *femme de chambre* attended to his every need. I spent my time trying to run an orderly household for my new family. I wasn't quite as successful at it as I had been in Aley, however. Assam couldn't speak French and I couldn't speak Chinese so it was impossible to get her to cook French food or, indeed, anything that wasn't Chinese. Eventually she left and I had to manage on my own until we were transferred to Saigon.

Nicolas had a new job working in the bureau of the colonel, which was a big change for him, and I was happy to be closer to the doctors and the hospital, with a small baby in a tropical climate. In fact, I needn't have worried. François was a bouncing baby boy. We lived on the out-skirts of town in a small concrete villa with a verandah and a garden. The Legion camp was close by, at a place called Djadine just outside the city.

Saigon was much more cosmopolitan than the bush and

I got to know it well, doing all my shopping and much of my socializing in town. My friends Madame de Sairigné (François's godmother) and Madame Geoffrey both had small babies the same age as mine. Together with our children we'd travel to Da Lat for the weekends and short holidays, while our husbands remained in the city. It was a happy and peaceful period and one in which I experienced the joys of motherhood for the first time.

It was in Saigon that I decided to leave the Legion, resigning my commission so that I could concentrate on being a mother and wife. Army life had given me the most marvellous opportunities to do exciting things, opportunities I'd grabbed with both hands, and now all of that was over. I had no regrets. Not only had I become the first woman legionnaire, but I was the first legionnaire to marry another legionnaire, fall pregnant and have a baby. Still technically in the Legion and being paid during the pregnancy, I had officially been on leave until I handed in my resignation.

'Was it all worth it?' Commandant Arnault asked me when I went to tell him. 'I mean, are you glad you joined?'

'Oh, yes, sir,' I enthused. 'If I had to do it all over again, I wouldn't change a thing.'

We spent two years in Indo-China and, by and large, it was a very happy time. Nicolas and I were in love, we had a beautiful son and we were surrounded by friends. The only sadness came in March 1948. Gabriel de Sairigné, hero of Bir Hakeim, was en route to the hill station at Da Lat to join his heavily pregnant young wife and little girl for a short break. They had gone ahead, flying to avoid any dangers, and he followed on, driving his jeep as part of a large convoy of eighty vehicles protected by a company of legionnaires. In another jeep were Lieutenant Hugo Geoffrey and his wife and son, who were planning a short holiday in the mountains.

The Viet Minh placed a tree across the road, blocking it, and then attacked the civilian vehicles first. Men, women and children were strafed with gunfire and their vehicles set on fire. Snipers hiding in the thick forest picked off those fleeing to safety, and grenades and mines did the rest. Prisoners were snatched and used as human shields in the fighting which raged for two hours. Some two thousand Viet Minh and twenty machine-guns were used in the attack. More than a hundred French were killed and wounded, including women and children. Some forty vehicles were destroyed. More than a hundred prisoners were taken, among them Lieutenant Geoffrey, his wife and son (who all later escaped).

Gabriel de Sairigné was shot in the head and mortally wounded. A sergeant dragged him from the car and into some bushes, where he later died. A great soldier and an old friend of both Dimitri Amilakvari and General Koenig, Gabriel had been much loved. He was one of the last links I had with those at Bir Hakeim. I attended his funeral with a heavy heart.

In 1948, having served the mandatory two years in Indo-China, after which the men were allowed a two-year break from the relentless climate, Nicolas was transferred to the Legion base at Meknès in Morocco, and François and I moved with him. Morocco had been occupied by the Allies during the war, as they drove the Germans out of North Africa. After the war, Sultan Sidi Mohammed ben Youssef led an independence movement, which threatened to turn into a savage guerrilla war like the one that was to convulse neighbouring Algeria. In both countries, it became the task of the Legion to maintain a French pro-tectorate and keep order.

But before we started a new life back in North Africa, I went home to England with my husband and child for a brief visit to my ageing parents. We had kept in touch by letter and they knew that I was married and had a child, but had never met either of them. Arriving in Kent, where they now lived in a little house near Seal, I laid my baby son in Father's arms.

'Here you are, Grandfather,' I said. 'Meet your first grandchild.'

He looked at the wriggling infant and then up at me, and said nothing. But, somewhere deep within his watery old eyes, I thought I could tell that I had finally made him proud.

Mother was delighted with her new grandson and couldn't wait to hold him. I suppose it brought back fond memories of baby Laurence. But she was less kind to Nicolas, whom she believed to be below my class.

'I should have thought you could have done better than an NCO,' she told me in the parlour as Nicolas and Father walked in the garden. I stared at her with quiet contempt and said nothing. A few days later, we left. I never told her that I was pregnant with my second child.

Arriving at Meknès in Morocco and posted to the garrison village of El Hajeb above the town with Nicolas and François, I hoped for a peaceful two years there with my new and growing family. Morocco was not entirely pacified, but the pro-independence activists were not causing too much trouble at that time, and I didn't expect my husband to be away very much, which was just as well because the people at the camp were not nearly as friendly or welcoming as we had hoped they would be.

On 6 April 1949 our second son came into the world. Tom was a beautiful, happy child whom everybody adored, and I hoped that with Nicolas's help we would soon be able to settle in a bit better to life in this strange land.

But it was not to be. The situation in Indo-China worsened considerably, with French forces being squeezed tighter and tighter by the Viet Minh. More legionnaires were desperately needed and in May 1949 – six weeks after Tom was born – Nicolas was summoned back to the front lines as part of the 4th Regiment. He left me alone with François and Tom, surrounded by strangers. Sitting on the steps of our little house, watching the convoys of lorries leaving, I threw my arm around Rebecca's shaggy neck.

'Now, *chérie*, we're all alone,' I told her.

I didn't have any friends in Morocco. Being an officer myself but married to an NCO, I was accepted by neither side. The officers' wives thought I was beneath them and the NCOs thought me stuck up. I had fallen between two stools and people were very unkind. I lived in a tiny house with a small garden, right on the road on the outskirts of the garrison, with only Rebecca and an Arab woman servant called Zena for company. Letters from Nicolas were few and far between and I often went for months without a word. My time in Morocco was one of the unhappiest periods of my life.

Left to cope on my own in the heat and hostility of North Africa with two demanding children, I had a recurrence of back problems I had suffered from in my teens. I had to have an operation and was in hospital for fifteen days. Without friends or family, I had to leave my children in the care of native women. The wives in the camp frowned on that, but none offered to take the children for me. 'It's just not done,' I heard one woman say about my temporary fostering arrangement, but I had to leave them with someone and there was no-one else around. In desperation, I'd written to my mother to ask her to come to Morocco and help me. To her credit she acquired all the necessary papers, but she never came.

When I was able to walk again, I returned home only to sit in a chair for several weeks, depressed and in pain. All I could do was drink sweet mint tea and watch Zena care for my two demanding children. François had reacted very badly to the absence of his father and when I came out of hospital he refused to have anything to do with me. He seemed to resent his younger brother tremendously. In his young mind, he'd associated Tom's arrival with Nicolas's departure and my debilitation. He would push his younger brother away and refuse to play with him. He cried all the time and wouldn't eat. I only hoped that when Nicolas returned, which I expected to be sooner rather than later, the boy would be happy once more.

But Nicolas, after six months in Lang Son, deep in the northern jungles of Indo-China, was taken seriously ill. The initial diagnosis was amoebic dysentery, but it soon became apparent that it was something far more serious than that. He'd been sent back to the tropics too early; his body had been given no time to build up a resistance to disease. The letters I received from the hospital gave little indication of how ill he was.

'*This is to inform you that your husband is in hospital and being treated for amoebic dysentery,*' the letters read. '*He is being well cared for and sends his love.*'

There was never any mention of when he was coming back. I learned later that Nicolas had very nearly died and was in hospital for almost a year. Eventually, eighteen months after he'd left me and our two children, he was shipped home.

I was so excited. With Zena's help, I cleaned and tidied the house, prepared some nice meals and made myself look my most presentable. Driving to the camp to meet him off the truck, I looked forward to seeing his face once more. When the truck came to a halt, I fully expected to see him jump down from the back as usual. Others did, men whose faces I recognized as having gone with him, but there was no sign of my husband. Confused, I stepped closer. A nurse was helping a little old man off the truck. Suddenly I realized that the 'little old man' was my Nicolas.

I barely recognized him. The last time I'd seen him, he'd been healthy and very good-looking. Now he was pale and sallow and terribly thin. His eyes had sunk into their sockets and his skin was grey. He could hardly walk. There was no romantic homecoming or rushing into each other's arms. He looked, and smelled, like a sick old man. I was unable to hide my shock.

'Hello, darling,' I said, taking his hand, but his eyes looked blankly at me.

320

The Nicolas I brought home was completely different from the man I'd waved goodbye to. Tucked up in bed, or in a chair under a blanket, he was barely able to feed himself. He slept a great deal and clearly needed peace and quiet, and our two noisy toddlers hardly provided that. François no longer knew his father and Tom never had, but they were both very excited at having a man in the house and wanted nothing more than to clamber all over him. Unable to cope with them or me, Nicolas booked himself back into hospital in Meknès to convalesce. He remained there for several weeks, and I visited him as often as I could, hoping to see some gradual signs of improvement.

'How are you feeling today?' I'd ask cheerfully, bringing him fruit and pleased to see that he'd gained a little weight.

But turning his head away to look out of the window, he'd shrug and mumble something, his eyes still dead to me.

One day I went to visit him and his bed was empty, the sheets removed.

'Where is my husband?' I asked the matron. My heart was in my mouth.

'He's been posted back to his regiment,' she replied. 'Didn't you know?'

Having been discharged from hospital, Nicolas had elected to move back into the barracks instead of coming home.

I followed him and found him in the mess, stirring a cup of coffee.

'What's going on?' I asked, a little fearfully.

'I don't think things are going to work out between us,' Nicolas said, rather coldly. 'I think maybe it would be best if we ended this before anyone gets hurt.' He lifted his head and stared at me for the first time in weeks.

Fighting to hide my feelings, clenching my hands together until my knuckles showed through the skin, I listened to what he was trying to tell me.

'Why?' I asked, after a time.

'Because everything's changed,' was all he said. He went back to stirring his coffee.

Silently, I picked up my bag and coat and left the room.

All the way home, I berated myself. 'You should never have expected happiness,' I said aloud. The marriage I'd longed for seemed doomed.

But my happiness was not the only thing that bothered me. If I was no longer married to Nicolas, then I was also homeless, along with my two children. There would be no place for me in the Legion camp. I had no money and no other options. I would have to return to England and live off the charity of my parents, a thought which filled me with dread.

After several days of agonizing about my future, I went to see Nicolas again.

'This is ridiculous,' I said, in feisty mood. 'You're on your own here and miserable, and I'm on my own and miserable at home, and it will all have been for nothing. At least for the sake of the children, can't we try again?'

There was no-one else involved, and Nicolas admitted that he was missing his sons, the thought of whom had sustained him in Indo-China. Eventually he agreed to move back into the garrison house, chiefly for the children's sake. I have no idea what took place in the Far East, or what change his illness brought about in his mind, but the result was that we were no longer the same as a couple. Clinically, sensibly, as parents and adults, we'd resolved to settle down and remain together. But we were never as close again.

Nicolas had also lost his love of the Legion. Not long afterwards we were transferred to Algeria so that he could play his part in crushing the bitter war of independence, but he found it almost impossible to return to service life or communicate with his fellow soldiers. Within a few months, his enlistment period was up and he decided not to sign up for another five years.

Contacting an old friend, an officer from the Legion, he

322

managed to secure himself a job as an archivist for the company which later became Elf Petroleum in Montpellier in France. It was 1950 when he first donned a suit and went to work as a civilian, in a position he was to keep for eighteen years.

Living back in France was a considerable culture shock after a decade in Africa and the Tropics. I had no choice but to become a housewife and mother. I had a *femme de ménage* but my new role was to stay at home and care for my young children while Nicholas went off to work each day. It took a great deal of getting used to at first, but with two demanding children and the company of the ever-faithful Rebecca, I was able to keep myself from going mad with boredom.

When Elf transferred to Villennes and then Paris, Nicolas moved with them and commuted into the city each day by train. Later, he got a desk job with the Banque Franco-Allemande, coming home on the same train every night to have supper, watch television and help me wash up the dishes. He became nothing more than a face in the crowd, another office worker going to and from work in a suit and hat. Few who'd seen him would have thought him anything more remarkable than a clerk.

Nicolas and I weren't ones to dwell too deeply on our previous lives and reminiscences and I told Nicolas little about my earlier life. I didn't see the point. It would only have hurt him and, if he'd ever heard rumours of my affair with Pierre, he never mentioned them. As the boys grew up, they sometimes listened to our anecdotes, but they learned not to ask too many questions. They knew we'd been in the Legion and in North Africa, but few of the details.

In 1952, my father died. He was ninety. The last time I'd seen him, he'd been confined to his bed and even more grumpy than usual. Nothing meaningful was said between us. I knew he was dying and so did he, but this didn't seem to be the moment to try to open long-closed lines of communication.

'Goodbye then, Father,' I said, my manner as awkward with him then as it had been when I was a child.

'Adieu,' he replied, as I kissed him lightly on the cheek.

I'd spent so much of my life seeking his approval that having never really obtained it, his death only left me feeling more empty. Any chance to impress him now was gone, and I felt cheated.

I asked my mother if I should come home for the funeral, and she told me not to bother. I tried to analyse my lack of tears, and wondered at the hardened woman I must have turned into. I think from an early age I had learned to harden my heart to protect myself from my father's coldness.

Visiting my mother in England a few months later, I tried to broach the subject with her.

'Do you miss Father?' I asked.

'Not terribly,' she replied.

'Neither do I,' I said honestly. 'I'm not sure he was a very good father, you know.' I watched her face.

'Perhaps you weren't a very good daughter,' Mother replied stiffly.

The wounds between us had never really healed. She died of a heart attack a few years later, not long after her beloved sister Hilda. I went to her meagre funeral in Folkestone and didn't cry then either. My brother Laurence was there as well, looking much older and greyer. It was one of the last times I was to see him alive.

By the time I reached middle age, a little disillusioned with life and feeling tired, I went on my annual 'cure' to the spa of La Preste in the Pyrenees, for three weeks' rest. My parents were dead, my children were in school, and Nicolas and I were alone.

I took with me the secret war diaries I had written in Tunisia shortly after joining the Legion, an aide-mémoire of my adventures from West Africa to Bir Hakeim. I'd found them in the bottom of a cupboard when I was packing and decided to take them along. Much of my time in

324

that hotel room that spring was spent systematically rewriting them. I sanitized every aspect of my life before Nicolas, so that I was left with a historical but rather impersonal account of my experiences during an extra-ordinary time. Tearing up the original diaries, I burned them in the grate in my hotel room.

Although neither Nicolas nor I had been very good at keeping in touch with our former colleagues from the Legion, we received the regular Legion newsletter, the *Kepi Blanc*. Nicolas was always more interested in it than me, reading out the latest news about who was where and doing what. He even told me that Pierre had been elected to the National Assembly, becoming Minister of National Defence in two successive cabinets. I barely listened. I had banished many of my memories from my mind. They were still too raw to dwell on and I didn't believe in looking back. I had led an interesting life and now I didn't. It was a simple fact.

In any event, things could have been a great deal worse. Nicolas was a good man. He worked hard and looked after me and the children well. He was a kind father who protected us all. He had been honourable enough to marry me when I became pregnant and had done right by me ever since. I, in turn, was very fond of him and grateful for his care. It was no longer the passionate relationship it had been when it began, but we got on well enough.

There were occasional, unexpected reminders of the past. Someone alerted me to an article about Père Mallec, the Yugoslav chaplain who'd been with us at Bir Hakeim. After the war he'd left the Catholic ministry, got married and had children. He was living in Australia and had been awarded the Légion d'honneur for his services during the war. Rightly so. No man there had seen more suffering than him.

Then, walking through my home town of Villeuus one day, my shopping in my hands, I was nearly knocked over by a man who emerged from a side door which opened onto the street. After he'd apologized and helped me with my scattered shopping, we looked at each other properly. It was Monsieur Celerier, the dentist with whom I had travelled so many miles in Italy and France.

'Goodness gracious,' I exclaimed, lapsing momentarily into English. 'How extraordinary!'

He took a few seconds to recognize me, but then his face broke into his customary grin and he embraced me warmly.

'Can it be? Is it Adjudant-Chef Travers?' he asked, beaming. 'Tell me, did you ever find your eggcup?'

Shaking my head and laughing, I told him I hadn't, but holding up a box of eggs in my shopping bag, I added, 'I have one at home, though.'

We chatted companionably together and went for a coffee to catch up on all the news. By sheer coincidence, he now had his own dental practice in Villennes and lived not far from me. I was delighted to see him and hoped that we might be able to resume our friendship. But he was officer class; married with children and living in a very grand house. Nicolas and he had never known each other and didn't really get on. Although Monsieur Celerier was to remain my dentist for many years – until he retired to the French Riviera – we were never able to pick up the threads again.

I also kept in touch with Eka Dadiani, the Georgian princess and former sister-in-law of Dimitri Amilakvari. She lived in a flat near Les Invalides in Paris, keeping her word to remain close to the Legion her brother-in-law so adored. Poor Eka, not only had she lost Dimitri but her sister (Dimitri's wife) had been killed in a car accident along with their other sister a few years after the war. They were on their way to visit the Legion in Provence when the accident happened. Unable to let go of the past, she was always pleased to see me on my occasional visits to her flat and to reminisce about what she called '*les années dorées*'.

Early in 1956, I received a letter from the Legion, inviting me to Paris. I studied it carefully and waited a day or two before telling Nicolas.

'I am to be awarded the Médaille Militaire,' I told him. 'To go with my Croix de Guerre and my colonial war medals. They want me to go to Les Invalides to receive it.'

Nicolas was delighted. 'It is a great honour,' he said gravely. 'You must accept.'

We travelled to the capital with our two sons, aged seven and nine, that bitterly cold winter of 1956 and drove to the place I hadn't seen in over a decade. There were hundreds of people there, including former legionnaires from all over the world summoned back to receive medals for their part in the Second World War.

I wore a purple beret at an angle and a thick black coat which flared out at the bottom. Pinned to my breast were my earlier medals. An official told me to take my place in the middle of the large square, the majestic cobblestone Cour d'Honneur, centuries old and surrounded by crenellated battlements and ancient cannon. French troops have paraded there since the days of Napoleon.

Standing to attention behind me was a company of modern-day legionnaires, formed up in ranks, their rifles on their shoulders. Alongside them was a military band, and the friends and families of the waiting recipients lined the edges of the square and filled the upper balconies. I felt very self-conscious among all these people, standing in the great square, flanked by grand arches, bristling with cannon and watched over by a statue of Napoleon, 'the little corporal', in his old grey coat and hat. The bugle band struck up, the first strains of the Legion's refrain '*Le Boudin*' rang out, and we were ordered to take our positions, a few at a time, marching in unison to the centre of the square in readiness to receive our awards.

A winding procession began to emerge from a side door off the square as the various commanding officers and military leaders of the wartime campaigns slowly marched out towards us, the medal-bearers carrying velvet trays behind them. I caught Nicolas's eye. He was standing under an arch a few hundred yards away, his large hands resting on the shoulders of our two sons. The French love the Legion; it means so much to them and it meant a great deal to Nicolas now, proudly watching me standing in line.

Listening to the sombre music and longing for it to be over before I caught my death of cold, I stood to attention, hands at my sides, eyes forward. Into my view gradually came the line of men approaching at the special slow rate of Legion marching – eighty-eight paces to the minute instead of the usual one hundred and twenty. Suddenly I felt my heart lurch within my chest. Coming straight towards me, in full military uniform, was a lone general. It was Pierre. Older, greyer and slightly thicker round the middle, he was nonetheless unmistakable. General Marie-Pierre Koenig, hero of Bir Hakeim, Minister of Defence, was about to present me and two fellow legionnaires with our medals.

I could hardly breathe. The music stopped and citations were read, but I was too busy concentrating on Pierre to take in what they were saying. Taking a medal from the blue velvet tray, he lifted it gently in his fingers and walked towards me, his head down, his eyes fixed firmly on the ribbon. I wondered if Madame Koenig was in the square somewhere, watching from an upper balcony perhaps with the other generals' wives.

'For bravery in the face of the enemy at Bir Hakeim,' the sergeant major was saying, his words echoing off the stone walls, 'the Médaille Militaire to Madame Susan Schlegelmilch, née Travers.'

My hands clenched into fists, I stood stiffly to attention and gazed into the middle distance as Pierre approached. I felt his hands fumbling to pin the medal to my coat. Unable to look away any longer, I stared into his face, and our eyes locked.

Looking at Pierre now, it was hard to imagine the life we had briefly led together, the places we had been and things we had seen. The Syrian campaign, Damascus, Beirut, Aley, Libya, Bir Hakeim. *We have been through a great deal together and I think we should make a good match,* he'd told me that day in the car in Paris. I had never wasted time wondering what life would have been like had I become *Madame la Maréchale*, the wife of the Governor of Paris, the second Madame Koenig, but – for that brief moment as I looked up into his eyes – I did.

From a distance, there was nothing unusual about our appearance. We seemed to be nothing more than a respected general congratulating his dutiful former underling. But as Pierre finished pinning the medal to my coat and leaned in towards me as if to say something, his eyes betrayed his emotions, as did mine. In that second or two of closeness, I was able to inhale his scent, the way his skin smelled, and a flood of memories threatened to overwhelm me. I stood stock still and waited.

'I hope this will remind you of many things,' he said finally, his voice tired but his eyes as alive as ever. 'Well done, La Miss.'

He stepped back and gave me a brisk salute. I returned it just as briskly, my eyes full of tears as he marched away. It was the last time I was ever to see him.

The ceremony over, I rushed across to my husband and children and showed them my award. It had taken on a new significance, and I was as proud of it as Nicolas clearly was. Nothing was said, no reference was made to the general and when I prepared to leave I looked around to see if I could see him. But he had gone.

16

DRAWING TO A CLOSE

In September 1970 the general died after complications following a routine hip operation in a Paris hospital. I learned of his death from Eka, a woman who'd always held her brother-in-law's best friend in the highest regard.

'Pierre died yesterday,' she told me on the telephone one morning. 'I thought you'd like to know.'

Slumping into a chair, I held the telephone close to my heart and shut my eyes.

I didn't go to see him or to the funeral. I didn't think it was my place to do so. Madame Koenig was still alive and I knew she wouldn't have wanted me there.

Eka went. Visiting his body as he lay in a darkened chapel of rest on the eve of his burial, she leaned over and kissed his forehead gently – for Amilakvari, for me and for herself. She was startled to hear a woman's voice say softly, 'Thank you, Eka,' and looking up, realized that Madame Koenig was sitting in a corner of the room, alone in the dark.

It was to be many years before that redoubtable woman was able to join her husband in the family crypt. I read in the newspaper that she'd died and felt sad.

A year after his death, General Koenig's memoirs were published in a book called *Ce Jour-là*. In it, he had written that I was 'respected and well loved by the whole division', and adopted by them as 'an honorary male of exceptional courage'. He described me as 'more disciplined than some of the men'. It was the highest accolade.

Three years later, in 1974, I was invited to attend a special ceremony for the general in which a square directly behind the main government buildings in Paris was named after him. They'd elevated him posthumously to the rank of field marshal. Watching the ceremony from a distance, hearing the many words of praise, I wondered what it all meant to the hundreds of people rushing past on their way to work, men and women, their heads bent against the chill wind, too busy to stop and listen to the citations to a brave man now dead. Most people had forgotten his great moment of glory – our great moment – thirty years before. If they gave the ceremony any thought at all, they probably assumed that he was some Gaullist who'd done well enough to have a plaque put up in his honour. Ask any Parisian and they'll tell you that the giving of the name 'Bir Hakeim' to the old Grenelle Bridge and the Métro station in the shadow of the Eiffel Tower was most likely due to some politically correct pandering to the French colonies. They know nothing.

I lived companionably with Nicolas for the next twenty years, seventeen all in the same house. We didn't go out much, he didn't like to socialize, and he never fully recovered from the illnesses of Indo-China. At his insistence, the children had been sent to a boarding school at nine and ten. He wanted them to be brought up Catholic and to experience boarding-school life. Because of their English heritage, we sent them first to St Bede's in Staffordshire and then to Ampleforth in Yorkshire. As a consequence, however, I only ever saw my children during the school holidays after that.

When their schooling was over, the boys grew up and moved away. François lived in Paris and has three children. Tom went to live in Australia and has two children. All my grandchildren are handsome and intelligent and fine. They are everything a grandmother could wish for.

My brother Laurence became destitute in his old age and wrote to me when we were living in Villennes, asking if he could come and live with us. I hadn't seen or spoken to him since my mother's funeral and I told him no. He ended up living in a monastery run by the Greek Orthodox church. When he died, the monks wrote and told me. I sent flowers.

Nicolas and I never travelled again and spent most of our time at home enjoying our dogs and reading. I was a good and faithful wife and I cared for him until his death, of liver cancer, in 1994. Towards the very end, when he was ill in hospital and François took me to see him, I think we became close again. He had no idea he was dying; nobody did, and I fully expected him to come home.

We buried him in the little cemetery in Villennes and put a cross over his grave. I didn't cry at his funeral. I couldn't. The last time I'd cried publicly was when my beloved Rebecca had died, at our home in Villennes. She'd been with me through so much – Tunisia, Indo-China and France. She felt like my last link with my former life. After I'd dried my eyes, I vowed never to cry again and I didn't. Not even for poor Nicolas. In a strange sort of way, his death didn't seem to matter very much. We were both old and we knew that one day we'd die. His time was then. Mine is yet to come.

Nicolas had qualified for a full military pension from the Legion, but I never had because of the itinerant nature of my service, despite Nicolas's repeated protests to the French authorities on my behalf. With scant income and my own health failing, I moved into a small flat in a sheltered home south of Paris near François and sold off most of my things. I gave Tom the lovingly oiled Beretta pistol and the shotgun I was given in Eritrea.

Among the precious belongings I kept for my tiny room was the beautiful chest of drawers, inlaid with mother-of-pearl, which had taken pride of place in the cottage I shared with Pierre at Aley. I also kept the ornate Middle Eastern chest that had been in our living room

332

there, the book *Said the Fisherman* which I'd read so many times at Bir Hakeim, and the bronze Foreign Legion statues which had belonged to my grandfather.

In 1996, I received a letter from General Hugo Geoffrey to tell me that he had nominated me for a medal. It was the Légion d'honneur – the French Foreign Legion's highest military medal. I tried to recall the fresh-faced young man I'd first met on the boat to Italy and wondered what I'd done to impress him so. A few weeks later, during a simple ceremony at my nursing home, attended by my family, the general made the presentation.

The official announcement in the Legion newspaper read:

> *The* Kepi Blanc *is pleased to inform you of the nomination to the grade of Knight of the Legion of Honour for Adjutant-Chef Susan Travers, married name Schlegelmilch, the only woman to be part of the history of the Foreign Legion (regimental roll number 22166). She served during the Second World War as the driver of General Koenig and as a nurse in the Far East and North Africa.*

A special reception was held for me and a few old friends, people I hadn't seen for years, came to pay their respects. There was Jean Simon, now President of the National Association of the French Foreign Legion; Bernard Saint-Hillier, who'd first told me of the Italian propaganda broadcasts after El Alamein, and who was now a general; and Lieutenant Rosenzweig, the NCO I'd taken my nightly meals with in the pointed store tent at Bir Hakeim, now very high up in the Legion and in charge of training. There were others too, men I vaguely recognized, whose names ignited old memories. Sweetly, the daughters of Gabriel de Sairigné came along also. There was even a bugler to play '*Le Boudin*', an incongruous sound in an old people's home.

* * *

Last year, a friend took me to Les Invalides to see the military exhibits in the Army Museum.

Pushed along the echoing, empty corridors in a wheelchair, I resolved beforehand not to be unduly affected by my memories. To begin with, I wasn't. There were route maps and charts, faded photographs and the usual memorabilia. But as we approached the glass display case devoted to Bir Hakeim, I found myself staring up at a portrait of Pierre, next to his familiar khaki uniform pressed behind glass. Beside his image were those of Amilakvari, de Sairigné and others, along with Pierre's toy lion, and a small container of grey sand dug up from that Libyan hell-hole. Ghostly images overwhelmed me. The screaming of the Stukas, the rat-a-tat of the guns, the stench of death and burning rubber. Studying Pierre's uniform, I was transported back to Aley, to the sight of it hanging on the wardrobe door. I remembered how I sewed on his stripes. The toy lion, dishevelled and faded from the sun, proudly presented to him by the men along with the little rabbit. The photograph of Amilakvari, proud and tall, sleeves rolled up, giving instructions to his men. The memories were strong, stronger than ever. They crowded in on me, threatening to engulf me in a wave of emotion and nostalgia. Wiping away a tear, I asked to be wheeled further on.

I hadn't expected there to be a mention of me in the rows of glass cabinets, and there wasn't one. But deep within one display, half-concealed by a tattered military pennant bearing the Cross of Lorraine, I spotted a fading sepia photograph of the general, standing up through the sunroof of the old Ford Utility. Almost hidden from view was a shadowy figure, its right arm resting on the window. It was me, sitting in the driver's seat.

THE END

ACKNOWLEDGEMENTS

This book became possible because Richard Filon and Ted Demers sought me out and persuaded me to speak after many years of silence. I thank them for their persistence and I'm grateful to them for bringing my story to the world. Wendy Holden, my co-writer, sat with me for hours on end throughout 1998 and 1999, listening to me rambling while she took notes and astutely asked questions. She was always most respectful of my age, tiredness and lamentable memory lapses. Without her gentle probing, extensive background research and ability to put it all together, I would have been unable to fulfil my ambition – to record the experiences of my life before I die. My one wish, I told her, was to let my grandchildren know what a wicked grandmother they had. I believe that she will grant that wish.

Val Hudson led Wendy to me via Alan Nevins at AMG/Renaissance in Beverly Hills. Alan deftly master-minded the process, along with his business partner Joel Gotler and Wendy's agent in London, Mark Lucas. I must also thank the attorneys in France and Los Angeles, Jean-Pierre Dagorno and Steven Brimmer respectively. To Anne Gray, who helped Wendy, we owe an enormous debt of gratitude for her kindness and efficiency in translating and transcribing so many documents with such expertise and enthusiasm. Jan Rose was also extremely efficient and supportive. Special thanks to Sergent-Chef Emilio Condado Madera, commander of the Foreign Legion Museum in Aubagne, France, for his time and help. John Forsey helped with book loans and military knowledge and Brian Silk gave his invaluable support and recommended reading lists. In the bibliography, I have tried my best to credit as many as possible of the myriad authors and books we've read or referred to, in order to help endorse my failing memories and to make sense of some of the details. Above all I am grateful to my dear sons François and Tom, and their families, and most of all to the French Foreign Legion and the people of France for embracing me as one of their own and allowing me to serve in some small way. Thank you. To those whom I may have inadvertently overlooked, I offer my humblest apologies.

Susan Travers

BIBLIOGRAPHY

Barker, A. J., *Eritrea 1941*. Faber, 1966.

Bauer, Lt Colonel E., *The History of World War Two*. Galley Press, 1984.

Beevor, Anthony and Cooper, Artemis, *Paris after the Liberation 1944–1949*. Penguin, 1995.

Bramall, Field Marshal Lord (ed.), *The Imperial War Museum Book of the Desert War, 1940–1942*. Sidgwick & Jackson, 1992.

de Gaulle, Charles, *The Complete War Memoirs of Charles de Gaulle*, translated by Jonathan Griffin and Richard Howard. Carrol & Graf Publishers, 1998.

Debay, Yves, *The French Foreign Legion Today*. Windrow & Greene, 1987.

Doherty, Richard, *A Noble Crusade, The History of the Eighth Army 1941–45*. Spellmount, 1999.

Fraser, David, *Knight's Cross, A Life of Field Marshal Erwin Rommel*. HarperCollins, 1994.

Geoffrey, Hugo, *Sur le Chemin des Etoiles: La Légion Etrangère*. Gérard Klopp, Paris, 1997.

Geraghty, Tony, *March or Die, France and the Foreign Legion*. Grafton Books, 1986.

Hamilton, Nigel, *Monty, The Making of a General*. Hamish Hamilton, 1981.

Hasey, Lieutenant John F., *Yankee Fighter*. Little Brown, Boston, 1942.

Holmes, Richard, *Bir Hacheim: Desert Citadel*. Pan/Ballantine, 1972.

Koenig, General, *Ce Jour-là: Bir Hakeim*. Robert Laffont, Paris, 1971.

McGuirk, Dal, *Rommel's Army in Africa*. Airlife Publishing, 1987.

Macksey, Kenneth and Woodhouse, William, *The Penguin Encyclopaedia of Modern Warfare*. Viking, 1991.

Majdalanay, Fred, *Cassino, Portrait of a Battle*. Longman, 1957.

Mercer, Derrik (ed.), *Chronicle of the Twentieth Century*. Longman Chronicle, 1988.

Moorehead, Alan, *African Trilogy*. Cassell, 1998.

Parker, John, *Inside the Foreign Legion*. Piatkus, 1998.

Parrish, Thomas (ed.), *Encyclopaedia of World War Two*. Secker & Warburg, 1978.

Porch, Douglas, *The French Foreign Legion*. HarperPerennial, 1991.

Robert Young, John, *The French Foreign Legion*. Thames & Hudson, 1988.

Rondeau, Daniel and Stephane, Roger, *Des Hommes Libres: La France Libre par ceux qui l'ont faite*. Grasset & Fasquelle, 1997.

Seeger, Alan, *Poems*. Charles Scribner & Sons, New York, 1916.

Selwyn, Victor (ed.), *The Voice of War, Poems of the Second World War*. Penguin, 1995.

Staff, Chester, *From Salerno to the Alps*. Battery Press, 1986.

Taylor, Eric, *Women Who Went to War, 1938–46*. Robert Hale, 1988.

Tibawi, A. L., *A Modern History of Syria*. Macmillan, 1969.

To War with Whitaker, The Wartime Diaries of the Countess of Ranfurly 1939–45. Mandarin, 1995.

Upton, Anthony F., *Finland 1939–40*. Davis-Poynter, 1974.

Windrow, Martin, Braby, Wayne and Lyles, Kevin, *French

Foreign Legion Paratroops. Osprey Publishing, 1985.
Windrow, Martin and Chappell, Mike, *The French Foreign Legion since 1945*. Osprey Publishing, 1996.

Extracts from Second World War poems are taken from *The Voice of War*, edited by Victor Selwyn for the Salamander Oasis Trust (Penguin 1995). The quotation from Wilfred Owen on p. 198 is taken from 'Dulce et Decorum Est', *Poems* (1963).

INDEX

342

THE PAST IS MYSELF
by Christabel Bielenberg

'It would be difficult to overpraise this book. Mrs Bielenberg's experience was unique and her honesty, intelligence and compassion makes her account of it moving beyond words'
The Economist

Christabel Bielenberg, a niece of Lord Northcliffe, married a German lawyer in 1934. She lived through the war in Germany, as a German citizen, under the horrors of Nazi rule and Allied bombings. *The Past is Myself* is her story of that experience, an unforgettable portrait of an evil time.

'This autobiography is of exceptional distinction and importance. It deserves recognition as a magnificent contribution to international understanding and as a document of how the human spirit can triumph in the midst of evil and persecution'
The Economist

'Marvellously written'
Observer

'Nothing but superlatives will do for this book. It tells its story magnificently and every page of its story is worth telling'
Irish Press

'Intensely moving'
Yorkshire Evening News

0 552 99065 5

DAUGHTER OF PERSIA
by Sattareh Farman Farmaian

'Once upon a time, long before fatwas and ayatollahs, the daughter of a *shazdeh*, or prince, grew up in a Tehran harem. Sattareh lived with numerous mothers, more than thirty siblings and some thousand servants. . . Sattareh's father may have been autocratic, infuriatingly stingy and over sixty at the time of her birth, but he was also unusually enlightened. His motto "education is everything" applied as much to daughters as to sons. It paid off, for Sattareh provides an accomplished portrait of a childhood enriched by nightingales and bazaars, politics and family romances. More impressively, she broke with tradition to study in California, returned to found the Tehran School of Social Work and, after the Shah's downfall, survived execution by a whisker'
She Magazine

'This entralling account . . . confirms my conviction, learned from experience, that idealism does not die. Indeed, the human spirit can still triumph, however brutal the tyranny under which so many are destined to live out their lives'
Christabel Bielenberg

'A wonderful book to read and own; a treasury of human experience'
Fay Weldon

'Her memories of her childhood . . . are lyrical and enchanting . . . beautifully written'
New York Times Book Review

0 552 13928 9

THE HOUSE BY THE DVINA
A RUSSIAN CHILDHOOD
by Eugenie Fraser

A unique and moving account of life in Russia before, during and immediately after the Revolution, *The House by the Dvina* is the fascinating story of two families, separated in culture and geography, but bound together by a Russian-Scottish marriage. It includes episodes as romantic and dramatic as any in fiction: the purchase by the author's great-grandfather of a peasant girl with whom he had fallen in love; the desperate journey by sledge in the depths of winter made by her grandmother to intercede with Tsar Aleksandr II for her husband; the extraordinary courtship of her parents; and her Scottish granny being caught up in the abortive revolution of 1905.

Eugenie Fraser herself was brought up in Russia but was taken on visits to Scotland. She marvellously evokes the reactions of a child to two totally different environments, sets of customs and family backgrounds. The characters on both sides are beautifully drawn and splendidly memorable.

With the events of 1914 to 1920 – the war with Germany, the Revolution, the murder of the Tsar, the withdrawal of the Allied Intervention in the north – came the disintegration of the country and of family life. The stark realities of hunger, deprivation and fear are sharply contrasted with the day-to-day experiences, joys, frustrations and adventures of childhood. The reader shares the family's suspense and concern about the fates of its members and relives with Eugenie her final escape to Scotland.

'Eugenie Fraser has a wondrous tale to tell and she tells it very well. There is no other autobiography quite like it'
Molly Tibbs, *Contemporary Review*

'A wholly delightful account'
Elizabeth Sutherland, *Scots Magazine*

0 552 12833 3

NOT WITHOUT MY DAUGHTER
by Betty Mahmoody

'You are here for the rest of your life. Do you understand? You are not leaving Iran. You are here until you die.'

Betty Mahmoody and her husband, Dr Sayyed Bozorg Mahmoody ('Moody'), came to Iran from the USA to meet Moody's family. With them was their four-year-old daughter, Mahtob. Appalled by the squalor of their living conditions, horrified by what she saw of a country where women were merely chattels and Westerners are despised, Betty soon became desperate to return to the States. But Moody, and his often vicious family, had other plans. Mother and daughter became prisoners of an alien culture, hostages of an increasingly tyrannical and violent man.

Betty began to try to arrange an escape. Evading Moody's sinister spy network, she secretly met sympathisers opposed to Khomeini's savage regime. But every scheme that was suggested to her meant leaving Mahtob behind for ever. . .

'The horrific situation in which Betty Mahmoody found herself would give any loving mother nightmares. Hers is an amazing story of a woman's courage and total devotion to her child that will have you rooting for them along every inch of their treacherous journey'
Susan Oudot, *Woman's Own*

0 552 13356 6

A SELECTED LIST OF NON-FICTION TITLES AVAILABLE FROM CORGI BOOKS

99065 5	THE PAST IS MYSELF	*Christabel Bielenberg*	£7.99
13337 X	THE PROVISIONAL IRA	*Patrick Bishop & Eamonn Mallie*	£6.99
14750 8	BLACK HAWK DOWN	*Mark Bowden*	£5.99
14493 2	THE JIGSAW MAN	*Paul Britton*	£6.99
14093 7	OUR KATE	*Catherine Cookson*	£5.99
99091 4	ANIMALS IN WAR	*Jilly Cooper*	£6.99
14465 7	CLOSE QUARTER BATTLE	*Mike Curtis*	£6.99
13582 8	THE GOD SQUAD	*Paddy Doyle*	£7.99
14239 5	MY FEUDAL LORD	*Tehmina Durrani*	£5.99
13928 9	DAUGHTER OF PERSIA	*Sattareh Farman Farmaian*	£6.99
12833 3	THE HOUSE BY THE DVINA	*Eugenie Fraser*	£8.99
14539 4	THE DVINA REMAINS	*Eugenie Fraser*	£6.99
14760 5	THE CUSTOM OF THE SEA	*Neil Hanson*	£5.99
14185 2	FINDING PEGGY: A GLASGOW CHILDHOOD	*Meg Henderson*	£6.99
14694 3	VIEW FROM THE SUMMIT	*Sir Edmund Hillary*	£7.99
99744 7	CHARLES: A BIOGRAPHY	*Anthony Holden*	£7.99
14164 X	EMPTY CRADLES	*Margaret Humphreys*	£6.99
14680 3	FARAWAY	*Lucy Irvine*	£6.99
13943 2	LOST FOR WORDS	*Deric Longden*	£5.99
14544 0	FAMILY LIFE	*Elisabeth Luard*	£6.99
13356 6	NOT WITHOUT MY DAUGHTER	*Betty Mahmoody*	£5.99
13953 X	SOME OTHER RAINBOW	*John McCarthy & Jill Morrell*	£6.99
14127 5	BRAVO TWO ZERO	*Andy McNab*	£6.99
14137 2	A KENTISH LAD	*Frank Muir*	£7.99
14288 3	BRIDGE ACROSS MY SORROWS	*Christina Noble*	£5.99
14632 3	MAMA TINA	*Christina Noble*	£5.99
14607 2	THE INFORMER	*Sean O'Callaghan*	£6.99
14709 5	THE YAMATO DYNASTY	*Sterling and Peggy Seagrave*	£7.99
14763 X	HIGH SPIRITS	*Joan Sims*	£6.99
14767 2	. . .AND JUNE WHITFIELD	*June Whitfield*	£6.99